W9-BUR-200

Is That Weird Story I Just Heard a "Classic" Urban Legend?

Some folklorists narrowly classify urban legends as follows: compelling stories of unknown or enigmatic origin that spread in various forms—and that may use humor or terror to deliver a lesson (often one involving punishment for violating a social code). These are "classic" urban legends.

Okay, but Is That the Only Relevant Standard for Determining Whether a Story Is an Urban Legend?

Nope. Lots of other stories are commonly referred to as urban legends. Even though they may not be up to formal academic snuff, many of these stories are worth considering and analyzing on their own merits.

Is There, Perhaps, a Handy Eight-Point Checklist to Use to Spot These "Nonclassic" Urban Legends?

Glad you asked. You could do worse than to consult the eight questions that follow, each of which focuses on a factor shared by the stories contained in this book. Not every story between these covers possesses all eight factors, but most display at least two or three.

- ❏ Is the story presented as having been experienced or seen by a "friend of a friend"?
- ❏ Does the teller seem a little too eager in his or her insistence that the story is true?
- ❏ Does the story play to a common fear or concern?
- ❏ Is the story demonstrably false?
- ❏ Has the story appeared in multiple versions?
- ❏ Does the story carry an important lesson or warning?
- ❏ Has the story been around for a really long time?
- ❏ Is the story "too good not to pass along"?

alpha
books

Hey, Have You Passed Along Any of These Memorable Stories?

Who's the ultimate authority figure? Mom and Dad, right? We can't let *them* off the hook. Among the most memorable stories of demented parental oversight are those concerning poor naming choices, including these:

❑ Long Dong (an unfortunate and elusive youth of Asian descent)

❑ Nosmo King (supposedly inspired by a "No Smoking" sign in the hospital lobby)

❑ Urine (pronounced YOU-REEN, an elegant female appellation inspired by a label on a hospital vial placed near a particularly unimaginative new mother)

❑ Oranjello and Lemonjello (allegedly the product of a new Louisiana mother of twins who just liked the sound)

As fascinating as the stories are, no one with a legal name corresponding to these has ever been tracked down. But there's always that next trip to the maternity ward ....

How Many of These Stories Have You Heard from a "Friend of a Friend"?

Widespread (and demonstrably untrue) urban legends include:

❑ Jerry Mathers of *Leave It to Beaver* was killed in action in Vietnam. (See Chapter 7, **"The Family Hour (Not): Twisted Legends About Your Favorite Children's Television Stars."**)

❑ Albino alligators prowl the sewers of New York. (See Chapter 9, **"All Creatures, Great and Small."**)

❑ The FCC is planning to tax e-mail transmissions. (See Chapter 11, **"The Government Is Out to Get You."**)

❑ Microsoft programmers placed a racial slur in millions of copies of the company's popular word processing software. (See Chapter 15, **"Authority Figures Lose It."**)

❑ Crazed AIDS victims are sabotaging public places with infected needles, hoping thereby to spread the disease. (See Chapter 17, **"Hazardous Amorous Duty."**)

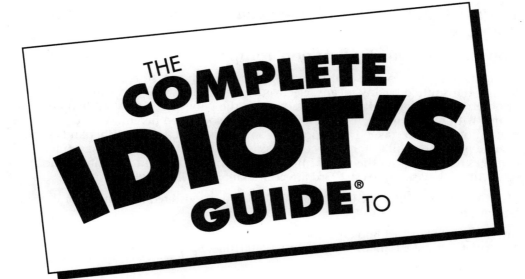

THE

COMPLETE IDIOT'S GUIDE® TO

Urban Legends

by Brandon Toropov

alpha books

201 West 103rd Street
Indianapolis, IN 46290

A Pearson Education Company

To Mom. If that's not too weird—considering, you know, the subject matter.

International Standard Book Number: 0-02-864007-1
Library of Congress Catalog Card Number: 2001088752

03 02 01   8 7 6 5 4 3 2 1

Interpretation of the printing code: The rightmost number of the first series of numbers is the year of the book's printing; the rightmost number of the second series of numbers is the number of the book's printing. For example, a printing code of 01-1 shows that the first printing occurred in 2001.

Printed in the United States of America

Note: This publication contains the opinions and ideas of its author. It is intended to provide helpful and informative material on the subject matter covered. It is sold with the understanding that the author and publisher are not engaged in rendering professional services in the book. If the reader requires personal assistance or advice, a competent professional should be consulted.

The author and publisher specifically disclaim any responsibility for any liability, loss, or risk, personal or otherwise, which is incurred as a consequence, directly or indirectly, of the use and application of any of the contents of this book.

Publisher
Marie Butler-Knight

Product Manager
Phil Kitchel

Managing Editor
Jennifer Chisholm

Acquisitions Editor
Randy Ladenheim-Gil

Development Editor
Deborah S. Romaine

Production Editor
Katherin Bidwell

Copy Editor
Krista Hansing

Illustrator
Jody Schaeffer

Cover Designers
Mike Freeland
Kevin Spear

Book Designers
Scott Cook and Amy Adams of DesignLab

Indexer
Tonya Heard

Layout/Proofreading
Cynthia Davis-Hubler
John Etchison
Susan Geiselman
Brad Lenser
Lizbeth Patterson

Contents at a Glance

Contents

6 Did Catherine the Great Really Do It with a Horse?   57

7 The Family Hour (Not): Twisted Legends About Your Favorite Children's Television Stars   69

Part 3: Paranoia 95

21 The Hazards of the Big, Bad World: Urban Legends About College and College Students 247

22 Maniacs, Unlimited 255

23 Too Disgusting for Words 265

24 Some Final Thoughts 277

Appendixes

Foreword

Northrop Frye once confessed, "I certainly do rewrite my central myth in every book; I would never read or trust any writer who did not do so."

The latest "hot" urban legend can be seen as a revision of somebody else's central myth when we hear it—and (not infrequently) as a revision of our own central myth when we pass along an embellished version to someone else. Between these covers you will find a whole lot of rewrites of a whole lot of peoples' central myths. I just want to go on record, however, that *I* had nothing to do with circulating any of the really icky bits that appear in this book.

The stories you'll find in this authoritative overview of the urban legend phenomenon are by turns weird, appealing, appalling, absurd, and hilarious. They're also highly addictive. Fortunately, there's a bunch of them to devour!

Let's face it: This book covers a strange subject. As luck would have it, though, Brandon is a strange person; I don't think he or anybody who knows him well would dispute that contention. His fascinating and supremely readable volume, which I think represents his very best work, seems to have made him a little stranger than usual—but that's his problem.

As for you, you've got a massively entertaining book to explore—and, perhaps, a few myths of your own to rewrite. Enjoy.

Leslie Hamilton

Coauthor, *How to Impress Anybody About Anything* (Citadel Press, 1998)

Introduction

You're no idiot. You know there's more than meets the eye to urban legends.

These stories—fascinating, enduring, and, more often than not, unforgettable—aren't just outrageous bits of eye-popping small talk. With the rise of the Internet, they've become inescapable reference points of modern life, shared bits of mythology to be forwarded, debated, debunked, analyzed, and endlessly, and I do mean endlessly, re-circulated. (A side note: At various points in the text, I've included classic "hyper-forwarded" e-mail messages that have, in recent years, given rise to various urban legends. These have been edited both for space and for style.)

Some of the stories under discussion in this book have become surrealistic cultural icons. If you haven't found yourself transfixed by the cute child star who allegedly ate too many Pop Rocks ... or the guy with the hook said to hang out in the shadowy recesses of Lover's Lane ... or the albino alligators that supposedly prowl the sewers of Manhattan—well, you're about to. (And, by the way, where were you when everyone else in the office was sharing these heartwarming tales during coffee break?)

You're also about to find out some of the possible *reasons* these stories—and their many counterparts—resonate so strongly with us. That's just as interesting.

Five (Count 'em, Five) Sections

In this book, you'll find five sections, each devoted to some element of the ongoing, ever-expanding urban legend phenomenon. Here's a quick breakdown:

Part 1, "This Really Happened!" This part of the book offers an overview of what urban legends are, why we keep coming back to them, and what their distinctive characteristics and challenges are.

Part 2, "Famous Figures." Here you'll find strange, persistent, and not always flattering legends about celebrated personages.

Part 3, "Paranoia." Having trouble sleeping? Eager to continue that white-knuckled bout of insomnia until daylight? Boy, have you come to the right place.

Part 4, "Intimate Entanglements." Here we conclude that many of us must possess profound misgivings about the human libido and its excesses.

Part 5, "Nasty Business." Fans of legends involving death, lies, manipulation, violence, and gross-out episodes will have plenty to leaf through here.

About the Sidebars

Throughout this book, you'll find helpful text boxes that will make it easy for you to get yourself up to speed on urban legends past and present. Here's what you'll come across as you read:

Fable Facts

Here you'll find supporting information and interesting trivia related to the legends or themes under discussion. Sure, you *could* skip this stuff—but why would you?

Strange but True

These boxes feature extended anecdotes, case histories, or other tidbits of interesting information. They're usually tangential extensions of an idea, story, or incident discussed in the main text.

Don't Believe It!

Urban legends have a fascinating way of convincing people that things that didn't really happen actually did. (They have an equally fascinating way of convincing people that things that *did* really happen actually didn't.) In this box, you'll get the "straight skinny" on stories that are a little too weird to be true.

Legend Lingo

These boxes include the definitions of vocabulary words, including jargon, slang, and any other terms and abbreviations that may be unfamiliar to you.

Acknowledgments

Judith Burros provided invaluable research and administrative and emotional support as I wrote this book; although no sentence of thanks here can do her efforts justice, this one will have to do. Randy Ladenheim-Gil and Debbie Romaine put up with my many eccentricities, which is saying something. David Toropov was there when I needed him. Bert Holtje continued to solidify his reputation as the most thoughtful, intelligent, and supportive agent on the planet. Glenn KnicKrehm made it all possible. Elvis Costello and the Attractions provided the working soundtrack via *Get Happy,* that illimitable redemptive force so often mistaken for a simple rock-and-roll album. And my wife, Mary Toropov, saw me, yet again, through another period where I couldn't seem to stand up for falling down.

Trademarks

All terms mentioned in this book that are known to be or are suspected of being trademarks or service marks have been appropriately capitalized. Alpha Books and Pearson Education, Inc., cannot attest to the accuracy of this information. Use of a term in this book should not be regarded as affecting the validity of any trademark or service mark.

Part 1
"This Really Happened!"

What exactly are these strange stories that we keep insisting to each other are "real"?

Even urban legends that can be traced to actual events have a dreamlike tendency to reinvent themselves, retaining their essential elements but constantly reapplying themselves to new situations and new audiences. In this part of the book, we take a close look at the fundamental questions behind these pervasive universal metaphors for an uncertain modern life.

Chapter 1

What Is an Urban Legend?

In This Chapter

➤ Defining the classic urban legend

➤ The eight standards of an urban legend—questioning "those weird stories"

➤ The power of fear

➤ Urban legends as social lessons

What is an urban legend? When asked this question, most people respond with examples:

➤ "Oh, you know, it's one of those weird stories—like the one in which the kid ate so many Pop Rocks that he died."

➤ "Well, it's kind of like—you know how they say there are alligators prowling the sewers of New York City? But really there aren't ..."

➤ "An urban legend is one of those creepy yarns people tell, like the one about the guy with the hook who hangs out on Lover's Lane."

Louis Armstrong once told someone who asked him to define the word *jazz* that if the guy didn't know it when he heard it, there was no use trying to explain it. The "definition" of an urban legend is a little easier to pin down—but only a little.

In this chapter, we'll come closer to understanding exactly what we mean when we talk about "those weird stories."

Calling All Folklorists

If you're an academic researcher or a folklorist, you're likely to categorize an urban legend as a kind of modern *myth* that carries certain distinctive attributes. The "classic" *urban legend* is a compelling story of unknown or enigmatic origin that spreads in various forms and may use humor or terror to deliver a lesson (often involving punishment for violating a social code). Many stories that vary from the classic formula but that nevertheless capture the popular imagination are also considered urban legends by nonacademics.

Nonacademics—that's most of us—tend to take a somewhat more open-ended approach than that suggested by the definition of the "classic" *urban legend*. And frankly, not everyone agrees on criteria, even among people devoted to the topic. So once we step out of the academic realm (and who wants to hang out there all the time?), we're talking about a range of relevant standards.

Legend Lingo

A **myth** is a story or legend rooted in tradition that helps the hearer come to terms with some unexplained or challenging aspect of the human experience.

Legend Lingo

Urban legend is defined in different ways by different groups of people. One way to understand the term as it's generally used is to think of the urban legend as a newfangled myth with a contemporary setting, spread in a way that includes face-to-face discussion. (But see the main text for a discussion of the cautionary "classic" urban legend.)

Eight Standards to Assess Urban Legend Status

Perhaps you've heard a story and wondered whether it meets the standards (formal or otherwise) for an urban legend. Although the eight questions that follow aren't carved in stone, each focuses on a factor common to urban legends. Not every urban legend possesses all eight factors, but most display at least two or three.

Is the Story Presented as Having Been Experienced or Seen by a "Friend of a Friend"?

How often does someone pull you aside and say, "Hey, the most amazing thing happened to me this morning—I personally saw an albino alligator crawling out of the sewer on Fifty-Fourth Street and Seventh Avenue. I even snapped an instant photo with my trusty Polaroid. Here, take a look—physical evidence that I, Joe Smith, collected on the first of February, and had dated and notarized. Cool, eh?"

Not too often.

Much more likely is the claim, "A buddy of mine *knows* someone who saw an albino alligator lurking beneath the surface of the Big Apple." This is known as the "friend of a friend" (or *FOAF*) attribution, and it's a common feature of urban legends. Actually, what often shows up is attribution to someone who knows the friend of a friend, which would be a FOAFOAF, but that's a little cumbersome.

Consider the following initial paragraph of an e-mail message warning of a government plot to impose martial law in the United States on January 1, 2000:

```
I met a man last night that used
to go to my church. Brandon moved
last year before I started attend-
ing. But several people, including
the pastor, say that Brandon is to-
tally honest and does not "go off
half-cocked." Brandon told me that
his wife received a call from her
cousin last week ….
```

(Author's note: It wasn't me—honest.)

The message goes on to describe the cousin's "eyewitness" account of a truck that overturned, spilling its contents of signs reading "This City Under Martial Law" and proposing the ominous date of January 1, 2000, as the date when the clampdown was to be initiated. Despite such fourth-hand assurances (endorsed by a pastor, no less!), martial law in the good old U.S. of A. retains its status as one of those horrible things that *didn't* happen as Y2K dawned.

Does the Teller Seem a Little Too Eager to Insist That the Story Is True?

This is often a tip-off that you've entered Urban Legend Land. In personal accounts, the teller may swear up and down that a reputable source (a local news station, the White House, or the College of

Legend Lingo

FOAF stands for "friend of a friend," the common—and impossible to verify—attribution associated with countless urban legends.

Fable Facts

For a full discussion of the "friend of a friend" syndrome—and the urban legend phenomenon as a whole—check out the works of Jan Harold Brunvand, the acknowledged expert in the field. His superb book *The Vanishing Hitchhiker* (New York, W.W. Norton, 1981) is an excellent place to start.

Cardinals) has verified whatever strange tale follows. Via e-mail messages, you may see something like the following, any one of which is likely to initiate some completely bogus pronouncement:

➤ This really happened!

➤ This is a true story.

➤ I heard this one in a National Public Radio report a long time ago.

➤ This story was told to me by a friend who heard it on the news on the radio a year or so ago. It is a factual account.

Et cetera, et cetera, et cetera. The teller doth protest too much, methinks.

If your source gets similarly emphatic about the factuality of a strange story but provides no verifying details that you can actually confirm (a photocopy of an article from the *New York Times*, say), you should probably start wondering whether you're being passed an urban legend.

Fable Facts

Most, but not all, urban legends are completely false. They persist for many reasons, but most often because they resonate within the popular imagination or focus on an area of shared anxiety or insecurity. See Chapter 2, "Urban Legends as Collective Dreams."

Strange but True

"Friend of a friend" stories that "really happened!" used to be transmitted (and revised) primarily by means of one person telling another person the story, face to face. This still happens, of course, but nowadays the Internet and e-mail have entered the mix. In addition to providing an instant, worldwide means of spreading an urban legend, e-mail provides "sourcing" details that make a legend sound legit. Among the touches used to impart that all-important sense of realism are these:

➤ Two messages composed at the same time, the first a shocked confirmation of the details of the "forwarded" message that follows

➤ The inclusion of links to Web sites that actually exist but for some strange reason don't contain the factual verification promised by the e-mail message

➤ Misleading or downright false references to actual mainstream news stories

➤ Reference to nonexistent stories in actual mainstream publications or broadcasts

Does the Story Play to a Common Fear or Concern?

Whether the tale originates in the mists of decades past or was just cooked up this morning by some Internet crank, one thing's for certain: If it's making the rounds, there's a reason. Often that reason is all too obvious: The story hits us right where we live. Consider the following widely circulated (but bogus) e-mail warning, which owes its popularity to the near-universal concern for the safety of children:

```
Subject: Fwd: WARNING: WATERPROOF SUNSCREEN LOTION

If you have kids, this is a must read! Sunscreen danger.

To my friends with children or who are soon to have children …
this was passed on to me by my best friend who works for
Boeing in Seattle, his own true story … FYI.

I wanted to tell you a story about a very serious thing. We
still use sunscreen on our whole family, but we are more cau-
tious now. I tell you this only to make you more aware and
use caution. When Zack was 2 years old, I put on the water-
proof sunscreen, like I always had. I don't know how, but he
got some in his eyes—most likely from his hands. It happens so
easily at that age, or any age really. He started screaming!!!
So I tried to flush it out with water. But guess what? Didn't
matter ….

Remember, *WATERPROOF*. So I just held him and let him cry,
thinking that the salty tears would flush it all out. But it
```
got worse. I called the poison con-
trol center. They told me to RUSH
Zack to ER NOW!!! I was surprised.
I got him there, and they rushed me
back without a second to spare.
They started flushing his eyes out
with special medications.

Anyway, I found out for the first
time that MANY kids each year lose
their sight to waterproof sunscreen. It burns the eye, and they
lose complete sight!!! I was ap-
palled. I could not believe that
the sunscreen we use to help keep
our kids safe from skin cancer can
make them go blind!

Don't Believe It!

Note to concerned parents and caregivers: The chilling "warning" concerning the supposedly blinding effects of children's sunscreen lotion has been thoroughly debunked by the American Academy of Ophthalmology.

Well, I made a big stink about it. I wrote the sunscreen company, and they admitted to the problem but said something to
the effect that the seriousness of getting skin cancer is much
worse than the chance of going blind. I think it's wrong if
just one child goes blind!

They should change ingredients or should at least have a huge
warning on the bottle. But they claim that if you put a huge
warning on it, then parents won't use it due to fear. I kind
of get that, but there needs to be a change.

We did this huge article in our big city and went on the
news, warning parents—education, along with the importance of
using it. Well, anyway, Zack did go blind for two days—it was
horrible. So please be careful!!! Don't stop using sunscreen,
but just be very careful that your children don't touch their
eyes for at least 15-20 minutes after you put it on! And if
your child does get it in his or her eyes, then get to the
emergency room at once!

PASS THIS WARNING ON!!!

Is the Story Demonstrably False?

Surprise: Not all urban legends are completely specious, although the vast majority are. Some cautionary stories that are circulated and assimilated by good-sized chunks of the world at large have some basis in fact. (See, for instance, the reports of naked guests locked out of their motel rooms in Chapter 16, "Humiliation Is a Many-Splendored Thing.")

For the most part, though, urban legends are stories that people insist are true in every meaningful respect—but aren't. The contention, for instance, that Paul McCartney died in 1966 and was replaced by a look-alike is pretty easy to refute. But the details surrounding this supposed cover-up are still fascinating (see Chapter 4, "Is Paul Dead? (and Other Burning Pop Music Questions").

Has the Story Appeared in Multiple Versions?

Urban legends are a modern equivalent of classic folk tales, and such stories tend to have a great many variants. (We often forget all the sifting, balancing, and consolidating work performed by people such as the Brothers Grimm in standardizing multiple versions of ancient folk stories.)

The ever-popular "hook" story, for instance, in which murderous disaster is narrowly averted on Lover's Lane, has taken many forms over the years. For two of the most popular, see Chapter 22, "Maniacs, Unlimited."

Does the Story Carry an Important Lesson or Warning?

Often, we pass along stories—not just urban legends—because we hope to communicate important morals, lessons, or cautionary notes contained within those stories.

The children's tale that we know as "Little Red Riding Hood," for instance, contains obvious warnings about the dangers of wandering away from the (literal) path that leads to one's destination. It also contains subtler lessons about the dangers of straying from the (metaphorical) path of parental authority and oversight into the uncharted adult world. An interesting and more recent parallel is the story of the Needle Man, who waits in darkened movie theaters to plunge his needle into the flesh of unsuspecting teenaged girls. The story has literal warnings (beware of wackos in movie theaters) and symbolic warnings (beware of guys who bring you into movie theaters). See Chapter 17, "Hazardous Amorous Duty," for more on the Needle Man legend and its many companion stories.

Fable Facts

Urban legends can cruise right past logic on their path to perpetual propagation. When asked for the umpteenth time whether Paul McCartney was dead (see Chapter 4), Ringo Starr took to replying, "I'm not going to say anything about this because nobody believes me when I do."

Has the Story Been Around for a Really Long Time?

The Library of Congress has been denying for years that it maintains a storehouse of records detailing the secret rituals of the nation's college fraternities (see Chapter 22). The myth appears to have been around for decades. No matter how many earnest, well-documented pronouncements the folks at the LOC put forward, the story keeps turning up.

As you will learn in the pages that follow, an urban legend can be awesome in its tenacity and endurance once it establishes itself.

Is the Story "Too Good Not to Pass Along"?

If the story you hear has a clear structure featuring unmistakable beginning, middle, and end sections; if it uses devices such as the "series of three" rule (three visits, three phone calls, three attempts to attain a goal, and so on); or if it features a "hero" who makes a fateful choice that ends up doubling back on him or her, then there is a good chance that what you're hearing is an urban legend rather than a factual account.

The vast majority of the stories that appear in this book are compelling and well-structured enough to inspire retelling. That's why they're here—people told (and still tell) them a lot!

And Back to Where We Started

Any number of urban legend enthusiasts might revise, expand, or otherwise amend the eight-point checklist proposed in this chapter, but it will serve as an adequate starting point for those new to the topic.

And now the stars of our show: the stories themselves.

The Least You Need to Know

➤ Remember that "those weird stories" are easy to discuss but somewhat more difficult to define precisely.

➤ Remember, too, the definition of the "classic" urban legend: a story of unknown or enigmatic origin that spreads in various forms and that uses humor or terror to deliver a lesson (often involving punishment for violating a social code).

➤ Bear in mind, however, that nonacademic types (that's you and me) classify many stories as "urban legends" that don't quite match the definition.

➤ When confronted with a story that you suspect may be an urban legend, check it against the eight standards.

Chapter 2

Urban Legends as Collective Dreams

In This Chapter

➤ Exploring Jungian archetypes

➤ Making sense of surrealism

➤ Examining dreamlike warnings

➤ Searching for lessons

In this chapter, you'll see how urban legends resemble communal dreams. We'll look at examples of legends that, like dreams, feature surrealism, Jungian archetypes, and, last but not least, important warnings about lessons ignored at one's own peril. And we'll start with a nursery rhyme.

"Row, Row, Row Your Boat ..."

A dream is a sequence of thoughts, ideas, images, and emotional responses that pass through the mind during sleep. Dreams are frequently considered symbolic indicators of the unconscious mind's warnings, concerns, and conclusions on important issues. Urban legends and other folk tales may be best understood as communal dreams, symbolic reflections of our own possible responses to common fears, challenges, and concerns.

In Urban Legend Land, the atmosphere is frequently dreamlike. It's so dreamlike, in fact, that the phenomenon of the shared urban legend resembles nothing so much as a series of communal dreams and nightmares. Maybe life is "but a dream" after all. That would mean, by definition, that urban legends are dreams, too, wouldn't it?

Strange but True

Carl Gustav Jung (1875–1961) was a Swiss psychiatrist whose massively influential work included the founding of analytical psychology. A contemporary and one-time ally of Sigmund Freud, Jung parted ways with Freud because of what he felt was an over-reliance on the role of sexual trauma as the root cause of human neuroses. Jung posited two ranges of the unconscious: a private realm and the archetypes associated with a common human (or "collective") unconscious. Jung emphasized the importance of attaining personal fulfillment by bringing about harmony between one's conscious and unconscious elements. The analysis of dreams and myths in this regard occupies an important position in his thought system.

Jungian Archetypes: Dream Casts

Jungian *archetypes* can be important tools in the analysis of dreams, literature, and cultural institutions. Consider, for instance, the archetype of the "shadow," which includes (among many components) the notion of a malevolent individual—Mr. Hyde—who also possesses a better nature—Dr. Jekyll.

Jung, who expanded the idea of the archetype well beyond the boundaries of its original meaning of "prototype," believed that archetypes reside in a "collective unconscious," a storehouse of shared human responses to certain patterns of experience.

Legend Lingo

An **archetype** is a pattern of ideas with parallels in every human culture. Archetypes are strongly associated with the work of Swiss psychiatrist Carl Gustav Jung.

Of Meanings and Interpretations

Some of the urban legends that appear in this book have obvious messages and warnings to deliver. The same, of course, can be said for dreams.

Some urban legends simply leave you with a feeling that something inscrutable but quite important is being worked through by the participants. The same is true of dreams, in which we often puzzle our way through the cast of characters in mysterious morality plays, only to learn that they and their lessons are components not of the outside world, but of ourselves.

Finally, some of the legends that appear in the pages that follow might leave you wondering, "What in the world made people want to repeat *that?*" Surely no dreamer has escaped the experience of awakening from a world that is not just different from the one encountered during the waking hours, but essentially impossible to decode.

Urban legends, like dreams, sometimes defy rational explanation. Both literal dreams and urban legends frequently inspire the betwixt-and-between emotional state best described as "This really happened—didn't it?" It is this common ground that causes experts to view urban legends as collective dreams—dreams that many people share.

Urban legends reflect our shared experiences, aspirations, and insecurities. Like dreams, they may be likened to a kind of "virtual reality" role-play exercise, in which strange ideas, flaws, dangers, and struggles are "tried on for size" as part of ongoing personal growth and development.

Legend Lingo

In C. G. Jung's 1927 work *The Structure of the Psyche*, he defined the **collective unconscious** as follows: "The collective unconscious—so far as we can say anything about it at all—appears to consist of mythological motifs or primordial images, for which reason the myths of all nations are its real exponents. In fact, the whole of mythology could be taken as a sort of projection of the collective unconscious."

Dreaming on Your Coffee Break

All three varieties of dream experience—the clear dream experience, the mysterious-but-engrossing one, and the one that leaves you just saying, "Huh?"—are valid. All three are worthy of honor and attention. That's true both in the individual realm (the dream that a single person experienced last night) and on the group level (the bizarre story attributed to a "friend of a friend" and shared with a co-worker during a coffee break this morning).

Are dreams "true"? In the sense that they reflect important conclusions and use potent symbols worthy of our attention, they certainly are. You would not, however, want to rely upon their literal interpretation when, say, developing a blueprint for a nuclear power plant during waking hours.

Are urban legends "true"? In the sense that they grab us by the scruff of the neck and make us look at—and work through—issues of importance, they certainly are. You

13

would not, however, want to base major (or minor!) life decisions on their literal, word-by-word "accuracy."

Strange but True

The desire to "nail down" the final meaning of a dream (or an urban legend) can be counterproductive. Some symbols are best allowed to float evocatively down the mental stream. Consider this observation from Jung: "The more the critical reason dominates, the more impoverished life becomes; but the more of the unconscious, and the more of myth we are capable of making conscious, the more of life we integrate. Overvalued reason has this in common with political absolutism: under its dominion the individual is pauperized" (*Memories, Dreams, Reflections,* Vintage Books, 1961).

Surrealism in Urban Legends

Jung's insistence on openness to "more of the unconscious" may be hard to understand at first. What he means is actually pretty simple: Attention to the implications of even the densely surrealistic imagery of dreams can be illuminating. For an example of such imagery in an urban legend, consider this story:

The Scuba Diver in the Treetop

If you think you're having a bad day ....

Fire authorities in California found a corpse in a burned-out section of forest while assessing the damage done by a forest fire. The deceased male was dressed in a full wetsuit, complete with a dive tank, flippers, and a face mask.

A post-mortem examination revealed that the person died not from burns, but from massive internal injuries. Dental records provided a positive identification. Investigators then set about determining how a fully clad diver ended up in the middle of a forest fire. It was revealed that, on the day of the fire, the person went for a diving trip off the coast—some 20 *miles* away from the forest.

The firefighters, seeking to control the fire as quickly as possible, called in a fleet of helicopters with very large buckets. The buckets were dropped into the ocean for rapid filling and then were flown to the forest fire and emptied. You guessed it! One minute our diver was making like Flipper in the Pacific, and the next he was doing a breaststroke in a fire bucket 300 meters in the air. Apparently, he extinguished exactly 1.78 meters (5 feet, 10 inches) of the fire.

Some days it just doesn't pay to get out of bed!

The diver-in-the-treetops story has no basis in fact, but it is still earnestly asserted on many fronts. It figured prominently in the opening sequence of Paul Thomas Anderson's 1999 movie masterpiece *Magnolia,* which starred Tom Cruise and Julianne Moore. Neither they nor the characters that they portrayed, however, ended up getting sucked into an airborne fire-prevention vehicle.

Salvador Dali, the preeminent *surrealist* painter, once asked why, when he ordered lobster in a restaurant, the waiter never returned with a flaming telephone book on a silver platter. Of course, waiters do show up with such orders in dreams—and urban legends do leave scuba divers who are minding their underwater business perched dead on treetops. From a certain point of view, such a legend is definitely about being sucked up in something that you can't understand or anticipate. But it is also about the perfect impossibility of its culminating image.

Legend Lingo

Surrealism is a style of art emphasizing the dreamlike juxtaposition of unlikely elements.

Archetypes in Urban Legends

Dreams feature archetypes, and so do many of the most memorable urban legends. Consider the following example, the plot of which centers on the prospect of being gobbled up by a vicious beastie.

This is a theme common (to give just two examples) to the book of Jonah in the Hebrew Bible (which tells of Jonah being swallowed by a "great fish") and the film *The Empire Strikes Back,* in which the Millennium Falcon mistakenly makes its way into the jaws of a huge space worm hidden within the heart of an asteroid.

So, swallowing monsters—on the golf course, no less ... is this a dream—or is it a nightmare? Read the story, and you decide!

Fable Facts

Archetypes common in modern urban legends include ghosts, corpses, and mad tricksters, all variants on the "shadow" figure. Jung argued that individuals share knowledge of such forms with the entire human race.

Unzipping Ole Mose

The first foursome of the day played together to the fifth hole, where one impatient golfer went ahead of the group. Thinking that the impatient golfer had finished without them and was waiting at the nineteenth hole, the remaining three weren't concerned with his absence. After waiting two hours for his return and finding his car still in the parking lot, the threesome notified the club. The search was on. Of course, the impatient golfer was not located, but his clubs were found on the seventh hole.

Three days later, Ole Mose was spotted on the seventh hole and was an immediate suspect. Ole Mose was an American crocodile that had been an infrequent course visitor for more than 20 years. Not too much concern was ever given to Ole Mose, who had always made a hasty retreat whenever he saw anyone coming. To make a long story even longer, the course officials, the SPCA, several lawyers, citizens groups, the mayor, the Palm Beach Police Department, and the American Crocodile Association of South Florida decided that to put everyone's mind at ease, Ole Mose should be unzipped.

Did it happen? Naaah. The e-mailed story concludes with a gruesome photograph, but the beast in question is a salt-water croc native to Borneo, not the fresh-water variety found in Florida. In dreamland, though, man-eating brutes lumber not in faraway lands, but along the local golf links, waiting to swallow someone whole—maybe you.

Fable Facts

"Vanishing hitchhiker" stories precede the automobile itself. Early versions of the story featured warnings from ghostly figures taken on as passengers on horses, wagons, and the like. The story appears to date back at least several centuries. For more on this fascinating complex of legends, see Jan Harold Brunvand's *The Vanishing Hitchhiker* (W.W. Norton, 1981).

Lessons in Urban Legends

Did you ever have one of those dreams that caused you to wake up certain of a change (big or small) that had to be made in your life?

The most notable dreams, according to Jung, contain not just random information, but important advice on how to live. The same is true of many urban legends. They use bold, sometimes startling and horrifying effects to draw our attention to warnings. In dreams, we are always in danger of overlooking critical lessons. Much the same thing can be said of many of the most popular urban legends.

Consider, for instance, the complex of legends involving the so-called "vanishing hitchhiker." In one of the most common variants of this story, a traveler picks up a hitchhiker (often a strikingly beautiful young woman) at a certain dangerous intersection. The traveler strikes up a conversation with his passenger, who assumes the back seat instead of sitting next to the driver. The young lady offers an address and convinces the driver to go out of his way to drop her off at her home.

The driver arrives at his passenger's home, turns to tell her goodbye, and sees that the back seat is empty. Mystified, he makes his way to the front door of the house and knocks on the door. The owner of the home opens the door, but the driver has hardly completed his story when the man at the door interrupts him.

The homeowner's daughter, we learn, is dead. She was killed at the very same intersection where the traveler picked her up. Her ghost now makes a habit of taking late-night travelers out of their way—the better, perhaps, to help them avoid her violent death.

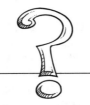

Strange but True

In some versions of the "vanishing hitchhiker" legend, the passenger is (or resembles) Jesus. This is perfectly appropriate, given the story's strong New Testament resonances. In the twenty-fourth chapter of the Gospel of Luke, Jesus makes a dreamlike appearance before two apostles. Jesus is not recognized. He journeys with them for a time, reveals secrets from the Holy Scriptures, and breaks bread with the two travelers. An awakening follows: "Then their eyes were opened, and they recognized him." Jesus vanishes.

A "Dream Outline"

The "vanishing hitchhiker" story, one of the most famous urban legends of them all, is an open-ended "dream outline" that has been used for centuries to warn innumerable listeners about innumerable hard-to-see dangers waiting just beyond the next curve.

It is both specific and universal, both a creation of the subconscious and (in each specific variant) a carefully conceived literary creation. Like many of the most compelling urban legends, it assumes a reality of its own—and expands to include what we most need it to mean the next time we tell it.

Warnings from Another Realm

The endlessly revised story of the "vanishing hitch-hiker" is often built around a specific (real) intersection of some nearby local thoroughfare. However, it also has been adapted to incorporate specific warnings "from beyond" about these topics:

➤ The outcome of military conflicts

➤ Forthcoming natural disasters

➤ Agricultural ups and downs (compare Joseph's interpretations of Pharaoh's dreams in the Book of Genesis)

➤ The end of the world

➤ And so on

On one level, the story is "about" whatever hazard, local or metaphysical, is specifically linked to the hitchhiker's visit. On another, it's fair to say that the story is also "about" listening to a voice from within our own psyche that has something important to say to us.

"Never Unequivocal"

In *Modern Man in Search of a Soul* (1933), Jung wrote that "(a) great work of art is like a dream; for all its apparent obviousness, it does not explain itself and is never unequivocal."

He was writing about works such as novels and paintings, but he might just as easily have been writing about those compelling true-yet-false stories that we can't seem to avoid telling each other over the water cooler at work.

Jung has been called a "rational mystic" because of his willingness to see virtually any intellectual process as a vehicle for encountering the authentic, informed voice of the unconscious. (See, for instance, his foreword to the superb Wilhelm/Baynes translation of the *I Ching*.) He would have had a field day with the legends that appear in this book.

The Least You Need to Know

➤ As you make your way through this book, consider the possibility of examining urban legends as though they were collective dreams built around shared challenges, concerns, and patterns of thought.

➤ The work of psychoanalyst Carl Jung has many applications to the study of urban legends.

➤ Surrealistic monsters populate urban legends just as they do ancient myths.

➤ Many urban legends feature dreamlike lessons from "beyond" the world of daily consciousness.

Chapter 3

Questions, Frequently Asked and Otherwise, About Urban Legends

In This Chapter

➤ Why they're called "urban" legends

➤ The lowdown on legends that are disgusting, lurid, or downright irresponsible

➤ The role of the Internet

➤ What constitutes folklore

➤ What you can do to check the accuracy of a story you've just heard

➤ Alphabet soup: IPJIEPTs

➤ Can a story be true—and still be an urban legend?

➤ Devices and motifs to watch for

Before you make your way into the main section of this book, you should get provisional answers (at least) to some of the most absorbing questions about urban legends.

Some of these questions are common. Others are likely to occur to you only after you've read or heard a couple thousand of these stories over a period of years. Questions in the second category are posed here, along with informed (if not necessarily definitive) answers. Why? Because the questions and their responses shed more light on the topic, because they may aid you in assessing what follows, and, well, because they've been on my mind.

What's So "Urban" About These Legends?

The best answer seems to be that the most familiar versions of the stories under discussion reflect themes, motifs, and obsessions consistent with a modern—and, by extension, presumably urban—sensibility. (Also relevant is the fact that storytelling itself has historically taken place in communal settings, which tend to be urban nowadays.)

One common story—shared in a later chapter for your reading pleasure—is about a (nonexistent) genetic research project adapted to fast-food production techniques. This kind of legend reflects an uncertainty about the excesses of modern technology.

Not many fast-food outlets are placed in the middle of a wheat field or in the secluded hollow of a meadow, right? So, it fits—kind of.

Actually, though, the settings are not *always* urban. Given the profusion of ominous dilemmas set in fast-food restaurants, multiplexes, and shopping-mall parking lots nowadays, you could argue that a far better name for this kind of story would be "*sub*urban legend." But that's not quite as catchy.

Another more thoughtful label to consider is "modern myth." Many folklore enthusiasts prefer this term. Your humble author is one of them. But because "urban legend" has caught on, that's the designation used here. (Hey, it's popular enough to have spawned a successful slasher-flick series; when in doubt, give the public what it wants.)

Fable Facts

Although the term "urban legend" is routinely applied to modern tales that circulate mysteriously, some of these stories are retellings of narratives that are centuries old.

Not for the Squeamish

There's no escaping the manipulative, excessive approach taken by many of these stories. There are a couple of possibilities to explain this tendency.

First, a classic preoccupation of the urban legend (and of folklore in general) is the establishment and perpetuation of social standards and rules. Sometimes, people with character flaws such as vanity, pride, or aggression violate these daily rules—or even flout fundamental *taboos* that we'd all like to think people would follow automatically. Many legends make sure that the violators receive their comeuppance in a way that emphasizes the corruption they've brought upon themselves and their loved ones.

Legend Lingo

A **taboo** (also **tabu**) is a fundamental proscription—forbiddance—of activities associated with uncleanness or corruption. Taboos against murder, incest, and adultery are common in most cultures. In its original sense, a taboo could also entail the prohibition of the use of sacred words or objects.

Second, people remember gross stuff. So, the legends that stick around and get told over and over again are often the ones that feature the most, well, memorable elements.

Third, there's a long and grand tradition of R-rated imagery in folk mythology to uphold. Much of what Americans think of as "mythology" is in fact quite sanitized. If you doubt this, pick up an unexpurgated copy of *Grimm's Fairy Tales* and read, say, the story of Faithful John. This heartwarming children's tale culminates with a king's decision to butcher his two children and smear Faithful John's stone image with their blood! Sure, the kids are put to rights again when the stone image springs magically to life … but only so they can be locked in a trunk for a time while the king plays a trick on his queen.

Back in those days, it was a tough gig being the child hero of a fairy tale.

Don't Believe It!

The most popular modern versions of classic folk tales like *Cinderella* generally aren't the "real thing." They tend to be sanitized versions of considerably franker, earthier stories.

Strange but True

Gross-out plot lines have been a part of folk mythology for as long as anyone can remember. Consider the unedited version of the Cinderella story: The vain, cruel stepsisters have their eyes plucked out by birds. Or, go even farther back: The haughty king Oedipus plucks out his *own* eyes when he realizes that he has married (and had children with) his own mother—and killed his father. Or, go farther back still: The goddess Athena is born from the head of her father, Zeus, with an assist from her brother-god Hephaestus, who helpfully grabbed his metal-working tools and used them to open up Dad's skull.

Plot Elements for Your Edification

Like fables of old, urban legends employ certain plot elements to make sure that everyone "gets" the point of the story. If you identify the elements, you'll know the moral (although you'll still want to read or hear the story, just for entertainment value).

Mirrors and Notes: Self-Revelation

These plot elements often highlight a moment of realization (usually none too pleasant) experienced by the central character in the story. Sometimes there's a mirror that *bears* a note written in, say, blood, or lipstick. This is the point at which everything in the story becomes clear—perhaps a little too clear.

Fable Facts

Notes and mirrors that serve as the "punch line" for urban legends may constitute dreamlike invitations to take a long, hard look at ourselves and our life choices. They appear to be analogous to the "moment of realization" in classical Greek tragedies such as *Oedipus Rex*.

Revenge and Comeuppance: Punishment

People make mistakes and pay heavy prices for those mistakes in some urban legends. In other legends, people make mistakes and *almost* pay heavily, often watching in horror as someone just like them gets the just dessert that they, too, had coming. (Somehow, the stories in the latter category tend to be more chilling.)

Kurt Vonnegut once remarked, "Revenge is the most powerful story of all." It's not surprising, then, that the stories we tell and retell and tell again often emphasize either the revenge of one human being taken out on another or the *prospect* of society taking out its dire revenge on someone whose errors in judgment recall our own.

Arbitrariness: A Random Universe

Punishment for a clear transgression is one thing. Some of these stories take people who haven't done *anything* (obviously) wrong and subject them to horrific mistreatment. What's up?

The real world, that's what. Fear of arbitrary, inexplicable runs of disastrously bad luck is a common preoccupation of urban legends. Bob Dylan once warned us all to look out because of "something" we did. God knows when we did it, but whatever it was, we're apparently doing it again—and again and again—in urban legends.

The Verification Paradox

If someone tracks down a verifiable account that seems to match the details of an urban legend, does that mean that the story isn't an urban legend anymore?

Not necessarily.

What it means is that the story *may* have been initiated by the actual event (assuming, of course, that the verified incident predates the first appearance of the legend). Finding out whether there's a clear cause-and-effect relationship between the two is the business of dedicated souls with vast reserves of patience, pluck, and (not infrequently) good fortune.

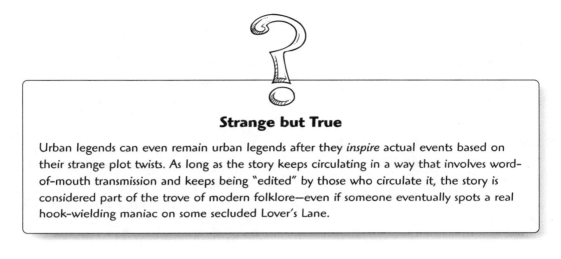

Strange but True

Urban legends can even remain urban legends after they *inspire* actual events based on their strange plot twists. As long as the story keeps circulating in a way that involves word-of-mouth transmission and keeps being "edited" by those who circulate it, the story is considered part of the trove of modern folklore—even if someone eventually spots a real hook-wielding maniac on some secluded Lover's Lane.

This kind of detective work may be fun, but it's actually not as relevant to the "is-it-a-legend-or-isn't-it?" question as many people imagine. Let's assume that, on the way to work this morning, I *see* you seduce a zebra in the middle of Grand Central Station. Let's assume, too, that I gather photos, mainstream news accounts, and signed affidavits from eyewitnesses proving that this event took place. Proof or no proof, people can (and probably would) keep telling the story to people they meet. They might do so for years into the future, altering details in the process.

A few years later, the story might hold that you seduced the zebra in the middle of Red Square in Moscow. Or that someone else seduced the zebra. Affidavits or no affidavits, the story would still be an example of contemporary folklore.

File the whole thing under *"true legend problem,"* and be done with it.

Modern Storytelling: Around the World in a Flash

There's a whole new species of legend to contend with: those that are circulated via World Wide Web sites or e-mail. As we've seen, these typically take the form of earnest "warnings" and "alerts" that have less to do with the real world than might at first appear to be the case.

Legend Lingo

The **true legend problem** arises when people assume (erroneously) that the term "urban legend" is always synonymous with the term "false." The vast majority of such legends are false—but that's a side point. If a story is still circulating and still undergoing popular revision, it's folklore.

Even when there's someone sitting at a keyboard composing or revising a legend, though, a lot of stuff stays the same:

Fable Facts

When people start spreading stories face to face, and changing or revising the stories as they do so, they've entered folklore territory, regardless of where they heard the stories in the first place.

➤ For the legend to circulate, it must touch on a common concern or insecurity of the audience it reaches.

➤ When people read an e-mail or Web "warning" or "alert," they're very likely not only to forward the legend to others via the Internet, but also to talk about it with the people in their circle of friends and acquaintances. As they do so, they're likely to revise, expand, or alter the message, perhaps without even realizing that they're doing it.

➤ In passing along the stories, both teller and listener "work through" the problem raised—obscurely or otherwise—in the story.

Strange but True

These days, lots of people make up stories out of whole cloth and unleash those stories on the world via the Internet. These circulators of carefully crafted bits of Internet paranoia don't provide any helpful advice for dealing with the "crises" that they identify. They do, however, provide an opportunity for people to address fears in a given area and move forward in their lives by internalizing and processing the myth. This doesn't make Internet rumormongers public servants, of course. Much of what gets circulated via e-mail is inflammatory and downright irresponsible. Nevertheless, it's interesting to notice *which bits* of inflammatory, irresponsible storytelling are seized upon and circulated by the online community—and turned into dinner-table conversation for the world at large.

How Can You Find the Truth on the Internet?

Yeah, yeah, yeah—insecurity, taboos, processing, "working through," purgation, social boundaries. It's all very interesting, but there's a point to address that's a little more immediate. If *you* get a heart-stopping e-mail message, how can *you* determine whether it's legit and worthy of being circulated to everyone on your personal "cc" list?

The very act of posing such a question makes you a good citizen of the Internet. Pose it frequently, and see Chapter 24, "Some Final Thoughts," for a list of sites and newsgroups that you can check to get the latest on the ever-expanding list of Internet legends, frauds, and hoaxes.

What the World Doesn't Need Now Is More IPJIEPTs

One final plea before we leave the subject of the Internet. This takes the form of a deposit in the Good Karma Bank: Please, please, please don't let anything that follows in this book persuade you to launch an IPJIEPT of your own. (That's my acronym for Internet Practical Jokes in Exceedingly Poor Taste, of which there are many examples online.)

Leave that to the knuckleheads who perversely delight in getting folks worked up with bogus charitable efforts for sick kids, racist rumormongering, and unwarranted assaults on the hard-won reputations of successful businesses.

Why Bother with Any of This?

Impossible conspiracies. Lunatic coverups of events that never took place. Fantastic horror stories are being circulated, and probably will continue to be circulated as long as humans endure on this planet without listeners asking questions like these:

➤ Do any of these stories actually *matter*?

➤ Is there any point in cataloging group hallucinations?

➤ Isn't this a waste of time and effort?

The conclusion that urban legends actually *do* matter, and that discussing them is a worthwhile endeavor, tends to come later. It is based on two major realizations.

Realization No. 1: The Stories Are Pretty Entertaining

Sometimes urban legends are hilarious. Sometimes they're disgusting. Sometimes they're terrifying. Sometimes they're a mixture of all three. But one thing that the most persistent urban legends *aren't* is boring. These stories stick around for a reason: They hold people's attention. For that reason alone, they're worth comparing and discussing.

Realization No. 2: They're Not About Us ... But They Are About Us

The process of working through fear and anxiety is constructive (and revealing) in and of itself. When we examine urban legends closely, we realize that some of them strike a nerve. We know that they're bogus. We know that they don't "matter" in the way that a news story on the front page of the *New York Times* "matters." But for some reason, a particular story keeps coming to mind again and again. Suddenly we realize that, even though the tale is "false" and has "nothing to do" with us, it contains important symbolic elements that we must need to examine on some deep level.

I'm not going to bore you by telling you which of the bizarre stories that follow left *me* feeling that way. I'm just going to guess that you'll have a similar reaction.

Good luck. And have fun at that next therapy appointment.

The Least You Need to Know

➤ Urban legends are really a form of modern mythology.

➤ Steel yourself for legends that are disgusting, lurid, or downright irresponsible when presented as literal fact.

➤ The Internet has affected the way urban legends are now developed and circulate.

➤ The Internet also gives you a way to check the veracity of stories that you're not sure about.

➤ Although most urban legends are false, falsehood is *not* a requirement for a story entering the realm of folklore.

Part 2
Famous Figures

Herbert Beerbohm Tree once observed, "The only man who wasn't spoiled by being lionized was Daniel." Yet if celebrities are often spoiled by their fame, they must from time to time be utterly mystified by the urban legends that they inspire.

The subjects of the following stories are famous folk who probably weren't all that flattered by the bizarre stories that mysteriously started circulating about them—and kept circulating as though powered by the Energizer Bunny. Some of the protagonists in question had passed to the Great Beyond when we started saying strange things about them. The rest—unlucky as they were—had to put up with enduring mass hallucinations and constant questioning about why they did things that they never did—like, for instance, pass on to the Great Beyond. (Just ask Paul McCartney.)

Chapter 4

Is Paul Dead? (and Other Burning Pop Music Questions)

In This Chapter

➤ The "clues" regarding Paul McCartney's "death" that are supposedly scattered throughout the Fab Four's post-1966 recordings and jacket art

➤ The Beatles' role in the development of the "Paul's dead" legend

➤ Elvis Presley "sightings"

➤ Jim Morrison's "suspicious" death

➤ More than you probably wanted to know about Mr. Greenjeans

In the fall of 1968, did John Lennon mutter, "Paul is dead, man, miss him, miss him," into an Abbey Road microphone while recording *The White Album?* Did the Beatles include intentional visual symbolism within their albums to suggest that McCartney had collected his eternal reward—and been surreptitiously replaced by a double? Or did millions of Beatles fans around the world just go a little nuts?

In the annals of popular music, no urban legend has proved to be more enduring, more intricately debated, and (at least to Beatlemaniacs) more fascinating than this one. The tale of Paul McCartney's supposed death and replacement by a clone within the Fab Four refuses to go away. For most observers, though, the pertinent question isn't "Is Paul McCartney dead?" but "Where on earth did this story come from?"

That's a pretty interesting question, as it turns out. In this chapter, we'll look closely at the obsession that was (and is) known colloquially as Paul Is Dead, as well as some other strange rumors about other pop stars that have become nearly as popular over time.

Fable Facts

The precise origins of the Paul Is Dead obsession appear to date from the late 1960s and must have come about after the release of the *Sgt. Pepper* album. (That's the first treasure trove of "clues.") Beatles experts are still debating the date of the first appearance of the myth.

Fable Facts

Many figures in popular culture have been the subject of false death rumors. See the Jerry Mathers urban legend that appears in Chapter 8, "Other Celebrity Legends That Sound Too Weird to Be True (and Are)."

The Mother of All Rock-and-Roll Urban Legends

Let's begin with the biggie among rock's urban legends—the one that virtually everyone who enjoys the music of the Beatles has, at the very least, heard of. To this day, this mass hallucination-meets-parlor-game attracts a huge number of passionate adherents.

The controversy (if that's the proper word) surrounding Paul McCartney's "demise" was initially just one of one of those bizarre but not at all uncommon press events in which a celebrity must reassure a mistaken reporter or two that he is indeed still among the living. These come up all the time.

In our own era, baseball great Joe DiMaggio had the unnerving experience of watching a television network flash a bulletin that he had passed on to the Great Beyond. He issued a terse denial. Mark Twain had a similar problem when a newspaper ran his obituary prematurely. He laid the issue to rest with a now-famous custom-built quip: "Reports of my death have been greatly exaggerated."

What *is* uncommon is for the celebrity's denial to result in *more* rather than less anguished questioning about his or her death. When the first wave of the speculation around the supposed Paul Is Dead clues reached a fever pitch, McCartney felt obliged to emerge from a brief hiatus in Scotland. He issued a statement, updating the Twain remark, in an attempt to reassure nervous fans that he was still very much above ground.

He may have thought that would be the end of the matter. It wasn't.

Three Mysteries (Not Four)

Thirty-plus years on, people are still putting Beatles album photos under magnifying glasses and listening to songs backward. The McCartney death legend boasts a seemingly endless popularity, as evidenced by postings of Talmudic length and complexity posted on any number of Beatles-oriented World Wide Web sites. The story's hardiness seems to be attributable to its unique "triple-mystery" structure; this structure gives fans lots to theorize about—and urban legend sleuths lots to debunk.

Basically, the Paul Is Dead nonsense—er, mystery—boils down to three fundamental questions, each of which has been fodder for hardcore fans since the late 1960s. The issues that Beatles fans have been wrestling with for three decades are these:

1. Do "clues" suggesting McCartney's demise really appear in the Beatles songs and album jackets?

2. If so, did the Beatles place these hints deliberately?

3. If not, what gives? How did the "clues" get there? Were they all examples of coincidence?

A fourth "mystery"—"Was Paul McCartney actually decapitated or otherwise dispatched to the hereafter in an auto accident in 1966?"—can be safely disregarded.

Strange but True

In interviews, Ringo Starr has attributed the earliest reports of the Paul Is Dead rumor to American disk jockeys. This would make sense, inasmuch as they would have been likelier than the average college student to have the tape equipment necessary to play bits of Beatles music backwards.

Three and a Half Decades in the Life (or, We Read the News Today, Oh, Boy)

For those requiring an update, the "cute Beatle's" post-1966 agenda has been pretty full. It has included a prolific second half with the most successful rock group in recording history; a stormy breakup and exit from said band; a *second* career establishing McCartney as one of the most successful solo artists in recording history; and, among many, many other things, knighthood.

Much of this post-1966 activity occurred in front of witnesses, including skeptical journalists, business associates, music industry insiders, politicians, tens of thousands of paying concertgoers, and the Queen of England. At least a few of these people, it is safe to assume, were capable of spotting a phony McCartney at close range.

All of this post-1966 activity occurred while the world press was poised to report everything of interest (and, indeed, much that was dull) about each of the Fabs. If

there were *anything* remotely factual about the world's Paul-as-clone compulsion, aside from its status as interesting party chatter, rest assured that you would have heard about it by now.

Here's the bottom line: If Paul McCartney's life since the Johnson Administration has been conducted by a cunningly selected double from Central Casting, I will buy you a drink. But that doesn't have to keep us from talking about the moped crash that started this fascinating story, which has emerged as one of the most intriguing and longest-running urban legends of them all.

Truth Is More Drab Than Legend: The Moped Accident

The Paul Is Dead (or *PID,* among those in the know) phenomenon did in fact arise from a 1966 Beatles-related vehicular accident, but not the gruesome auto crash so frequently alluded to. The mode of conveyance was far more modest, and the outcome was considerably less grisly. According to Ian MacDonald's fine book *Revolution in the Head* (Henry Holt, 1995), McCartney, who was out riding with a friend while high on marijuana, crashed his moped and sustained minor injury.

However, he was soon up and about doing distinctly Beatle-y things (such as growing his *Sgt. Pepper*–era mustache and recording "Penny Lane"). Word about the accident eventually got out, and fans started talking about Something Ominous Having Happened.

Who Blew Whose Mind Out in a Car?

It's tempting to conclude that the emerging legend—which began circulating around the time the *Abbey Road* LP was released in 1969—was influenced by the earlier Beatles song "A Day in the Life." This landmark tune was based in part on a January 1967 newspaper account of the death of Tara Browne, a rich young acquaintance of the Beatles. (Browne, who may or may not have been under the influence of hallucinogens at the time, ran a red light in his sports car and hit a van.) The lines about someone having blown his mind out in a car were frequently cited as somehow referring to McCartney.

The First Mystery: So Many Clues

Here is a (nonexhaustive) list of images, verbal references, and sonic manipulations that Beatles fans have cited over the years in support of the Paul Is Dead legend. There's probably enough of this stuff out there to fill a whole book this size, but these 15 items are the most commonly cited pieces of "evidence."

1. The band is arranged as though for a funeral on the cover of the *Sgt. Pepper* album. (Note the eerie presence of somber "early Beatles" wax figures on the left.)

2. McCartney appears with his back turned on the reverse of the *Sgt. Pepper* album.

3. McCartney's band uniform is emblazoned with the ominous legend "O.P.D.," interpreted as "Officially Pronounced Dead."

4. Lennon mutters something that sounds like "I buried Paul" at the conclusion of "Strawberry Fields Forever."

5. Someone says "bury my body" near the end of "I Am the Walrus."

6. McCartney wears a black carnation, while the other three Fabs sport red ones, during the "Your Mother Should Know" sequence of the film *Magical Mystery Tour;* a photo of the incriminating sequence is reproduced on the soundtrack album sleeve.

7. Lennon includes a confusing, vaguely menacing "the walrus was Paul" clue in the *White Album* track "Glass Onion."

8. Starr hints coyly at decapitation and car crashes in the *White Album* track "Don't Pass Me By."

9. Lennon mumbles incomprehensibly at the conclusion of the *White Album* track "I'm So Tired." Played backward, the passage sounds like "Paul is dead, man, miss him, miss him."

10. When played backward, Lennon's chaotic *White Album* track "Revolution 9" sounds like "Turn me on, dead man."

11. McCartney appears barefoot on the cover of *Abbey Road,* supposedly mirroring an Italian practice of burying corpses without shoes.

Legend Lingo

Beatles fans referring to "the O.P.D. patch" are talking about insignia that Paul sports on his day-glo *Sgt. Pepper* uniform. It was thought by many to stand for "Officially Pronounced Dead." (Actually, it stands for "Ontario Police Department.")

12. If that's enough for you to accept McCartney as a dead body, then you probably already noticed that the other three Beatles represent members of a funeral party: Harrison (in blue jeans and a work shirt) as the gravedigger; Starr (in black) as the mourner; and Lennon (in white) as the officiant.

13. McCartney is out of step with the other three Beatles on cover of *Abbey Road.*

14. A car (presumably representing the one that struck McCartney) is pictured as speeding off into the distance in the very lane that Paul occupies—to his peril!—on the cover of *Abbey Road.* Bear in mind that the photo was shot in England, where people drive on the left.

15. Immediately behind Paul on the *Abbey Road* cover is a white Volkswagen Beetle bearing the license plate 28 IF, indicating that McCartney would have been 28 had he lived until 1969, the year of the record's release.

Paul Is Alive, Man ...

It's true. Each and every one of the 15 items just cited (with the intriguing exception of no. 7—more about that later) really was a coincidence. You want specifics? Here you go ....

By 1967, the Beatles had stopped touring. They wanted, among other things, to announce a change in direction with their new album—hence the inclusion of the "old" Beatles on the *Sgt. Pepper* cover, along with many, many other influences. The image as a whole is meant to evoke a gathering in a park—after a performance of Sgt. Pepper's band—for one of those circa 1900–style group photographs. If those trippy uniforms and that Mae West wax figure say "funeral" to you, feel free to take another hit off the bong.

Strange but True

The "bury my body sequence" is a taped excerpt of a BBC performance of *King Lear* that fades in and out of the conclusion to "I Am the Walrus." If you're interested in following along at home, you can find the scene in your collected Shakespeare and track it as it wafts through the mix. The scene in question is Act Four, Scene Four. According to Mark Hertsgaard's book *A Day in the Life,* the performance happened to be on the radio on a night when Lennon was in the studio recording the song.

As for Paul's turned back, Lennon always insisted in interviews that his former partner had a peculiar habit of finding *some* way to stand out in many of the group's photographs. The rear cover of *Pepper* (like the black carnation and the bare feet in the later album photographs) seems to bear this idea out.

It's worth noting in support of Lennon's claim that a widely distributed early photo of the group during its lovable-moptop period includes Paul—and only Paul—smoking a cigarette. John was frequently paranoid, but he may have had a point here.

The various mumblings-as-ominous-clues examples don't hold water, either. That strange stuff at the end of "I'm So Tired" is just John trying to sound as though he's not quite awake. (He succeeds.)

Strange but True

At least one Beatles record features a real hidden message. Upon the "reunion" release of the John Lennon composition *Free as a Bird* by the three surviving Beatles in 1996, reporters around the world announced—accurately—that they had discovered an *actual* backward message to Beatles fans. At the conclusion of the track, a computer-reconstructed version of Lennon's own voice can be heard saying, "Made for John Lennon." Played backward, the snippet yields Lennon saying, "Turned out nice again, didn't it?"

The "I buried Paul" remark never even existed. The release of the second *Beatles Anthology* CD features a crystal-clear version of the same section, unobscured by a fadeout, that is clearly recognizable as "cranberry sauce," not "I buried Paul." Note, too, that Lennon was big on putting meaningless things into Beatles records. The game began at least as early as 1964, when he hid the sound of barking dogs in the fadeout of the group's hit song "I Feel Fine."

The "number nine" snippet was part of an old EMI tape that Lennon appropriated for his sound collage. The fact that it sounds like something else when you play it backward is one of those strange but not particularly meaningful coincidences that people tend to celebrate when they've had too much mescaline.

As for the "bury my body" business, that's part of a British Broadcasting Corporation broadcast of *King Lear* that the band saw fit to mix in and out of the tumultuous conclusion of "I Am the Walrus." So unless Shakespeare had the foresight to be in on the gag in 1608 ....

What About the Album Covers?

All—repeat, all—of the supposedly ominous visuals on the *Abbey Road* cover are the inventions of fans with overactive imaginations.

The tantalizing 28 IF car is particularly inconvenient for Paul Is Dead proponents, as it should read 27 IF, given McCartney's actual date of birth. The photographer, Iain MacMillan, laughingly dismissed the contention that any sublayer of symbolism appears on the album cover. It's four guys walking across the street outside their recording studio, wearing whatever they happened to be wearing that day. One of them, known to enjoy attention, took off his shoes beforehand. That's it.

The Second Mystery: Was It Intentional?

We come now to the most interesting question pertaining to the whole Paul Is Dead business. Did the Beatles contrive all this silliness? The answer is no, with one fascinating qualifier. (See the third mystery that follows.)

Strange but True

At the height of the first wave of Paul Is Dead hysteria, UPI reported that a Florida acoustic analyst had determined that the McCartney voice on certain early Beatles recordings did not match the McCartney voice on certain later Beatles recordings. Left unexplored was the question of whether the engineer had taken into account the varispeeding and other studio trickery common on post–*Rubber Soul* Beatles records.

All four Beatles earnestly maintained that the rumor was entirely the creation of fans with a lot of time on their hands to turn innocuous recording details and graphic extracts into "clues." The best reason to believe them: You can "prove," just as persuasively, that each of the other Beatles was replaced by a stand-in. Consider, for instance, the telltale "I may be asleep" vocal from George on the funereal "Blue Jay Way." Or the somber *black* turtleneck sported by the wax Ringo dummy on the cover of *Sgt. Pepper*. (The other three Fab waxwork likenesses on the cover sport proper shirts and ties.) Or the fact that Lennon mutters "shoot me" ominously (and, alas, prophetically) during the opening seconds of "Come Together."

Lennon, as usual, had the most pragmatic assessment of the whole phenomenon. In 1969, when pressed for a comment about the rumor, he observed that "Paul McCartney *couldn't* die without the world knowing it ... he can't go on holiday without the world knowing it. It's just insanity. But it's a great plug for *Abbey Road*."

Strange but True

In an interview, John Lennon dismissed the Paul Is Dead hysteria as "made up" (presumably by someone other than the Beatles) and complained about people who "have nothing better to do than study Bibles and make myths about it, and study rocks." He never, however, appears to have discussed the group's role in inspiring such phenomena, which was indirect but significant. For a brilliant analysis of how the Beatles' dalliance with self-referential songwriting and "random" creative exercises appealed to the predominant "clash between logical/literal and intuitive/lateral thinking" of the late 1960s and early 1970s, see Ian MacDonald's *Revolution in the Head*, one of the best books ever written about the group.

The Third Mystery: Was Paul the Walrus?

That leaves us with just one major unexplained "clue"—the strange lyric in "Glass Onion" about Paul being the Walrus.

Leaving aside the usual doubletalk about the walrus symbolizing death in some foreign land, one has to ask, "What the heck is this doing on the record?" What were they getting at? Why go to the trouble of including such a line at all?

The answer is both simple and complicated.

The simple answer: Lennon wanted to acknowledge his partner's efforts in holding the group together between 1966 and 1968, when *The White Album* was released. (He conceded this in post-breakup interviews.)

The walrus reference was a way to salute McCartney's many contributions and organizational efforts in a suitably vague, self-referential style. This made a certain amount of sense, given that "Glass Onion" is an ambiguous Beatles song about, um, other ambiguous Beatles songs. One of these, "I Am the Walrus," was, of course, a creative high-water mark for Lennon.

Now for the complicated answer: Ever since the release of *Revolver,* the Beatles had inclined toward obscurity and "random" elements in their recorded output, their public posturings, and their album designs. To put it plainly, they sometimes enjoyed playing games with and confusing their audience.

Quite often, this purposeful ambiguity yielded spectacular compositions, such as "A Day in the Life" and "Come Together." Yet this approach also had the effect of inviting people to find whatever significance they chose in the group's work. The Paul Is Dead phenomenon is just one example of such meaning-searching obsession run amok. Tragically (considering the manner of Lennon's death in 1980), it is not the most extreme example.

Other Urban Legends About Pop Stars

The strange, persistent history of Paul McCartney's "death" illustrates a larger principle that we would all do well to observe. If you want to be absolutely sure that no one ever says anything dumb about you, do yourself a favor and stay out of the rock-star business.

So for your reading pleasure, here are a few of the more outlandish urban legends that have arisen from the contemporary music scene.

Fable Facts

The tabloid newspaper *Weekly World News* has contributed to the nation's long-running chain of Elvis sightings by providing many vivid accounts of close encounters with the King. Each new, fascinating, and journalistically suspect account of Presley's reappearance has been carefully targeted to a readership that relies on supermarket checkouts for its news—or its entertainment.

Did Elvis Presley Really Die?

This one represents the flip side of the McCartney myth. Instead of obsessing over the death of a live rock star, fans obsess that a genuinely dead one may be walking among the living.

Did Elvis Presley really move on to that Great Vegas Gig in the Sky? Yep. Presley died in August 1977 after a period of sustained and massive abuse of prescription drugs.

A cynic might note here that this is the man Richard Nixon appealed to as a role model for America's youth during early days of the government's war on drug abuse. Your humble author, however, has nary a cynical bone in his body, and so will simply return to the point that Presley died in 1977—and stayed dead in all subsequent years.

That fact, however, hasn't stopped countless Elvis fans from reporting the King's post-1977 activities. As part of a national "can-you-top-this" game that has elevated the King to mythical (or is it pseudoreligious?) status, Elvis has been "sighted" (or nearly sighted) while ...

➤ Cruising through a service station in Chattanooga, Tennessee in his black Oldsmobile Aurora.

➤ Sipping coffee in an upper room in Graceland, in "an area forbidden to tourists." (The parallel with the Last Supper is perhaps too obvious to be belabored, but I'll note it for the record anyway.)

➤ Acting as silent benefactor to an entire town in rural Mississippi.

➤ Performing at a wedding reception for two lucky Elvis-obsessed fans.

➤ Providing sperm for artificial insemination at an unnamed Southern fertility clinic.

If you are so inclined, you can find a lot of this kind of stuff on the World Wide Web under the category *E.S.P.C.C.* (for "Elvis Sightings, Paranormal, and Conspiracy Claims."). Such surfing, though, can certainly yield an interesting comparison of obsessive fan bases. Quentin Tarantino was right: You will never mistake a Beatles fan for an Elvis fan.

What does that mean? Well, none of the Elvis-is-still-among-us material on the Internet evidences the exciting pseudological rigor with which Paul Is Dead sleuths cite their endless stream of sources, theories, and "evidence."

Make no mistake. Both camps can come across as half a bubble off center. The Paul Is Dead believers, though, tend to write as though they're trying to impress a particularly demented college professor. The Elvis Is Alive faithful, on the other hand, write as though they have been traumatized by years of living in the constant, numbing fear of losing their electric hookups at the trailer park.

The ultimate Elvis "sighting" has to be the one that blazes the trail for a whole new genre: A dead pop star is really alive *and yet also* really dead. Bob Meyer's *Compendium of Elvis Sightings* informs us breathlessly:

> Jeff P. (not his real name) works at the city morgue in Washington, D.C. Two years ago, a man presumed to be Elvis was found dead in a used car lot. Instead of going through the usual identification process, the body mysteriously disappeared only an hour after its arrival [at] the morgue. When Jeff asked his supervisor about the disappearance, he was advised to "Forget about it …."

Legend Lingo

E.S.P.C.C. refers to "Elvis Sightings, Paranormal, and Conspiracy Claims," a category embracing a whole school of thought on the Internet. By entering these words in your favorite search engine, you may be able to track down Gail Brewer-Giorgio's book *The Elvis Files: Was His Death Faked?* (SPI Books, 1997) and Peter Eicher's book *The Elvis Sightings* (Avon, 1993).

Now, this may come as a huge surprise, but tracking down authors or witnesses to any of this stuff turns out to be a thankless and impossible task. Who is Jeff P., the morgue employee who saw Elvis's corpse? Don't bother trying to find out. The Powers That Be have apparently driven him into hiding.

By the same token, if you attempted to e-mail the woman who reported the strange goings-on in the upper room at Graceland, your message would bounce back to you within minutes. If you tried to visit the Web site that features "very convincing photographs" of the King performing at a wedding reception on September 14, 1996, you'd find a suspiciously dead link.

Still, you get the feeling that the truth about Elvis is out there. You develop an instinct, after you read enough of this stuff, that if you decided to wait faithfully for the King's black Oldsmobile to cruise through the service station in your own hometown, you would eventually attain deliverance. Or achieve remission for your sins. Or have 24-hour access to reruns of *The Andy Griffith Show*. Or something.

Did Jim Morrison Really Die?

Dead pop star isn't really dead after all, volume II: On July 3, 1971, legendary singer Jim Morrison was found dead in the bathtub of his Paris apartment. It was a stunning loss to the music world—and the best career move that Morrison ever made.

So many myths about Morrison's last days have been promulgated that obsessed fans of the Lizard King can pretty much take their pick. He faked his death and headed to Africa. He overdosed on heroin. He was assassinated by French intelligence. He had an advanced venereal disease. He had cancer. He drank himself to death. He went to Graceland to give the King pointers on escaping the clutches of demanding hordes of fans.

Okay, I made that last one up. But the rest of this has been earnestly and passionately maintained by various hordes of Morrison maniacs. What is known for sure is that Morrison is dead, that he is buried in Paris, and that no autopsy or police report has ever materialized. It seems most likely that his girlfriend, Pamela Courson, and/or the French medical examiner whom she appealed to, instituted an amateur news blackout, wary of the inevitable media storm. That ham-handed maneuver eventually invited fans who were inclined to smell some kind of rat to spread the word about various Dark Conspiracies and Mysterious Sightings.

Over the years, fans have certainly risen to the opportunity. One of the current Doors Web sites encourages visitors to pipe up if they've "seen Jim Morrison

Fable Facts

Oliver Stone's movie *The Doors* refrained from positing a convoluted series of conspiracies to explain singer Jim Morrison's death. Given the director's paranoid, quasihistorical, and utterly irresponsible account of the Kennedy assassination in the popular film *JFK*, this omission may have come as a disappointment to some Stone fans.

walking down the street." By all accounts, this appears to be a fairly common claim. Are such apparitions evidence of a massive hoax or of Morrison's supernatural status? Break on through to the other side to find out ....

Was Frank Zappa Related to Mr. Greenjeans?

The mistaken notion that Frank Zappa's father was the actor who played Mr. Greenjeans on the original *Captain Kangaroo* children's TV program appears to have arisen from a Zappa song title. The track "Son of Mr. Green Genes" appears on the offbeat rocker's classic album *Hot Rats*. (Can you imagine what fans would have come up with if he'd called the song "Son of Jim Morrison"?) Anyway, the late, great Zappa was in no way related to any member of the *Captain Kangaroo* cast or crew. There—one less mystery to lose sleep over.

With the breezy freedom from logic or sequentiality that typifies fast-moving urban legends, this tale eventually evolved into one claiming that rocker Ted Nugent was sired by Mr. Greenjeans. Prediction: The next twist is that Mr. Greenjeans, by an improbable twist of genetic fate, is revealed to be his own father and to have taken Paul McCartney's place in the Beatles in 1966. (See him there in the white Beetle on the cover of *Abbey Road?*)

Stay tuned—and keep on rocking.

The Least You Need to Know

➤ Don't worry—Paul isn't dead.

➤ Do bear in mind, though, that there are lots of pseudoclues to the contrary that have consumed the time of countless obsessive Beatles fans.

➤ In evaluating these clues, consider that the Beatles' own fondness for ambiguity and complex internal references may have had something to do with the popularity of this urban legend.

➤ Neither Elvis nor Jim Morrison is going to pull up in your driveway in a black Oldsmobile Aurora while on the run from French intelligence.

➤ Neither Frank Zappa nor Ted Nugent sprang from the loins of the actor who played Mr. Greenjeans.

Chapter 5

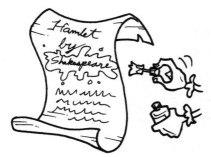

Did Shakespeare Write Shakespeare?

In This Chapter

➤ Everything your high school English teacher never told you about the Shakespearean authorship dispute

➤ The resolution of the "mystery" regarding who wrote the plays and poems

➤ The evidence relating to Edward de Vere, the seventeenth Earl of Oxford

➤ The evidence relating to Francis Bacon

➤ Why the controversy continues

We come next to a seemingly endless debate: the supposed "mystery" regarding the authorship of the writings attributed to William Shakespeare.

Is this an urban legend? This dispute differs in some notable ways from stories easily classified as "classic" urban myths. For instance, there is no single story line focusing on someone who is punished for transgressing the rules of the social order, and there is precious little in the way of humor or terror. (There is, of course, plenty of humor and terror in plays like *Richard III* and *King Lear,* but that's another story.)

However, the conflict is pretty entertaining when considered on its own terms. And like the best urban legends, it simply refuses to go away.

"Wherefore Art Thou, Walrus?"

Here's one good reason to look closely at the argument: The "did-Shakespeare-write-Shakespeare?" debate sometimes resembles nothing so much as a passionate argument about the cover imagery of Abbey Road among a particularly erudite gathering of Beatles fans. What's more, this long-running standoff, unlike the Paul Is Dead phenomenon, has continued to inspire heated discussions about the actual status of the person at the heart of the discussion.

In other words, most Beatles fans don't seriously believe that McCartney is dead. Yet a fair number of prominent people over the years (Sigmund Freud and Charlie Chaplin, for instance) have signed on to the idea that Shakespeare was a "front" for someone else—someone who didn't want the true authorship of the plays and poems to be discovered. That view remains fairly common today.

The presence of a chapter in this book about the ongoing authorship debate is based on the following interesting overlaps with other stories that fit into the category of urban legend:

Legend Lingo

Anti-Stratfordianism is the school of thought holding that someone other than William Shakespeare of Stratford-on-Avon wrote the plays and poems commonly attributed to him.

➤ The central contention is not true. (Partisans for the various candidates are, of course, free to disagree; open-minded readers are invited to judge the points discussed in this chapter for themselves.)

➤ People love to repeat and offer variations on the contention anyway.

➤ The myth has persisted. (For years, Shakespearean scholars have wistfully observed that being accosted about Bacon or the Earl of Oxford at cocktail parties must simply be accepted as a tiresome, long-term occupational hazard.)

So What's All the Fuss About?

Few subjects in English literature arouse quite the variety of sound and fury generated by the Shakespearean authorship debate. The identity of the "actual" author varies depending on the *anti-Stratfordian* you're reading or talking to. The two most commonly cited candidates are Edward de Vere, the seventeenth Earl of Oxford, and Francis Bacon, a philosopher, essayist, and politician of the era. (A side note: If you're looking for evidence of the decline of civility among supposedly intelligent people, all you have to do is log on to one or two of the Internet Web sites and bulletin boards focusing on this debate.)

The many versions of the anti-Stratfordian argument defy brief—or even extended—summary. The most common claims, that Edward de Vere or Francis Bacon wrote the works attributed to Shakespeare, are addressed in this chapter. For a look at the debates concerning other candidates, log on to the newsgroup humanities.lit.authors. shakespeare, where various authorship issues are discussed heatedly and in detail.

So, let's get down to business. A remarkably large number of books and essays have been written over the last 80 or so years defending the idea that William Shakespeare from Stratford-on-Avon, who was the son of the glover John Shakespeare, did not write the works that history has associated with him.

The "Looney Argument" and Other Challenges

The dispute began when one J. Thomas Looney (and, yes, that was his real name) put forth a work entitled *"Shakespeare" Identified* in 1920. In it, he argued that Edward de Vere, the seventeenth earl of Oxford (1550–1604), was the true author of Shakespeare's works, and he offered what appeared to be a number of biographical parallels between Oxford's life and the events of the plays.

Other candidates proposed over the years have included the politician, writer, and politician Sir Francis Bacon; the playwright Christopher Marlowe; Queen Elizabeth; the playwright Thomas Heywood; and a number of other contemporaries. Over the years, the most sustained arguments have surrounded the candidacy of Oxford, followed at some distance by that of Bacon.

In this chapter, the focus is on these two men and on the question, "Is there anything to these rumors?" The answer is pretty straightforward.

No.

Fable Facts

Although the renowned playwright Christopher Marlowe has occasionally been mentioned as a candidate as the "true" author of Shakespeare's plays, his death in 1593 presents what might charitably be called a major obstacle to his partisans. Most of Shakespeare's greatest plays were composed after this date.

Fable Facts

Despite reams of evidence to the contrary, seemingly intelligent people continue to maintain that an elaborate conspiracy concealed the true authorship of the plays attributed to Shakespeare. The great essayist, poet, lexicographer, and Shakespearean scholar Samuel Johnson wrote, "Many falsehoods are passing into uncontradicted history." He wasn't writing about the Shakespearean "authorship debate," but he might as well have been.

Fable Facts

Interestingly, the debate over authorship always seems to divide into two groups, with the Stratfordian side attracting far more people with academic credentials than the anti-Stratfordian side. Draw your own conclusions.

We're talking about a clear-cut "No," too. But you'd never guess that from the average response to the Shakespeare authorship controversy.

In fact, many people who know virtually nothing else about Shakespeare "know" that his plays may have been written by somebody else. And many people who know a whole *lot* about the plays in question get downright touchy when you ask them to supply some form of hard proof for their contentions.

The result: Some, but by no means all, mainstream Shakespeare scholars have simply *stopped* asking anti-Stratfordians to supply proof about anything. In fact, the scholars try to skip this subject whenever humanly possible. They don't do this because they are afraid that their arguments won't stand logical scrutiny. They do this primarily because they're tired of getting yelled at about something that, in their view, isn't a real academic debate and, as such, doesn't matter very much.

"Thou'rt Mad to Say It!" "Nay—'Tis Thou Who'rt Mad!"

Anyone who has followed this debate for a while can tell you that it has an interesting way of degenerating into name-calling. Some of the name-calling can get fairly energetic.

Because the "authorship mystery" has inspired such intense feeling over the years, and because your humble author has no particular interest in entering the fray with individual partisans, the following points merit special emphasis before we proceed.

➤ This chapter argues unapologetically in favor of the Stratfordian view that William Shakespeare wrote the works of William Shakespeare.

➤ Anti-Stratfordians are entitled to take exception to this; however …

➤ … those intent on disagreeing with this chapter before reading it should consider that each of the points put forward here in support of the Stratfordian position has been embraced by some of most respected scholars of the Elizabethan era.

So, before deciding to write an impassioned letter to the author care of the publisher, anti-Stratfordians could do everyone a favor by checking their preconceptions at the door and reading, in full, the definitive research available on *The Shakespearean Authorship Page*. This site, available for review at www.clark.net/pub/tross/ws, is one of the most exhaustively researched Shakespeare sites on the Web. It offers access to many superbly argued articles, notably those of Dave Kathman, who may well be the Internet's final authority on this endlessly debated subject.

After reviewing this site, if you nevertheless decide to write an impassioned letter to the author care of the publisher in favor of the proposition that the works attributed to William Shakespeare were not written by William Shakespeare, go ahead. Bear in mind, though, that this staff of one may take a while to get back to you.

Thank you. We now resume our program.

Candidate No. 1: The Earl of Oxford

Edward de Vere, the seventeenth Earl of Oxford, was a well-connected English poet. He was educated at Queens' and St. John's colleges, was a regular at court, moved in the highest social circles, and visited Italy. All these facts have led to speculation that he had the "right" educational and social background for composing Shakespeare's plays.

de Vere received some favorable notices from his contemporaries for his poems. He apparently was not regarded as any literary genius, however, although plenty of people in the Oxfordian camp have tried to suggest otherwise. The *Columbia Encyclopedia* describes him as simply "one of the court circle of writers."

Is It Plausible That the Earl of Oxford Could Have Written the Plays?

For most who are curious about this but are unfamiliar with the details of the debate, the central dilemma is a straightforward one. Does someone who argues that de Vere wrote Shakespeare possess any more credibility than, say, someone who argues that Elvis is still cruising through the rural South in a lime-green Cadillac?

Fable Facts

Among the most prominent books promoting the idea that Edward de Vere wrote the works published under Shakespeare's name are Joseph Sobran's *Alias Shakespeare* (Free Press, 1997), and Dorothy Ogburn and Charlton Ogburn Sr.'s *This Star of England* (1953). Challenges to the Oxfordian theory were cogently put forward in Irving Leigh Matus's *Shakespeare, In Fact* (Continuum, 1994), and in Dave Kathman's fine article "Why I'm Not an Oxfordian," first published in *The Elizabethan Review* in the spring of 1997.

Parallels Between Life and Play

The claim that the Earl of Oxford secretly wrote Shakespeare's works has set off countless hypothetical scenarios involving events from de Vere's life and their possible use as source material in the various plays and poems. There's a problem, though. These speculations have no more (or less) weight than any of the far-flung biographical theories that try to use the texts of the plays and poems to amplify what we know of *William Shakespeare's* life. They count for nada.

For both Stratfordians and anti-Stratfordians out to expand the biographical record, a tough fact remains: Simply finding an intriguing life history parallel within a favorite play or poem proves nothing. Disciplined historians have an obligation to search out hard evidence—fascinating ain't enough.

Don't Believe It!

The "burden of proof" in any authorship dispute must rest with the person attempting to prove that the historical record has been altered or is incomplete. Why? Because that record features more than enough specific contemporary references to William Shakespeare as actor, playwright, and theatrical professional to place him in the ranks of Ben Jonson, Christopher Marlowe, and the rest of the literary and theatrical luminaries of the era.

Legend Lingo

Elizabethan means of or pertaining to the reign of Queen Elizabeth I, who ruled from 1558 to 1603. **Jacobean** means of or pertaining to the reign of James I, who ruled from 1603 to 1625. Shakespeare, who died in 1616, was a subject of both monarchs.

Do Shakespeare's Plays Contain "Insider Knowledge" of Aristocratic Life?

The arguments of Oxfordians (and those of most people who challenge Shakespeare's authorship of the plays and poems) rely heavily on the idea that the author of such works as *Hamlet* and *Richard II* must have possessed firsthand knowledge of life as it was lived in a royal court in aristocratic households. Do the plays really carry the unique stamp of personal experience on this subject?

Nope. There is not a single contemporary reference indicating that people in *Elizabethan* or *Jacobean* England considered the depiction of court life in these plays to be factual. (Good thing, because it wasn't.) For that matter, they didn't consider *The Comedy of Errors* to be a literal depiction of life during Roman times. (It wasn't, either.)

Key point: An Elizabethan drama was entertainment, typically entertainment aimed at a large audience. It was not a documentary.

Don't take my word for this. Unfortunately for the Oxfordians, those who have researched the Elizabethan period have not been at all kind to the proposition that the plays were written based on "insider knowledge" of life as it was lived within the Elizabethan upper classes.

For instance, consider the following brief passage from social historian Muriel St. Claire Byrne's chapter "The Social Background" in the 1940 volume *A Companion to Shakespeare Studies.* Byrne discusses Shakespeare's portrait of Lord Capulet, Juliet's father in *Romeo and Juliet.*

> Shakespeare may label Capulet head of a noble household, who can treat Paris, "a young nobleman, kinsman to the prince," as his equal—but when it comes to a scene like Act IV, Scene iv, which shows the home life of this supposed nobleman, we realize the setting is not Verona but Stratford, and that the most likely person to have sat for that very realistic portrait is John Shakespeare, or any of the good burgesses who were William's father's friends. They probably got in the way of all their busy servants and kitchen staffs on the occasions of their daughters' weddings; but it is quite certain that an Elizabethan nobleman, with his retinue of anything from twenty to eight hundred gentleman officers ... did not himself have to issue orders for the quenching of fires and the turning up of tables.

—Muriel St. Claire Byrne in *A Companion to Shakespeare Studies,* 1940 (via "The Shakespearean Authorship Page")

Did Shakespeare Lack Access to Information He Would Have Needed to Write the Plays?

Those who argue that de Vere wrote the plays and poems that we customarily think of as Shakespeare's insist that the author of these masterpieces shows an intimate knowledge of legal matters, classical literature, and Italian customs. This knowledge, they argue, can be plausibly attributed only to a university-educated nobleman—someone like the Earl of Oxford. They also declare firmly that Shakespeare would never have been able to gain access to some of the books that serve as the source material for the plays.

Wrong again. Although it's true that Shakespeare did not have an extensive formal education, that fact on its own proves nothing. When has a university degree ever been an essential prerequisite for genius?

Don't Believe It!

Here's a fact that the anti-Stratfordians tend to skip over: A contemporary of Shakespeare, Richard Field, grew up near the glover's son in Stratford. He eventually became a prominent bookseller and publisher in London, releasing many of the volumes that served as source material for the plays.

51

Anyone who reviews the source materials for the plays with an open mind reaches one impossible-to-challenge conclusion: *Whoever* wrote these dramas must have been an exceptional reader, someone able to devour books quickly and to gather essential dramatic details that could be incorporated or expanded on within the plays. To argue that only a university-educated aristocrat could fit this description is not simply to stake out starkly elitist territory, but to maintain a deep and willful ignorance regarding the capacity of the human imagination.

Those who have reviewed the record at some length have determined that the references within these works were derived from sources available to any bright Elizabethan male who had an interest in pursuing them. Shakespeare, as a professional dramatist, certainly had such an interest.

Strange but True

Did Shakespeare have to be a nobleman to write about nobles? Consider the following:

"Shakespeare learned how to squeeze the maximum amount of knowledge out of a minimum of experience. Henry James once commented that a good novelist could talk to a soldier for ten minutes and then write a novel about military life. The same could be said about Shakespeare."

—Norrie Epstein, in the article "Who Was Shakespeare?" from *Living in a Shakespearean World,* Wordbeat, 1999

Was Shakespeare's Death a Nonevent at the Time?

Those who argue that de Vere (or anyone other than Shakespeare) was the true Bard often maintain that the death of "the Stratford man" in 1616 went curiously unregarded by his contemporaries. This is simply not true.

The problem here is that Oxfordians seem to believe that a genius is always recognized as such and treated accordingly—and as a member of the highest level of his or her society. As Hamlet might say, "Would that 'twere so!"

The facts are these: At the time of Shakespeare's death, it was indeed common for noblemen to be eulogized in print. But it was *not* common for playwrights and poets to be so honored; memorial poems for these figures tended to be circulated in manuscript form. Dave Kathman has studied the issue extensively and theorized that, when compared *to his colleagues in the theatre,* Shakespeare attracted a remarkably high number of contemporary writings honoring his passing.

Strange but True

Oxfordians who make a big deal out of the fact that English society didn't convulse in national paroxysms of grief at Shakespeare's death commit two major errors. First, they assume that theatrical professionals of the time were held in very high esteem—probably because of the godlike status that many people came to assign centuries later to the author of the world's greatest plays.

Actually, people who worked in the theater in Elizabethan and Jacobean England were anything but high-ranking at the time. Let's face it—they were forced by law to do their business outside the city limits, and they competed for popular attention (and cash) with people who tortured and killed bears. Theatre pros, of which Shakespeare was one, were often regarded as impious lowlifes.

What Was That About Death Notices?

Oxfordians don't do their own cause much good by focusing on who died when and what that means about authorship. Edward de Vere, the seventeenth earl of Oxford, is known to have died in 1604.

That leaves him inconveniently dead during the final 12 years of William Shakespeare's life, a period when such works as *King Lear, The Winter's Tale, The Tempest,* and many other plays are known to have been performed for the first time.

Hmmm ... Sounds Serious

It is.

The fact that de Vere shuffles off this mortal coil more than a decade too early for the composition of a significant number of major plays is the most damaging blow to the Oxford candidacy. It's what moves the "authorship mystery" out of the realm of "academic dispute about which informed experts disagree" and into the realm of "silly legend that doesn't stand up to scrutiny."

What Do the Oxfordians Have to Say About All This?

You mean, besides quoting that noted classical literary historian Ralph Kramden ("Hummana hummana hummana ...")?

The sad truth is, they generally try to change the subject. When pressed, they offer various solutions involving earlier composition dates for the plays than mainstream scholars accept. In short, they try to shift the relevant authorship dates into the dark backward and abysm of time by 12 years.

Does Any of That Date-Shifting Hold Up Against the Record?

Nope. Consider only the most unassailable chunk of proof: *The Tempest* uses as one of its sources a publication describing a real-life sea journey from England to Bermuda and back again. That journey took place in the years 1609 and 1610. If Oxford wrote about it, he did so from the grave, which *would* be quite a story.

This uncomfortable set of facts leaves the Oxfordians with three options:

➤ Accept that the author of *The Tempest* was someone other than the author of the earlier plays. (That's impossible for anyone on either side of the authorship debate, given the stylistic affinities and thematic resonances of the play with the rest of the works.)

➤ Accept that the author of *The Tempest* was in fact William Shakespeare. (This is a great option—unless, of course, you're dead set on proving that Oxford wrote the plays and poems, and are willing to fast-forward past any facts that blow your thesis to pieces.)

➤ Change the subject. (Again, this has been a clear winner among Oxfordians for some time now.)

Candidate No. 2: Sir Francis Bacon

Oxfordians aren't the only partisans in this crowd. You've also got your Baconians, who argue that the brilliant English philosopher and politician of the era is the only logical candidate for authorship of the plays and poems attributed to Shakespeare.

The case for Sir Francis relies almost exclusively on hidden "clues" within the printed texts of the plays and poems revealing Bacon as the true author. These coded messages are supposedly buried within the lines of the various plays and poems. (Yes, the proposition that Paul McCartney died and was replaced by a doppelganger has been established through similar methods. If you missed this, see Chapter 4, "Is Paul Dead? [and Other Burning Pop Music Questions].")

Over the years, the Baconians put forward various alphabetical code systems of great beauty and complexity that, when applied to the texts of the plays and poems, produce a huge number of variations on the word *Bacon*. For instance:

➤ baqin

➤ bekan

➤ biekon

And so on. The only problem, as Dave Kathman points out, is that the system produces exactly the same results with virtually any other extended text.

You might well ask, "Why so many variations? Why not limit the search to the single spelling of *Bacon?*" The answer: That doesn't produce enough references to Sir Francis Bacon to make the case, silly!

By accepting so many variant spellings of their candidate's last name, the Baconians dramatically increase the odds that a "clue" pointing toward Sir Francis will arise within the text passage in question. The only problem is, you can use the same method to "prove" that the Earl of Essex, or Mickey Rooney, or Roger Rabbit wrote the works of Shakespeare.

To make a long story short, the evidence that Baconians offer in favor of their man makes the average Oxfordian look like Sherlock Holmes.

Fable Facts

Authorship specialist Dave Kathman applied the Baconian codes to the four Gospels of the New Testament and "proved" that Bacon had written those as well. Not satisfied with his efforts, he turned his attention to the Whitewater report and discovered that Bacon had written that political-erotical-historical-pastoral masterwork, too. That's a neat trick, considering that Sir Francis had been dead for more than three centuries at the time of the Lewinsky affair.

So How Come People Get So Worked Up About All This?

Apparently, a fair chunk of the population simply likes to find a reason to believe that somebody other than Shakespeare wrote all those masterpieces. Maybe they actually believe that genius can arise only among the socially advanced and formally educated. Maybe they were brutally mistreated by English teachers many years ago. Maybe they get a strange thrill from challenging the "standard version" of anything. Maybe they delight in the possession of what they imagine to be special insider knowledge denied to the rest of the world.

Or maybe they just like the attention that they get from arguing with people who know the subject a little better than they do.

The Argument's the Thing

One thing's for sure: The more uncomfortable facts come up, the more intense the anti-Stratfordians get about their cause. That makes for some very entertaining discussions, but it sure doesn't make for good scholarship.

Shakespeare wrote of Cleopatra, "She makes hungry where she most satisfies." He meant that coming into contact with the Egyptian queen produced an even more insatiable desire for her company. The same thing can be said for those who argue that Shakespeare wasn't Shakespeare. They just can't seem to get enough.

The Least You Need to Know

➤ Don't worry—Paul still isn't dead.

➤ Before you buy into any elaborate Shakespearean authorship theory, you should probably take a look at the extensive research that has been done on the subject.

➤ Christopher Marlowe and Edward de Vere, the seventeenth Earl of Oxford, both died too early to have written Shakespeare's plays.

➤ Francis Bacon's authorship adherents place way too much emphasis on wacky cryptographical pseudoproofs.

➤ Anti-Stratfordians who get worked up about their chosen obsession tend to stay worked up about it.

Chapter 6

Did Catherine the Great Really Do It with a Horse?

In This Chapter

➤ Everything you know is wrong: why historical myths deserve examination

➤ The whole thing about the horse being lowered onto Catherine the Great

➤ Other (unhistorical) stories too good not to pass on

➤ Why you must, alas, continue to pay income tax

➤ A common thread among pseudohistorical myths

Does a persistent, inaccurate myth about a political or historical figure—or the structures of government itself—qualify as an urban legend? Well, why not?

There's no generally accepted governing authority to settle such vexing questions. There are, however, two big reasons to consider these enthralling (but untrue) stories about leaders and famous figures to be at least *closely connected* to today's urban myths.

Reason the First

Many of the modern stories that we instinctively classify as "urban legends" are in fact variations on folk tales, horror stories, children's stories, and cautionary parables that have been around more or less forever. So what's the big difference between a myth that pretends to be modern but isn't and one that pretends to be historical but isn't? Both echo endlessly down a tunnel that often spans generations, and both are reflections of our unconscious fears and fantasies.

Fable Facts

Excluding quasihistorical stories from a discussion of the urban legend phenomenon means rejecting one fascinating form of collective myth-making for another fascinating form of collective myth-making.

Fable Facts

Every tale in this chapter has endured for years, despite the best efforts of various responsible historians to correct common misconceptions. Why? At least in part, it was because each story was considered too darned good not to pass on. But none of them are true.

Reason the Second

People love repeating erroneous historical stories so much that the phenomenon really does deserve to be considered closely. In fact, this particular species of myth may be among the most popular variety of them all. If you disagree, ask yourself whether you ever "assumed" that Washington chopped down a cherry tree, or that Nero fiddled while Rome burned, or that Catherine the Great and a horse once ... on second thought, never mind.

Part of the appeal of an urban legend is the thrill that people get in passing on a memorable, if outlandish, story. When we circulate such a tale, we become one of the people "in the know" about an extraordinary (and supposedly true) event. Pretty soon, enough people are excited about being "in the know" to ensure that the story is broadly accepted as fact, even when the account is absurd. That's how classic urban legends spread.

Well, exactly the same principle applies to many of our most cherished beliefs about political and historical figures. You be the judge. If the stories that follow don't place us in the same territory as the story about Mr. Greenjeans being Frank Zappa's dad, what does?

Take Catherine, for example. Sometimes it seems that more people "know" that Catherine the Great died *in flagrante delicto* with a horse than can tell you who Catherine the Great actually was. For the record, she was the czarina of Russia between 1762 and 1796, and the wife of the eccentric Czar Peter III. She became sole ruler when a conspirator, who also happened to be her lover, arranged for Peter's murder. Catherine emerged as one of Russia's shrewdest, most autocratic, and most ruthless rulers, which is saying something. And yet ....

Yeah, Yeah—What About the Horse?

At one point or another, the question on everyone's mind is: Did Catherine the Great *really* die as the result of being crushed by a horse that her attendants were attempting to lower onto her during a kinky sexual escapade? The correct answer is "no." It sure is a hoot to pose the question, though, isn't it?

This particularly colorful (and remarkably persistent) rumor was initiated by Catherine's political enemies after her death, the better to capitalize on her acknowledged reputation as a lady who got around. That notoriety was valid enough, but it's nevertheless important to remember that, as far as the historical record reveals, Catherine appears to have stuck to her own species.

Has that inconvenient fact stopped people from circulating this account? Of course not. Do people ever bring up this lurid rumor simply for the amusement of conjuring up, yet again, a mental image of the despotic Catherine being crushed in pursuit of some new sexual thrill? It probably has happened once or twice.

Whatever unfounded suspense may have, er, mounted among the tale's countless listeners and circulators over the centuries, Catherine's story certainly passes the "too good not to repeat" test. That's why people repeat it—often with that classic introduction, "Well, someone who ought to know told a friend of mine that …."

For those with a tireless thirst for racy details concerning the Russian empress, the following tidbit may be of interest: She *actually* died after suffering an apparent stroke in the vicinity of the imperial commode in her St. Petersburg palace. The maid found her. That's unexciting, compared to the horse thing, of course, and perhaps even a little gross. It's true, though.

Don't Believe It!

The much-circulated rumor about Catherine the Great's fatal erotic predilection for horses was circulated by her political enemies after her death. The truth of the matter is this: She preferred men. Some of them, to be sure, may have been beastly at times, and you get the feeling that she may have returned the favor. But, strictly speaking, Catherine wasn't into bestiality.

Other Historical "Facts" That Aren't Factual

Catherine's rendezvous with a horse is by no means the only unhistorical "historical" anecdote that has gained wide acceptance over the years. Plenty of stories about notable figures were too delicious for writers to avoid incorporating, despite being (to put it politely) so much baloney.

Many leaders have been subjected to posthumous rumormongering campaigns. Shakespeare, for instance, accused the English monarch Richard III of having murdered his two nephews. Did he do it? Nobody's certain. What we do know for sure is that Richard had neither a pronounced hunch nor a withered arm, and that Shakespeare wanted to flatter the Tudor dynasty, which succeeded Richard.

Here's a brief sampling of political and social nonevents that got plenty of people—historians, nonhistorians, libertarians, and flat-earthers—all worked up. They never actually took place, but they sure sounded—and still sound—good in the telling.

Cleopatra Was Egyptian

The Egyptians that Cleopatra ruled considered her exalted family Greek. (And, make no mistake, people paid pretty close attention to the royal bloodlines back then.) Even though that family had been around for a while, it was all Greek to the subjects of the Queen of the Nile.

Cleopatra also appears not to have been half as active sexually as her modern reputation would suggest. A number of writers have concluded that Caesar and Marc Antony were probably her only lovers. Still, you have to give her credit: She could pick 'em.

Caligula Had His Horse Appointed Consul

How nutty do emperors get? Pretty nutty, if Caligula is any example. Yet the most famous story about that wild and crazy Roman ruler Caligula is totally unsubstantiated. Does that mean that people have been able to prove that he *didn't* try to have his horse named *consul?* Well, let's answer that question by posing another one. If someone tried to get you to believe that, say, Richard Nixon tried to get, say, Checkers confirmed as, say, Secretary of Commerce, wouldn't you want to see a little proof before enshrining the story as fact for generations to come?

The truth is that no one has been able to confirm the bizarre story about Caligula's horse. (What is it about bizarre horse-related stories that make for good historical myths, anyway?) The account first appears in the writings of Suetonius, and he wasn't too sure about it himself, being careful to identify it as an intriguing bit of gossip rather than historical fact.

Caligula was certainly not the kind of guy you'd want to invite over for a game of Monopoly. If you're looking for reasons to consider him a wacko, though, look no further than his (amply documented) yen for torture and execution as a form of entertainment.

Somehow, those evenings spent listening happily to the screams of political opponents and random bystanders haven't captured the popular imagination in quite the same way as the image of a horse attending important government meetings. At least nobody in Caligula's circle is accused of propositioning the beast.

Legend Lingo

A **consul** was a chief magistrate in ancient Rome. No one has ever been able to prove that Caligula's horse held the job.

Nero Fiddled While Rome Burned

This one comes up again every time someone uncovers new evidence that some politician somewhere has been neglecting the fundamental interests of the populace.

That happens a lot, so it's not that surprising that the fiddling-while-Rome-burned business comes up a lot, too.

It's not true, though. The Roman emperor Nero may not have won any points for etiquette (he had the young Britannicus poisoned, and he ordered the murders of his wife and mother), and he wasn't big on accountability (when half of Rome was consumed in a massive fire, he blamed the Christians). Nasty as he was, though, we can't hold him responsible for indulging his musical passions as his city burned down around his ears, because he didn't.

For the record, Nero didn't even know how to play the fiddle.

Marie Antoinette Said, "Let Them Eat Cake"

Jean-Jacques Rousseau attributed this hardhearted remark to "a young princess" who had just been informed that the populace had no bread to eat. Some wag whose name is now lost to history apparently thought that it was *precisely* the thing the French queen would have said during the French Revolution ... if she'd thought of saying it. She didn't, but the story stuck anyway.

File it under "If it isn't true, it ought to be," a common justification among myth-circulators.

George Washington ... (Insert Favorite Myth Here)

Once you start a country, people really get the legend machinery humming on your behalf.

There are so many myths surrounding the Father of Our Country that you can't really boil them all down into a single *uber*-myth. You can, however, summarize the most commonly circulated legends into a list.

It's not true that George Washington ...

➤ Chopped down a cherry tree and then 'fessed up about having done so. This falsehood can be traced back to a story circulated by Parson Weems. In that account, Weems tells of Washington's inability to tell a lie about *barking* the tree, not chopping it down. The whole tale, however, is dubious at best.

➤ Knelt in the snow to pray at Valley Forge, looking for all the world like the occupant of a secular Gethsemane. At least, there's no persuasive evidence that he did so. Our only source on this is Weems again, and even this account is presented as unsubstantiated hearsay.

➤ Stood heroically at the front of the boat as he crossed the Delaware. In reality, he was much too smart to pull such a stunt, which probably would have landed him in the drink. Credit an imaginative "historical" painter for the image that we all remember.

61

➤ Was elected to the presidency by a unanimous vote of all 13 of the original states. Washington did receive every vote cast in the electoral college, but because New York couldn't resolve an internal political conflict, it voted for no one in the election of 1789.

➤ Wore the morose expression of a disappointed deity most of the time. We just think he did because of all those sober paintings, especially the famous Gilbert Stuart portrait reproduced on the American dollar bill. By this time Washington was an old man whose dentures didn't fit very well. You'd have looked cranky, too, if you had to stand still for hours on end with cotton stuffed in your mouth.

How do these stories get started? Here's one theory: In the first century of our republic, everyone had a vested interest in Washington being not just a great man, but also a godlike figure.

Another commonly circulated but false story about Washington is that he was the ninth U.S. president rather than the first. There were, you see, eight presidents selected under the Articles of Confederation, which were adopted by Congress in 1777 and which the states ratified in 1781. Some nitpickers think this means that Washington wasn't really the first U.S. president. Said nitpickers conveniently overlook the primacy of the U.S. Constitution in defining the office we now call the presidency.

John Tyler Was Never President

Strike up the band and play "Hail to the Second Banana"! It's time to talk about the president who wasn't—or, at least, the president some people still *say* wasn't—John Tyler.

Fable Facts

At various points during his term of office, Tyler received mail from political opponents addressed to "Ex-Vice President Tyler" and "Vice-President-Acting President Tyler." He returned all this correspondence without opening it.

The myth surrounding Tyler's (alleged) nonpresidency arises from his special status in American history. With William Henry Harrison dying just a month after his inauguration, Tyler was the first vice president to take over the job after the death of the president. Here, as elsewhere, the Constitution is vague on an important question—in this case, what to *call* such a chief executive.

Not surprisingly, there was an argument at the time about whether Tyler was to be referred to as "president" or as "acting president." It may not surprise you to learn that the debate was finally settled in favor of the title "president," or that people since haven't wasted time getting twisted up in their shorts over this issue.

Historical troublemakers who take pleasure in confusing things, however, may cite contemporary news stories that refer to Tyler as "acting president" (or "His Accidency," another catchy nickname that stuck to Tyler). Troublemakers may also distribute quotes from one side of the debate and pretend that some fundamental constitutional question was at issue, or that Tyler's status was somehow more dubious than, say, Harry Truman's or Lyndon Johnson's. Wrong on both counts.

Strange but True

Is it a myth (urban, rural, suburban, or otherwise) that the United States once had a president named David Rice Atchison? The answer is ... murky. At the stroke of midnight on Saturday, March 3, 1849, James Polk's term as president expired. His duly elected successor, Zachary Taylor, strict observer of the Sabbath that he was, declined to be sworn in until Monday, March 5, 1850. Who, then, was president on March 4? Depending on which constitutional scholar you check with, the answer is either nobody or David Rice Atchison, then president pro tempore of the Senate—and next in line for the presidency under the laws in effect at the time.

Marconi Invented Radio

Ask a hundred people for the name of the person who invented radio, and odds are good that 90 of them will name Guglielmo Marconi.

Okay, okay—they probably wouldn't say *Guglielmo* Marconi because the Guglielmo part is a little hard to remember and pronounce. But the Marconi part would probably leap to the lips of 9 out of 10 people asked for the name of the person who invented radio.

The problem is, Marconi didn't do it. What Marconi managed to do was send *telegraph messages* without the use of wires. Years later, other people figured out how to send something besides Morse code over the airwaves.

What Marconi *did* do is run a company that had his name on it, and get a lot of press over the years for a breakthrough that eventually made radio possible. Those are certainly noteworthy accomplishments, but they're not the same as inventing the radio. That doesn't bother the people who give out Marconi Awards to prominent people in the radio industry.

Besides, it takes longer to say that Ernst Alexanderson and Reginald Fessiden, while under the employ of General Electric, overcame previously insuperable technical obstacles and allowed Jack Benny, Charlie McCarthy, and fireside chats to be ushered into the living rooms of America.

In America, we love the story of the lonely inventor who strikes it big. That may be why we prefer Marconi over Alexanderson and Fessiden. We also love short names that are relatively easy to pronounce—which is, as we have seen, why people tend to skip the Guglielmo part.

The 16th Amendment Is Invalid

Fasten your historical safety belts—the Complete Idiot's Guide advisory board cautions that the following entry may well cause temporary brain damage in some readers. Proceed at your own risk.

Somehow, when all the i's were being dotted and t's were being crossed back in 1803, Congress forgot to actually admit Ohio to the Union. You read right. Congress okayed the boundaries and gave the thumbs up to the Buckeye State's constitution, but it never actually passed the legislation formally admitting Ohio as a state.

Apparently, no one actually noticed this until 1953, when 150th-birthday celebrations for the state (territory? ersatz state?) were well underway. When Congress finally realized its oversight, there was a lot of good-natured chuckling on both sides of Pennsylvania Avenue. Eventually, a new bill formally authorized Ohio's admittance to the Union, retroactively, 150 years late. But what's a century and a half among friends?

Don't Believe It!

Think twice before you shred that tax bill. Various fascinating arguments attacking the legitimacy of the 16th amendment were briskly dismissed in Porth vs. Brodrick 214 F. 2d 925, 6th Circuit 1954. The IRS won—doesn't it always?—and you probably shouldn't hold your breath waiting for Porth to be overturned.

With apologies to humorist Dave Barry, I must pause here to assure you that I am not making any of this up. We really and truly haven't yet gotten to the urban legend part of this story.

Okay, here it comes. Every six months or so, some self-appointed constitutional scholar/overheated party guest declares that the federal government has no legal right to tax its citizens. Why not? Because, you see, the 16th amendment to the Constitution is invalid. Why, you may ask, is it invalid? Because Ohio approved the amendment but was technically (or so the argument goes) not a state when it did so.

What these folks ignore is the inconvenient fact that, even if one excludes Ohio from the equation, there were more than enough states in favor of the 16th amendment to secure its passage. You have to admit, though, that as attempts to abolish the central government's taxing authority goes, this is a pretty nice try.

There's also a desperate-sounding backup argument that holds that William Howard Taft, under whose administration the 16th amendment originated, was never really president. The tortured logic follows: Taft came from Ohio, and you have to be a naturalized citizen to be president; since he couldn't have been a naturalized citizen, what with the whole *Ohio problem,* yada yada yada, please shut down the Internal Revenue Service.

For some reason, this elegant reasoning hasn't swayed the feds.

Time out for a quick question. Why do you suppose, of all the amendments to the Constitution, the 16th is the one around which a legend like this has arisen? Why haven't people used the Ohio-wasn't-a-state argument to, say, challenge the 25th amendment's procedure for nominating a new vice president when a vacancy in that office arises? Could the petty financial interests of the legend perpetuators possibly be playing a role?

Perish the thought! This is strict constructionism at its finest!

Thrilling as the prospect of padlocking the doors on the local IRS office may be, the sad fact remains that the courts have looked askance at this attack (and even weirder attacks) on the taxing authority of the federal government. None of it has ever held up in court. But if you feel like making the case yourself during your next audit, be my guest.

Legend Lingo

The **Ohio problem** refers to the formal admission of the state of Ohio to the Union. Even though your almanac or history book may tell you that this occurred in 1803, Congress had to correct a little-known legislative oversight and admit Ohio retroactively in 1953. This gave desperate critics of the government's taxing authority a couple of extremely feeble arguments against the validity of the 16th amendment.

JFK Would've Lost Without the Daley Machine

Over the years, there has been a lot of speculation about the role that Chicago Mayor Richard Daley (the first one, that is) played in the outcome of the 1960 presidential election. People sometimes nod sagely and pronounce that, without Daley's "help" in the city of Chicago, John F. Kennedy would have lost the state of Illinois, the electoral college vote, and the presidency to Richard Nixon.

Whatever shenanigans Daley may or may not have been responsible for in Chicago, those shenanigans *didn't* win the 1960 election for Kennedy. The Democrat from Massachusetts pulled a total of 303 electoral votes that year. Take away 27 votes from Illinois and give them to Nixon, and Kennedy still ekes out a victory in the electoral college with 276 total votes.

Why do people keep spreading this one around? Who knows? Conspiracies *are* fascinating (especially ones involving a Kennedy—see Chapter 11, "The Government Is Out to Get You"). And maybe a rigged presidential election is more interesting than one in which the right candidate wins.

The Trilateral Commission's Silent Global Coup

In 1973, banking magnate David Rockefeller assembled a couple of hundred big shots from the United States, Japan, and Western Europe to discuss grave challenges facing developed economies. He did this, presumably, on the theory that a couple of hundred heads are better than one, especially when it comes to the discussion of grave challenges.

A cynic might note that Rockefeller was launching a think tank of interest to movers and shakers in the three most important market regions for his humble family business, Chase Manhattan Bank. (Let's just say that the guy knew how to network.) The organization he formed, dubbed the Trilateral Commission for its emphasis on the three geopolitical areas just referenced, pursued ominous activities such as circulating newsletters, holding seminars, and holding power lunches.

In the early 1980s, extremists on both the left and the right started to comb through the membership list of the organization and fomented various complicated theories of a shadowy plot for world domination. (The fact that there *was* a membership list to comb through didn't seem to make the alleged conspiracy any less shadowy.)

Fable Facts

Nervous defenders of democracy prepared for the worst when Ronald Reagan held a White House reception for Trilateral Commission members in 1984. Somehow, the republic survived. (Reagan, by the way, was never a member of the Trilateral Commission.)

You still hear ominous talk about the Trilateral Commission from time to time. Paranoid right-wingers tend to see the dreaded onset of One-World Government taking place before their very eyes. Paranoid left-wingers tend to see the various members of the "power elite" getting a little too clubby for comfort and pulling puppet strings on behalf of a secret but powerful international fascist oligarchy.

Both sides are at least half a bubble off center. These folks meet once a year and pass out press releases. If you doubt it, check out their Web site (www.trilateral.org). While you're at it, take a long, deep breath.

You read it here first. The Trilateral Commission *doesn't* subvert the electorate and corrupt the democratic process. (That's the job of the electoral college.) For more fevered theorizing on the supposed behind-the-scenes influence of the Trilateral Commission in shaping political events, see Chapter 11.

A Constitutional Loophole

Energetic detractors of the former president from Arkansas—of which there were and are quite a few—started circulating this one on the Internet and over the nation's airwaves during the last year or two of Bill Clinton's term. "Hold on to your hats," they warned the faithful (in so many words), "Clinton's making plans to seek the White House once again in 2004. True to form, he has found a loophole in the Constitution. By waiting four years, he's planning to get around the *22nd amendment*, which the nation passed back in 1951 to avoid just such an eventuality."

Now, saying this sort of thing is certainly an effective way to ensure that angry people without a full complement of chromosomes will pick up the phone and call your talk show. Once they do, you can listen attentively as they natter on endlessly about, say, their plan for the evacuation and demolition of every federal building with an address ending in an even number. Of course, the third-term rumor is not true. If you run a lively enough talk show, though, you won't let a little obstacle like that bother you.

Some variations on this urban legend posited a situation under which Clinton planned to assume "emergency powers" in order to run for a third term so that he and he alone could deal with the (predicted) chaos surrounding the Y2K bug crisis. It's all banana oil. Neither Clinton nor any other president can be elected to the office more than twice. Period. Flip to the 22nd amendment to the Constitution if anyone tries to run some jive past you about there being a loophole of some kind allowing people to run for president three times or assume emergency powers. There isn't.

Legend Lingo

The **22nd amendment** is a revision to the U.S. Constitution, passed in 1951, setting term limits on the office of President of the United States. It forbids anyone from being "elected to the office of president more than twice."

Some Final Thoughts

Have you noticed a pattern here? People tend to circulate historical myths to perpetuate some version of world events that they *wish* were true, or because they have a bizarre vested interest in convincing others this version *is* true. (Let's not get started on Holocaust revisionism; it's too ugly.)

The moral: Everyone's got an angle. You should probably ask your grade school teacher to come clean about that cherry tree thing.

The Least You Need to Know

➤ The story about Catherine the Great and the horse is a lot of malarkey.

➤ Many commonly circulated stories about Nero, Marie Antoinette, and other historical figures are a lot of malarkey as well.

➤ Keep paying your income taxes because the 16th amendment is still in effect.

➤ Don't worry about Clinton—or anyone else—being elected to three terms as president; the 22nd amendment is still in effect.

➤ When someone tells you something extraordinary about a political or historical figure, be ready to ask yourself, "What's the angle here?"

Chapter 7

The Family Hour (Not): Twisted Legends About Your Favorite Children's Television Stars

In This Chapter

➤ The Steve Burns/Mr. Rogers/Mr. Greenjeans syndrome

➤ The "dark side"

➤ Stories about tragedies that supposedly befall child actors

➤ Important updates on the Brady girls

Some urban legends thrive on an intriguing mixture of what is welcome and familiar to us and what is dark and unknown. Often we hear a strange story about someone we don't know personally but have heard of or have a strong positive emotional association toward. Because the story offers a host of surreal (and even nightmarish) details about the person in question—details that may play to some insecurity or fear that we hold at a very deep level—we're riveted by the account. Who can resist passing the tale along?

Many legends gain stunningly wide circulation because of this kind of stark contrast. They complete the connection between the appealing surface of some public personage and the sinister truth that supposedly lies beneath the image. Strangely, or perhaps predictably, beloved personages from television programs aimed at children frequently play lead roles in these urban legends, which I call *"TV legends."*

"Guess What a Friend of a Friend of Mine Heard About (Insert Kids' TV Star Here) ..."

In this chapter, we look at television stars whose appeal to children has unexpectedly brought them a kind of fame that they probably never thought (or wanted) to win.

Legend Lingo

A **TV legend** can be an urban legend about someone who has appeared on a television show; it can also be a legend about an outrageous episode that people believe to have seen but haven't because no such episode ever existed.

In most of these stories, the actors or personalities associated with the shows have been credited, if that's the word, with strange, often disturbing deeds. The stories have nothing to do with the lives of the stars or the events depicted on the kid-oriented show on which they appeared. In fact, the stories completely *subvert* the themes of the show. And that, apparently, is the whole point.

Read on if you're interested in setting the record straight—and explore why, precisely, we are so quick to circulate dark and ominous stories about people whom kids love and trust.

Did Steve Burns, the Star of *Blue's Clues,* Die of a Drug Overdose?

To begin with the most recent, ludicrous, and easy-to-refute legend, let's look at Nickelodeon's critically praised, endlessly licensed television program *Blue's Clues.* The innocuous show would seem to be the least likely source for a national news story about heroin addiction, yet that's what it became.

In the late 1990s, tongues started wagging with a haunting and sensational story: The show's kid-friendly host, Steve, played to perfection by actor Steve Burns, was a heroin addict and had recently suffered a fatal overdose.

Fable Facts

Shades of Paul McCartney! Despite a nationally televised appearance on *Today* and an equally prominent guest slot on Rosie O'Donnell's program covering the same territory, rumors of *Blue's Clues* host Burns's addiction and demise continued to make the rounds. People still encounter it on the Internet from time to time.

This was news to the show's producers, the network, and Burns, who was (and is) alive, kicking, and drug-free. In a joint appearance with *Blue's Clues* creator Angela Santomero, the actor took to the airwaves on NBC's *Today* to debunk the myth and offer some advice to parents on the best ways to address the rumor with kids.

So How Did It Start?

The ghoulish story may have taken root from some child's (or adult's) garbled retelling of the story from a 1995 episode of NBC's *Law and Order,* in which Burns played an autistic kid who was *mistaken* for a drug user. The character died during the course of the show.

Alternatively, it may have been the product of people with nothing better to do than terrify and disorient vulnerable preschoolers. File under: Get a life.

Who's going to bet against the possibility of twisted grown-ups circulating this story in knowing and reckless disregard of the facts? Nobody who has sifted through a couple of thousand Internet hoaxes, that's for sure.

Anyway, Steve is fine. So is Blue. And so is Paprika. And, no, the handy-dandy notebook has never been pressed into service as a hash pipe.

Variations on a (Sick) Theme

The Steve Burns overdose story shares some interesting overlaps with the story about Mr. Greenjeans as Frank Zappa's dad, discussed in Chapter 4, "Is Paul Dead? (and Other Burning Pop Music Questions)." In both, a loving, trusted uncle figure strongly associated with children is linked with various unsavory images. We think we're talking about children's television, and suddenly we're talking about addiction, needles, and death (in the former legend), and the various envelope- and button-pushing works of the late Zappa (in the latter).

As rock fans will recall, Zappa won a passionate following in the 1960s and 1970s for his intricate, iconoclastic songs about (among other things) drug use, oozing television sets, and, um, sex. Nothing against the songs, mind you … most of them are witty, literate rock, and Lord knows we can't get enough of that. They're just not the first ditties that you'd instantly associate with kids' TV.

This brings us to the next bogus story about your favorite TV uncle figure, none other than Mr. Rogers. Among the strange stories being circulated about Fred Rogers—an ordained minister and a short-list contender for the title of World's Nicest Person—is the absurd allegation that he was forced to wear sweaters on his show to hide tattoos he had picked up during his past incarnation as an Army sharpshooter. Not true.

Odd stories about the Sesame Street gang have also made the rounds. (For the record, the puppets Bert and Ernie are not gay and have never been depicted as such.)

Strange Rumors About Nice People on Children's Programs

Mr. Greenjeans. Mr. Rogers. Steve, from *Blue's Clues.* Why have bizarre and totally untrue stories circulated like wildfire about three really nice guys whose primary characteristic is a love for children and an ability to communicate with them warmly and with honesty?

Don't Believe It!

Legends purporting to tell of the death of a child's television friend are no laughing matter. They can—and do—traumatize kids. If you hear one of these rumors or receive an e-mail outlining one, check it out before circulating it.

One theory: We are threatened, perhaps at a very deep level, by the possibility that people who appear trustworthy and whom we trust to form relationships with our kids are, in fact, weirdos.

The weirdo-abducts-my-kid possibility is a nightmare scenario that just about every parent has spun out privately at one point or another. Even if some bizarro creates these rumors for a dose of sick fun at the expense of innocent kids, isn't it possible that nervous parents play *some* role in the circulation of the stories?

Here's another way to consider the same question: When their kids are just beginning to interact with the outside world, do parents ever listen with a too-credulous ear to the latest paranoid fantasy involving someone they thought they could trust to hang out with our children? It's a possibility.

Watch That Caregiver!

When it comes to listening to and spreading stories like these, the adults (and particularly parents) may also be driven by their own insecurities concerning people who connect with kids better than they sometimes can—and who seem just a little too nice to be beyond suspicion.

True, Steve, Mr. Rogers, and Mr. Greenjeans all built "relationships" of the televised variety with most of the kids they influenced. And yet people have given at least some measure of credence to stories that turn these good men into iconic figures representing Dangerous Folks Who Want to Connect with Your Kids ... and then link those outsiders to the Dark Side.

Logical? No. Attention-getting? Absolutely.

Sad but True: Dark Stories About TV Friends Make Great Conversation

Urban legends often spring up from simple error or the erroneous retelling or interpretation of some innocuous detail. (Witness the genesis of the Mr. Greenjeans/Frank Zappa connection, which is based in the misinterpretation of a song title.) But the most unsettling of these stories have a way of acquiring the force and speed of malignant viruses when they touch on our most intense fears and uncertainties. Let's face it, there is a certain thrill to learning that someone we thought of as inherently good is being linked to something inherently evil. We almost can't help talking about the story once it surfaces.

Sadly, the three stories we've examined are not the only examples of manipulation of images and people beloved by children.

The Darth Vader Syndrome

Another kind of urban legend serves as a useful counterpoint to the ones falsely alleging that gentle, caring, kid-friendly uncle types are actually connected somehow to Very Nasty Business Indeed. This category involves those legends that the *kids* we came to know and fall in love with on television have, in adult life, been transformed into dark aggressors. Since we're talking about show business in the modern era, you'd *think* that there were enough stories of dark aggression to go around without dragging the kids into it. Apparently not, though.

Will the Real Marilyn Manson Please Stand Up?

Some part of the human psyche is endlessly fascinated with the idea that (for instance) lovable little Annakin is fated to be sacrificed to the Dark Side and be turned into the dark lord, Darth Vader. Stories following this pattern have been around for centuries and are potent enough to support multiepisode series of Hollywood blockbusters. We shouldn't be too shocked, then, when group hallucinations spawn them and cast our favorite young friends from TV land in the lead roles. Take, for example, the many (alleged) faces of shock rocker Marilyn Manson.

Did the actor who played Paul on *The Wonder Years* eventually become shock rocker Marilyn Manson?

No. The actor in question, Josh Saviano, is another person entirely, despite an alleged resemblance rendered inconclusive by Manson's trademark stage makeup.

Did the actor who played Kevin Owens on *Mr. Belvedere* eventually become shock rocker Marilyn Manson?

No. The actor in question, Rob Stone, is another person entirely, despite an alleged resemblance rendered inconclusive by Manson's trademark stage makeup.

Did the actor who played Eddie Haskell on *Leave It to Beaver* eventually become shock rocker Alice Cooper?

No. The actor in question, Ken Osmond, is another person entirely, despite an alleged resemblance rendered inconclusive by Cooper's trademark stage makeup.

Is a pattern emerging here?

Yes.

Does it have an intriguing variation regarding the actresses who played the daughters on *The Brady Bunch?*

Yes. Read on ....

Did Susan Olsen, who played Cindy on *The Brady Bunch*, ever pose in the altogether for photographers?

No. Cheesy publications may have attempted to capture the Cindy look in various pictorials, but the models pictured therein would be—surprise—other people entirely.

Did Eve Plumb or Maureen McCormick, who played Jan and Marcia, respectively, ever pose in the altogether for photographers?

No. Blah blah blah blah blah other people entirely.

Are you sure?

The question has been reviewed on the Internet at some length by a group of *Brady Bunch* fans best described as "extremely dedicated to the topic." Nobody has turned up anything reliable yet. And if any group is worthy of our trust in researching such matters, it's these folks.

Did Susan Olsen, Who Played Cindy on The Brady Bunch, Tragically Die?

Olsen has been dogged with questions for years about whether she's actually alive. She is on record saying she that is flattered by the implied comparison with Paul McCartney. At least nobody is accusing her of having covered up the identity of the person or persons who actually wrote the works of Shakespeare. Here are a few of the stories about her false demise.

Fable Facts

Susan Olsen, who played Cindy on *The Brady Bunch* and has been the subject of numerous death rumors, told *TV Guide*, "If you watch one of *The Brady Bunch* episodes backward, you can hear Greg saying, 'I buried Cindy.'" She was kidding.

Did Susan Olsen, who played Cindy on *The Brady Bunch*, commit suicide?

No. Tragically, that was Anissa Jones, who played Buffy on *Family Affair*.

Did Susan Olsen, who played Cindy on *The Brady Bunch*, die in the 1970s when she got her coat stuck in the door of a public bus?

No. This story arose from a tragic accident that involved another Susan Olsen who was, the record indicates clearly, an entirely different person.

A question: What do you suppose it is about the Bradys that launches multiple legends? Why didn't people ever spin out lurid, grim fantasies about, say, the kids who show up in some episode of Nickelodeon's *Double Dare*?

By now it should be pretty obvious where all this is going. There's nothing to any of these stories. For more lurid stories involving the Brady cast, see Chapter 18, "Private Parts in the Public Eye."

So did any former network child star go on to launch a highly visible, twisted variation on his or her past persona incorporating Marilyn Manson, Alice Cooper, a nude model, a porn star, or some intriguing variation of all of these possibilities?

No. This is not to say, of course, that every child star goes on to have a happy, well-adjusted adolescence and adulthood. Many face extremely tough challenges after their first rush of stardom fades. But the idea that yesterday's adorable moppet has morphed into today's latest parental nightmare is not fact, but a classic free-floating urban legend mirroring social insecurities about sex and the loss of innocence. The stories will doubtless continue to attach themselves to new child stars as the years pass.

Fable Facts

For those curious about the details of the more lurid manifestations of the (unfounded) legends in which a cute little kid gets very nasty indeed in front of the cameras, Chapter 18 offers an in-depth discussion of the phenomenon.

The Mikey Syndrome

A similarly bizarre series of stories surrounds kids we knew and loved on television who suffered terrible tragedies. Their fates often serve as grim contrasts to the themes of the shows on which they appeared, accounting for much of the conversational and Internet appeal of the stories in questions. Legends in this category have proved to be extremely popular.

Take a look now at some of the most widely circulated kid-TV-star-as-victim stories.

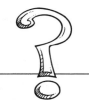

Strange but True

There are a number of variants on the Mikey Eats Too Many Pop Rocks legend, which is among the most famous all of urban legends. Sometimes Mikey suffers head injuries. Sometimes he simply chokes. Sometimes his stomach explodes. Sometimes it's not even Mikey. Not all variations on the rumor involve John Gilchrist, the child actor from the fabled television commercial. Sometimes it's an anonymous kid who consumes a fatal overdose of Pop Rocks.

Don't Believe It!

Unless you've got an etiquette problem with the occasional lusty burp, carbonated candy presents no problem whatsoever. No matter how much soda you mix it with, your head will remain where it belongs, positioned safely upon your neck.

Fable Facts

Contrast is everything. The more white-bread the television family, the grimmer the story people appear to be willing to believe.

Did the Kid Who Played Mikey Eat Too Many Pop Rocks, Thereby Causing His Head to Explode?

You'd be amazed how worked up a corporate P.R. department can get over a story like this. It's not true, of course. But that hasn't stopped people from breathing fresh life into the decades-old rumor that the actor who played Mikey, John Gilchrist, downed too many Pop Rocks and Pepsi at the same time, thus causing instant death attributed to a diversely reported variety of disgusting body reactions. Among the most common versions: Mikey blows his top.

The plot of the commercial, for those who have forgotten it or never saw it in the first place, is this: Skeptical big kids won't touch the cereal, but Mikey, who "hates everything," puts aside his finicky ways and tears into a bowl of Life with gusto.

The legend might mean to assign considerable danger to Mikey's choice to not be picky about what he eats. Is this legend a not-so-subtle commentary on the perils of unlimited sensory gratification? Or do young boys simply love telling disgusting stories to their companions?

The Mikey/Pop Rocks legend is representative of not one, but *two* unfortunate varieties of urban legend: the kid-you-loved-on-television-suffers-grisly-death variety, and the familiar-consumer-product-is-actually-lethal variety. For examples of the latter, see Chapter 10, "Brand-Name Nightmares."

"Tragedy" Strikes Other TV Families

Is it possible that the more impossibly wholesome a television family is, the more likely it is to serve as a breeding ground for strange rumors? Could this theory be verified by means of yet another bizarre urban legend centering on another impossibly perfect television family?

Oh, look. Here it comes!

Did Jerry Mathers of Leave It to Beaver *Die in Vietnam?*

No. Actually, most people now accept that Mathers, who played the Beaver, is alive and well. Like Susan Olsen, he was the victim not of violent death, but of a story founded on an innocent mistake. And like Susan Olsen, he had to stare in wonder as the country took that innocent mistake and ran with it.

The facts of the matter are as follows: Mathers, who served in the Air National Guard, appeared in uniform during the Emmy broadcast of 1967. A couple years later, someone with a similar name was killed in Vietnam. A news wire service erroneously reported the death of the 1950s television star, and the country was off to the races.

The rumor took on a surreal life of its own when actress Shelly Winters, who had read one of the inaccurate news reports, reported Mathers's "death" in front of a nationwide television audience during her appearance on *The Tonight Show* on December 22, 1969.

For a while, Mathers, following in McCartney's footsteps and preparing the way for Susan Olsen, had to keep reassuring skeptical news reporters that he was still alive.

And to continue the pattern of a picture-perfect family as a backdrop for bloody doom …

Was Eight Is Enough *Child Star Adam Rich Murdered by a Distressed, Unemployed Stagehand?*

No. Like the other former adorable child stars referenced in this chapter, Rich was still drawing breath without incident at the time the story started circulating. No word yet, though, on whether he's going to start putting on his Alice Cooper makeup and going back on the road.

Did Superman Fail a Superhuman Test and Prove His Mortality?

Another bizarre urban legend links an *adult* children's television star with grisly death. This one has it that actor George Reeves, who starred in the *Superman* show in the 1950s, died when he decided to test his superhuman abilities. Reeves did not leap from a tall building and plummet to his death, nor did he dare someone to shoot him in the chest.

There is a measure—but only a measure—of truth to the story. Reeves did commit suicide in 1959. Apparently dejected over setbacks in his career, the actor shot himself in the head.

Somehow, though, a personal or professional crisis is not enough of a reversal to satisfy the requirements of an urban legend illustrating the death of the actor who played the Man of Steel. To undercut the figure of invincibility effectively, the actor must be driven mad *and believe himself to be the role he plays*.

A separate version has a conscience-stricken Reeves die by his own hand after hearing one too many reports of children leaping out of apartment windows in imitation of Superman.

Creepy, huh? That's the idea.

Bottom Line: Innocence Is Unsettling

Apparently, wholesome TV fare is a little too wholesome for some of us. Anyway, that's one explanation for the legends discussed in this chapter and their seemingly endless variations,

Because one of the driving principles of good storytelling is the reversal of expectation, it's not really that surprising that television programs for and about children have served as fertile territory for the development of urban legends. Unfortunately, the stories that adults may regard as simply entertaining can carry serious emotional implications when they're expanded to include the kiddie-TV personalities of today.

In other words, let's leave Steve—and whomever else 4-, 5-, and 6-year-olds are watching right now—out of this.

The Least You Need to Know

➤ Don't worry—Steve isn't dead; Mr. Rogers isn't a tattooed, gun-obsessed former sniper; and Jerry Mathers didn't die in Vietnam.

➤ Anyone who tells you that (insert name of beloved TV moppet here) actually went on to become Alice Cooper or Marilyn Manson either is pulling your leg or is the victim of a misconception.

➤ Anyone who tells you that (insert name of beloved TV moppet or kids' show personality here) suffered a violent or tragic death may well be either pulling your leg or the victim of a misconception.

➤ Show skepticism when confronted with stories that the girls from *The Brady Bunch* engaged in various public forms of moral turpitude or met with grisly deaths.

➤ Do everyone a favor, and avoid spreading rumors about what may traumatize kids.

Chapter 8

Other Celebrity Legends That Sound Too Weird to Be True (and Are)

You knew all along that Neil Armstrong didn't *really* tell a dirty joke during his historic moon walk. And *you* knew that Oprah Winfrey didn't *really* order a famous fashion designer off her show for racially offensive remarks. And *you* knew that Mel Gibson didn't *really* star in *The Man Without a Face* because his own face was mangled beyond recognition years ago (and was later repaired by a skilled plastic surgeon).

This chapter is for everyone *else* who fell for these and other fascinating, totally bogus stories about celebrities—stories that make the latest gossip item from *The National Enquirer* look like a Pulitzer-contending piece of investigative journalism from *The New York Times*.

A reminder: As usual, there are way too many of these legends to incorporate within a single chapter of this book. What follows is a representative sampling that includes some of the most entertaining and interesting representative legends.

"He Said *What?*" "She Did *What?*"

There's an old show business saying, "It doesn't matter what you print about me, as long as you spell my name right." In today's age of chat rooms, e-mail rumor mills, and sick-and-twisted Web sites, though, you'd find very few celebrities who would sign on to that dictum. Too many salacious, cruel, or downright weird stories have been falsely attributed to the famous.

As the stories in this chapter suggest, in the Internet age, it often *does* matter when we get the facts wrong about famous people.

"One Small Step for Mr. Gorsky"

The following legend, reproduced in its most popular e-mail incarnation, is probably the most famous of the many urban legends involving a mythical celebrity quote.

> When Apollo Mission Astronaut Neil Armstrong first walked on the moon, he not only gave his famous "one small step for man, one giant leap for mankind" statement, but he followed it by several remarks, usual com traffic between him, the other astronauts, and Mission Control. Just before he re-entered the lander, however, he made the enigmatic remark "Good luck, Mr. Gorsky." Many people at NASA thought it was a casual remark concerning some rival Soviet cosmonaut. However, upon checking, there was no Gorsky in either the Russian or the American space programs. Over the years, many people questioned Armstrong as to what the "Good luck, Mr. Gorsky" statement meant, but Armstrong always just smiled.

> On July 5, 1995 (in Tampa Bay, Florida), while answering questions following a speech, a reporter brought up the 26-year-old question to Armstrong. This time he finally responded. Mr. Gorsky had finally died, so Neil Armstrong felt he could answer the question.

> When he was a kid, he was playing baseball with a friend in the backyard. His friend hit a fly ball that landed in the front of his neighbor's bedroom windows. His neighbors were Mr. and Mrs. Gorsky.

> As he leaned down to pick up the ball, young Armstrong heard Mrs. Gorsky shouting at Mr. Gorsky, "Oral sex! You want oral sex? You'll get oral sex when the kid next door walks on the moon!"

> True story.

Actually, not-so-true story. An extended review of the transcripts of the original moon landing yields two important conclusions. First, nobody should have to read extensively through the transcripts of the original moon landing. And second, Armstrong never said any such thing.

This is almost certainly an example of a joke that has been padded with specific-sounding but bogus time and place references (July 5, 1995; Tampa, Florida) by some anonymous legend-spreader in an effort to win credibility. Armstrong himself has recalled hearing the joke in a Buddy Hackett routine.

Don't Believe It!

Neil Armstrong did not send a sly, risqué message to an attention-starved former neighbor during the historic Apollo 11 moon walk.

More Nationally Televised Remarks That Weren't

The visceral thrill of "hearing" a public figure make a risqué remark is often enough to overcome any residual qualms that people have about spreading the story. If it sounds like the person *should* have said it, pass it on!

A Double Entendre That Wasn't

A remarkable exchange supposedly took place when Monica Lewinsky was chatting with Larry King on his CNN show. According to countless people who "actually saw" the interview, Monica tossed off a priceless (and unintentional) double entendre. The e-mail message alerting the nation to the exchange ran as follows:

> Here's the first quotable quote of the century:
> Monica Lewinsky (on CNN's *Larry King Live* discussing her miraculous Jenny Craig weight loss):
>
> "I've learned not to put things in my mouth that are bad for me."

Fascinating, right? And so, so *á propos!*

The only problem: A replay of the interview in question yields nothing remotely like this remark. It's another example of a too-good-to-bother-verifying celebrity quote. So, if you hear someone pass on this tale at the bar, or if you get an e-mail message with the same lame story, ponder the classic "sex-is-dangerous" motif for a moment, and then take a pass on circulating the yarn.

The Mythical Carson Zinger (Part One)

Did Zsa Zsa Gabor set up the raunchiest *Tonight Show* one-liner of them all?

Here's the story. Zsa Zsa is visiting *The Tonight Show* and has, for some reason, a cat on her lap. She smiles and asks Johnny Carson, "Would you like to pet my pussy?"

Carson grins wide, raises an eyebrow, and replies, "I'd love to, but you'll have to remove that darn cat."

Countless viewers claim to have seen this exchange. No one has been able to track down any video, though.

What gives? Well, consider the following.

The Mythical Carson Zinger (Part Two)

Did Johnny make a similarly outrageous off-color remark to the wife of golfer Jack Nicklaus?

Supposedly, Nicklaus's wife mentioned during a visit to *The Tonight Show* that, as a prematch good luck ritual, she took a batch of her husband's golf balls and bestowed kisses upon them. (You can see where this is going, right now, can't you?)

Ahem. Upon being informed that Nicklaus's wife kisses her husband's spherical playing implements, Johnny supposedly remarked, "That must make his putter flutter!"

You can almost picture Carson saying it, can't you? Can you picture Carson saying it to the wife of golfer Arnold Palmer as well? It must be pretty easy to do, because lots of people swear that they've seen the episode. Neither story, however, reflects an actual event on the show. If either did, surely some snippet would have shown up on a videotape anthology by this point.

So far, nothing, other than a sneaking sense that we must, on occasion, really want to see television personalities step right past the borders that they themselves have made a career of dancing around.

Did Oprah Toss a Racist Fashion Designer off Her Show?

Urban legends cynically designed to fan racial animosities often involve celebrities. Here's a classic, all-too-common example that was apparently designed to incite righteous indignation among blacks.

From the suspiciously chummy subject line onward, this crafty bit of cannily contrived hate mail gives every sign of being an attempt by someone who *isn't* an African-American to incite fury among people who are. (Compare the similarly cynical e-mail message claiming that the Voting Rights Act is due to pass into oblivion, in Chapter 20, "You've Got Mail [and It's a Scam].")

```
Subject: FWD: Tommy Hilfiger hates us …

Did you see the recent Oprah Winfrey show on which Tommy
Hilfiger was a guest? Oprah asked Hilfiger if his alleged
statements about people of color were true—he has been
accused of saying things such as, "If I had known that
```

> African-Americans, Hispanics, and Asians would buy my clothes,
> I would not have made them so nice," and "I wish those people
> would not buy my clothes—they were made for upper-class
> whites." What did he say when Oprah asked him if he said these
> things? He said, "Yes." Oprah immediately asked Hilfiger to
> leave her show.
>
> Now, let's give Hilfiger what he's asked for—let's not buy his
> clothes. Boycott! Please—pass this message along.

Unfortunately, the mythical dispute associated with the Winfrey show was taken as factual by many, and the rumor spread.

This message, with its hateful attempt at racial and social division, has a number of variant forms. (There is, for instance, a nearly identical tale involving Liz Claiborne.) All involve on-air spats with Winfrey; all are untrue.

Did Paul Harvey Reveal Startling New Facts About the Early Life of Mel Gibson?

Here's a widely circulated "transcript" supposedly taken from a recent Paul Harvey broadcast about a major celebrity. See if you can spot any flaws in the story (other than the style, punctuation, and spelling errors, that is).

Hot off the Internet—Mel Gibson's (Literally) Incredible Life Story

For those of you keeping track at home, "incredible" means "so extraordinary as to seem impossible," according to the unabridged second edition of *The Random House Dictionary of the English Language* (Random House, 1987).

> Subject: True Story
>
> Here is a true story by Paul Harvey. Pass it to anyone you
> think would find it interesting and inspiring. You will be
> surprised who this young man turned out to be. (Do not look
> at the bottom of this letter until you have read it fully).
>
> Years ago a hard-working man took his family from New York
> State to Australia to take advantage of a work opportunity
> there. Part of this man's family was a handsome young son who
> had aspirations of joining the circus as a trapeze artist or
> an actor. This young fellow, biding his time until a circus
> job or even one as a stagehand came along, worked at the local
> shipyards that bordered on the worst section of town.

Walking home from work one evening, this young man was attacked by five thugs who wanted to rob him. Instead of just giving up his money, the young fellow resisted. However, they bested him easily and proceeded to beat him to a pulp. They mashed his face with their boots, and kicked and beat his body brutally with clubs, leaving him for dead. When the police happened to find him lying in the road, they assumed he was dead and called for the Morgue Wagon.

On the way to the morgue, a policeman heard him gasp for air, and they immediately took him to the emergency unit at the hospital. When he was placed on a gurney, a nurse remarked to her horror that this young man no longer had a face. Each eye socket was smashed; his skull, legs, and arms were fractured; his nose was literally hanging from his face; all his teeth were gone; and his jaw was almost completely torn from his skull. Although his life was spared, he spent over a year in the hospital. When he finally left, his body may have healed, but his face was disgusting to look at. He was no longer the handsome youth that everyone had admired.

When the young man started to look for work again, he was turned down by everyone just on account of the way he looked. One potential employer suggested to him that he join the freak show at the circus as "The Man Who Had No Face." And he did this for a while. He was still rejected by everyone, and no one wanted to be seen in his company. He had thoughts of suicide. This went on for five years.

One day he passed a church and sought some solace there. Entering the church, he encountered a priest who had seen him sobbing while kneeling in a pew. The priest took pity on him and took him to the rectory, where they talked at length. The priest was impressed with him to such a degree that he said that he would do everything possible for him that could be done to restore his dignity and life, if the young man would promise to be the best Catholic he could be and trust in God's mercy to free him from his torturous life.

The young man went to Mass and communion every day, and after thanking God for saving his life, he asked God to only give him peace of mind and the grace to be the best man he could ever be in His eyes.

The priest, through his personal contacts, was able to secure the services of the best plastic surgeon in Australia. They would be no cost to the young man, as the doctor was the priest's best friend. The doctor, too, was so impressed by the young man, whose outlook now on life, even though he had experienced the worst, was filled with good humor and love.

The surgery was a miraculous success. All the best dental work was also done for him. The young man became everything he promised God he would be. He was also blessed with a wonderful and beautiful wife, many children, and success in an industry that would have been the furthest thing from his mind as a career if not for the goodness of God and the love of the people who cared for him. This he acknowledges publicly. The young man—Mel Gibson.

His life was the inspiration for his production of the movie The Man Without a Face. He is to be admired by all of us as a God-fearing man, a political conservative, and an example to all as a true man of courage.

And Now, the Rest of the Story

There's so much to go after here that it's hard to know where to start. Suffice it to say that Gibson may now regret mentioning a brawl that had preceded his audition for the 1979 movie *Mad Max* in a *Playboy* interview a few years back.

That account of the fight, which left Gibson with impressive but by no means disfiguring facial injuries, seems to have inspired the tall tale. Mel got the part, healed up, and eventually became a big-time movie star. No year in the hospital. No bouts of depression. No masterful plastic surgery.

Mel did direct and star in *The Man Without a Face* in 1993, but it wasn't based on his life story. Rather, it was based on a novel by Isabelle Holland that was written in 1972.

One final point about the Gibson myth: Nobody in the world of broadcasting loves a rags-to-riches story more than radio commentator Paul Harvey, but it's hard to believe that even he would try to deliver one with a wrap-up as shamelessly over-the-top as this one: "a God-fearing man, a political conservative"? Please.

Fable Facts

The gory details behind the bogus "true story" of Mel Gibson's early life make it all the harder to stop reading. Many urban legends about celebrities impart such explosive plot points. They grab attention but have nothing to do with the celebrity's actual experience.

Speaking of Politics ...

You wouldn't believe the outrageous things some politicians say.

And you certainly *shouldn't* believe the things some people *say* politicians say. Two examples involving former Vice President Al Gore should serve to make that point.

Urban Legend as Political Weapon

In 1999 and 2000, the right-wingers took Gore into the sights of their legend-creation machinery. Two memorable pieces of their handiwork follow.

Strange but True

Right-wingers spent years circulating absurd rumors about President Clinton, rumors presumably designed to incite fear among the G.O.P. flock. In so doing, they were a step ahead of most urban legend creators, many of whom seem to delight in spreading lies, fear, and panic for the sheer joy of doing so. By placing their calumny in a political context, the right-wing Clinton-haters were forwarding a political agenda. Given the use of similar tactics against Al Gore in 2000, Internet-supported urban legends now appear to be standard weapons in the right's national-campaign arsenal.

Does Al Gore Mess Up His Bible Citations?

That appears to be the point of the following attack e-mail:

> In an important speech given this week, Al Gore attempted to portray how important his faith is in his life. Of course, he was trying to apply what he has learned from his mentor Clinton. Here's what happened.
>
> In his typically stiff, condescending, and insincere manner, he said his favorite Bible verse is John 16:3.
>
> Of course, the speech writer meant 3:16, but he wasn't even familiar enough with this often quoted and of course often taken-for-granted Scripture to catch the error. Neither was Gore, and how incredibly appropriate it is.

> "And they will do this because they have not known the Father or me." John 16:3

The point, of course, was to paint Gore as a religious hypocrite wholly out of touch with Bible Belt voters, many of whom appear to have taken the story seriously.

This tale, which comes in many forms, would be more persuasive if the incident in question had been the result of a Republican slip of the tongue rather than a Democratic one. Author Cal Thomas attributes the 16:3 error to a 1990 discussion with George Bush in his book *Blinded by Might: Why the Religious Right Can't Save America* (Zondervan, 2000). In other words, someone apparently took a Bush blunder (presumably from Thomas's book), attributed it to Gore, and was off to the races. Hypocritical? Just a little.

Yet even *that* attack legend pales in comparison with the following.

Does Al Gore Think Christians Are Bad for the Environment?

Refreshingly free of subtext or subtlety, this crude lie was widely circulated during the 2000 presidential campaign. In fact, you can even make an argument that it *decided* that election. Don't laugh! Who's to say that it *didn't* turn the tide in the historic and bitterly contested 2000 presidential election, with its razor-thin margin in the Sunshine State? After all, if a couple of hundred on-the-fence Floridians happened to conclude that any of what follows was credible ....

You be the judge.

> Subject: AL Gore re: Christianity
>
> THE NOTORIOUS QUOTE OF THE DAY
>
> "Refusing to accept the earth as our sacred mother, these Christians have become a dangerous threat to the survival of humanity. They are the blight on the environment, and to believe in Bible prophecy is unforgivable."
>
> —VP Al Gore, in his book *Earth in the Balance*, p. 342

Predictably, the legend that Gore considered Christians to be threats to the survival of the human race took a number of strange forms. Consider the following, equally unfounded version:

> For Gore and other environmentalists, the Judeo-Christian faith is the source of ecological evil, from oil spills to global warming. He said, "Ignorant Christians who are afraid to open their minds to teachings first offered outside their

own system of belief by refusing to accept that the earth is our sacred mother, Christians have become a dangerous threat to the survival of humanity ... blights on the environment."

Can't you just hear the cogent pre-vote assessment from those undecided Floridians? "Wow. Page numbers, quote marks and everything. Even those three little dots you see in the newspaper sometimes. I guess he must have written it after all, Mabel."

Neither quote, of course, appears in Gore's book *Earth in the Balance,* or any of his other writings.

Could the fate of the republic actually have hinged on lamebrained pieces of political propaganda like this? The answer: Too close to call.

Enough politics. The author's computer is about to overheat.

Did Julia Child Drop a Duck to the Floor During a Program, Pick It Up, Dust It Off, and Say, "It's Fine"?

No. Child denies any such event, although she does admit to dropping a potato pancake *on the stove* during one episode and replacing it. But she never dumped the duck, this food legend notwithstanding. Nor did she take a pull from an opened bottle of cooking wine while the cameras were rolling, as another legend has it.

Fable Facts

Food legends are often nightmarish stories about things that are best not eaten or drunk. Legends involving food corruption or contamination are legion; they may reflect anxiety over our own social roles and obligations, or our lack of trust in others. Then again, they may just be a good way to get people to remember and pass along a story. See Chapter 13, "Tales of Hell from the Service Economy," and Chapter 24, "Too Disgusting for Words" for more examples.

Was Humphrey Bogart the Model for the Gerber Baby Food Baby?

This seems pretty unlikely, given that Bogart was born around the turn of the century, and the campaign using the now-iconic baby illustration launched in 1929. Some of the confusion giving rise to this popular story may be attributable to the fact that Bogart's mother was a commercial artist.

What makes the story fascinating is the possibility that the screen's ultimate tough-guy of the 1930s and 1940s could also be the emblem of innocence and guilelessness we all grew up with. Of such contrasts are urban legends born. See also Chapter 7, "The Family Hour (Not): Twisted Legends About Your Favorite Children's Television Stars," for the answer to the pressing question "Is Mr. Rogers a retired Army sniper?" (No.)

While we're on the subject ....

Was John Denver a Retired Army Sniper?

No. Same deal, just without the childcare angle. Take an entertainer with a gentle, peace-loving image, and attach the nearest violent image you've got access to.

Wait until the folks who engineered this legend come up with something for the late Mother Teresa. Can you imagine what they might use to elicit sufficient shock value? Are you sure you want to?

The Great *Newlywed Game* Controversy

Perhaps the most controversial of the celebrity-based legends, this one involves game show host Bob Eubanks, of the original *Newlywed Game*. The show, you'll recall, focused on embarrassing questions posed by Eubanks to a panel of newlyweds. Husbands were supposed to guess how wives would respond to the questions, and vice versa.

As we have seen, many television-based urban legends take the form of episodes and events that people swore they saw broadcast on television but couldn't have because they simply never happened. One of the most famous of these legends was thought to involve a episode of the *Newlywed Game*. As it turns out, though, the story in question may well have been inspired by an actual episode of that classic game show.

The Butt of the Joke

The disputed legend originally went as follows:

➤ Host Eubanks asks Guileless Young Wife to guess how Innocent Husband would have answered some variation on the question, "Where's the strangest place you ever made whoopie?"

➤ Guileless Young Wife thinks for a moment.

➤ After due consideration, Guileless Young Wife offers her answer: "That'd be the butt, Bob."

Predictably, the story came in many forms. Remember how urban legends often take varying forms? For many people, the shifting details of the *Newlywed Game* account suggested that it was unlikely to reflect an actual event.

Did anything like this exchange really happen? For years, host Bob Eubanks, heartily sick of confronting that question in interviews, not only swore that it didn't, but also offered a $10,000 reward to anyone who could offer proof that it had.

Censors, Start Your Engines

The story *seemed* to lack foundation ... until a tape from the honest-to-goodness *Newlywed Game* show featuring a very similar exchange actually surfaced. In the snippet, now available on the Internet (on the excellent site www.snopes.com), the woman answers a very similar question with the less quotable but more direct response, "In the ass?" and leaves the studio audience in stitches. The clip is indisputably genuine. Eubanks, as ever, remains unflappable; the hubby is pretty much floored, as were the censors, who bleeped over the words "In the ass?" (A replay and a little lip-reading, though, confirms that that is in fact what the wife, whose name is Olga, says.)

So, something very funny and very similar, but not identical, to the legend did take place—and was apparently broadcast. Did this incident serve as the inspiration for the (markedly wittier) "That'd be the butt" story? If so, how does one account for the fact that the show would have aired at a time when slow-motion replays of the sequence would have been much more difficult to obtain, and when the vast majority of the show's watchers would have had little or no idea what the audience was laughing at?

Fable Facts

There's a lot more where the material in this chapter came from. Virtually none of it's credible, though, and a lot of it's pretty rank. Celebrities like Richard Gere, Rod Stewart, and Jamie Lee Curtis have all been subjected to starring roles in lurid, hateful, and untrue urban legends. Makes you wonder whether God somehow has it in for talented people.

Did a separate urban legend arise that happened to coincide with an incident that simply slipped Eubanks's mind? Did Eubanks ever pay up? Did the couple in the actual videotape ever speak to each other again?

Some mysteries are perhaps better left undisturbed.

And Finally ...

After hearing so much that is lurid and off-putting about celebrities, we'll close with a legend that actually imparts a positive message of racial inclusiveness. It didn't actually *happen,* of course, but given some of the stomach-churning stuff that people decide to swear is above board about their favorite stars, the following is at least a step in the right direction.

> Having her hair done at a Dallas beauty parlor, a woman told a cautionary tale about racial prejudice. The story deserves a wider audience.
>
> On a recent weekend in Las Vegas, the woman related, she won a bucketful of quarters at a slot machine. She took a break from the slots for dinner with her husband in the hotel dining room. But first she wanted to stash the quarters in her room.
>
> "I'll be right back and we'll go to eat," she told her husband, and she carried the coin-laden bucket to the elevator. As she was about to walk into the elevator, she noticed two men already aboard. Both were black. One of them was big—very big—and was an intimidating figure. The woman froze.
>
> Her first thought was. "These two are going to rob me." Her next thought was, "Don't be a bigot; they look like perfectly nice gentlemen." But racial stereotypes are powerful, and fear immobilized her. She stood and stared at the two men.
>
> She felt anxious, flustered, and ashamed. She hoped they didn't read her mind, but she knew they surely did; her hesitation about joining them on the elevator was all too obvious. Her face was flushed. She couldn't just stand there, so with a mighty effort of will, she picked up one foot, stepped forward and followed with the other foot to get on the elevator. Avoiding eye contact, she turned around stiffly and faced the elevator doors as they closed. A second passed, and then another second, and then another. Her fear increased!
>
> The elevator didn't move. Panic consumed her. My God, she thought, I'm trapped and about to be robbed! Her heart plummeted. Perspiration poured from every pore.
>
> Then one of the men said, "Hit the floor." Instinct told her, "Do what they tell you." The bucket of quarters flew upward as she threw out her arms and collapsed on the elevator carpet. A shower of coins rained down on her. "Take my money and spare me," she prayed. More seconds passed.

91

She heard one of the men say politely, "Ma'am, if you'll just tell us what floor you're going to, we'll push the button." The one who said it had a little trouble getting the words out. He was trying mightily to hold in a belly laugh.

She lifted her head and looked up at the two men. They reached down to help her up. Confused, she struggled to her feet. "When I told my man here to hit the floor," said the average-sized one, "I meant that he should hit the elevator button for our floor. I didn't mean for you to hit the floor, ma'am." He spoke genially. He bit his lip. It was obvious that he was having a hard time not laughing.

She thought, "My God, what a spectacle I've made of myself." She was too humiliated to speak. She wanted to blurt out an apology, but words failed her. How do you apologize to two perfectly respectable gentlemen for behaving as though they were going to rob you? She didn't know what to say. The three of them gathered up the strewn quarters and refilled her bucket. When the elevator arrived at her floor, they insisted on walking her to her room. She seemed a little unsteady on her feet, and they were afraid that she might not make it down the corridor. At her door, they bid her a good evening.

As she slipped into her room, she could hear them roaring with laughter while they walked back to the elevator. The woman brushed herself off. She pulled herself together and went downstairs for dinner with her husband.

The next morning, flowers were delivered to her room—a dozen roses. Attached to EACH rose was a crisp $100 bill. The card said, "Thanks for the best laugh we've had in years."

It was signed,

Eddie Murphy and Bodyguard

An Elevating Tale

That elevator yarn also has been connected to Bill Cosby, Richard Pryor, and many other black celebrities over the years.

If you overlook the implausibilities (would *you* say "Hit the floor" instead of, perhaps, "Hit seven"?), and the narrator's ability to hear what the unnamed woman is thinking at any moment, the story is actually pretty positive. It seems to be saying, "Don't make unwarranted assumptions about people. Don't assume the worst. Don't be a racist boob." (That's refreshing, given the hateful contexts of many other urban legends dealing with racial insecurities.) And remember, celebrities are human, too.

The Least You Need to Know

➤ If you were considering feeling sorry for Mr. Gorsky, don't—the story is bogus.

➤ If you were considering feeling angry at any fashion designer for harboring racial hatred that got him or her tossed off Oprah's show, don't—the story is bogus.

➤ If someone swears to have seen a celebrity say or do something strikingly unlikely on TV, consider asking for a video clip or a reference in a major media source.

➤ If you watch enough episodes of the *Newlywed Game* in search of the long-lost "butt" clip, strange things may happen to your mind, and then someone else will find it before you do, causing you significant psychological distress.

➤ If you're looking for a great tale to pass on, consider telling the Eddie Murphy/Richard Pryor/Bill Cosby story to your friends—but identify it as bogus, because it is.

Part 3

Paranoia

A popular saying has it that "what goes around comes around."

The stories in the following chapters demonstrate that we may be a little too concerned about things going around and then (gulp!) coming right back around at us. Here we have legends featuring marauding beasts, befouled consumer products, shadowy government conspiracies, ominous strangers, service staff with bad intent, crazed gang initiates, and representatives of the Establishment pushed past the brink of reason. What did we do to deserve their attention?

In the end, it may not matter. If these stories are to be believed, they are all out to get us after all.

Chapter 9

All Creatures, Great and Small

In This Chapter

➤ Why we can't get enough of legends about animals

➤ Dog legends

➤ Cat legends

➤ Bug legends

➤ Predator legends

It's often hard to resist passing on urban legends in which animals play a leading role. They're often impossible to forget—witness the long-running story about marauding alligators in the sewers of New York City (more about that later).

Here are two theories on why animal legends stick with us in the way they do: First, lots of us just plain love—or hate—certain animals from the word *go*. The animals in question are inherently attractive (think about puppies) or repellent (consider, say, rats or snakes or alligators). In other words, the animals themselves are *already* rich in associations, either positive or negative. That makes them prime candidates for starring roles in memorable urban legends.

Second, people have a habit of attributing many human qualities to animals. (Just ask the folks at Disney about the profitability of working *anthropomorphism* into animated feature films.) So, some stories that may seem at first glance to involve animals are *really* primarily about problems and challenges faced by human beings.

Whatever the reasons, stories involving our fellow creatures are at least as old as the Bible's account of Eve's chat with that crafty snake. In this chapter, we look at similarly captivating modern legends that involve run-ins with members of the animal kingdom.

Warning: Some of this gets a little dicey for the humans involved. Of course, the animals don't always make out well either, as illustrated by our first account.

Legend Lingo

Anthropomorphism is the act of projecting human attributes onto an animal or other non-human entity.

The Pooch in the Microwave

To begin, we'll look at one of the most persistent urban legends involving an animal—the microwaved poodle. Its grim but apt message for human beings (that they are capable of heedlessly destroying someone or something they love) may account for its popularity.

In the story, a woman gives her beloved poodle a shampoo but finds herself frustrated when she can't dry him off quickly enough with a standard towel. Then, after catching a glimpse of the microwave oven in her kitchen, she has a brainstorm. She'll pop the pooch in the oven, punch High, zap the animal for a minute or so, and be ready to roll.

When she does so, however, disaster unfolds. The poodle, alas, explodes, thereby providing an important, if grisly, object lesson in the improper use of modern cooking tools—and supplying the requisite "yuck factor" necessary for an enduring urban legend.

The pet owner's horror at having done in the poodle (or whatever breed is adopted for the purposes of the story) is usually the final image of the story. Sadder but wiser about the use of household appliances, the poor dog owner is left to mourn the loss of her pooch—and, presumably, apply a healthy coating of Formula 409 to the interior of the oven before using it to heat up a bowl of oatmeal.

Something akin to the pseudoparental horror of the poodle owner before the microwave is summoned in the following legend. It explores a similar "small-dog-in-jeopardy" theme, but it adds a dash of adorability to the mix.

Cute Puppies Are Counting on You

Did you ever see one of those television commercials urging you to spend a dollar a day to help save the life of a third-world child? Those are legitimate. The following "warning," which follows the same general theme, isn't—but neither that fact nor a certain friendly unintelligibility has kept the plea from being circulated far and wide via e-mail by unsuspecting dog enthusiasts.

Every day, hundreds of puppies are killed. Why? Because they are sick. They are kept in "puppy mills" and then are shipped to pet stores. If a dog is bought in a pet store, it can die easily. The poor puppies in the mills aren't even let out to go to the bathroom. They just go on each other. The food and water is scarce, too. Many die in the mills.

What can you do about it?

Just send this to as many people as you can. Then $1 will be donated to every person sent to. Remember, this is not your money! But it will help a lot.

Could you just spare 10–20 minutes of your time to save these poor puppies' lives? It will make a huge difference.

To help people send, the person who sends this to the most people can choose from these two prizes:

1. Receive an award that will be posted on many huge Web sites that demote dog cruelty
2. Have their choice of one of the many dog Ty Beanie Babies

Do this for the puppies. It can save their lives.

Don't Believe It!

Anonymous appeals on behalf of dogs trapped in "puppy mills" are bogus. Instead of spreading the rumor, make a donation to the American Humane Association, whose Web site address appears in this chapter.

Fable Facts

Puppies in jeopardy aren't the only way to get people to respond as though a helpless creature were in need of protection. For more examples of manipulative and dishonest e-mail campaigns that tell emotional tall tales, see Chapter 20, "You've Got Mail (and It's a Scam)."

What was that a minute ago about anthropomorphism?

The entreaty that appears here is perhaps the most ham-handed attempt yet to use the Internet to engender concern for a surrealistically nonexistent charitable effort. If you're concerned about the plight of puppies in pet stores, you're supposed to take 10 to 20 minutes of your busy day to ... do what? In order that the puppies might benefit ... how? And you'll be rewarded with ... huh?

Never mind. Puppies are lovable. Someone is doing something vaguely terrible to them. They need your help. Pass it on.

Meanwhile, back on planet Earth, people who are interested in actually improving the lot of victimized animals, including adorable puppies, can point their browsers toward the American Humane Association's Web site at www.americanhumane.org.

Sly Cats, Sleeping Babies

In the two legends we've just seen, cute little doggies function as stand-ins for endangered children. When it comes to cats, though, people seem more likely to take a different approach, casting felines as wily (or even other-worldly) aggressors.

This is an instance in which what once might have been called an "old wives' tale" is now being classified as an urban legend. Whatever you call it, the story goes as follows: An actual but anonymous baby in a forgotten or mysteriously undisclosed location was inattentively left to sleep in a room to which the family housecat had access. While no one was looking, the feline crept up into the baby's crib, licked its face, and then, quite literally, sucked the breath out of the child's body.

Fable Facts

Urban legends involving malevolent cats may have something to do with the celebrated standoffishness of felines. As writer Mary Bly put it, "Dogs come when they are called; cats take a message and get back to you."

The story is quite literally hundreds of years old; its origins appear to go back to the days when horrible events of the kind that we would now identify as crib death needed *some* kind of explanation, rational or otherwise. Cats have long been associated with witches and witchcraft; the idea that a kitty would turn to the Dark Side and hoover the life-breath from a sleeping infant might have passed muster back in the Middle Ages. It's still circulated widely now, however, despite earnest protestations that it's bogus from doctors who treat humans *and* doctors who treat animals.

Cats *do* like to sleep next to warm people, though—a fact worked into the following legend to ominous and humiliating effect.

Sly Cat, Nude Man

In this legend, the cat plays a (half-conscious?) role in bringing about the humiliation of the unwelcome human being with whom she's in conflict.

A man—presumably a houseguest—is sleeping late on a bed that's set up on the floor of a living room featuring a large picture window and a great big curtain covering it. The cat, who "owns" the house, decides to nestle nice and close—close enough to pee on the fellow's head, which she promptly does. Message: Intruders aren't welcome here.

That's not the most pleasant awakening in the world, and the gentleman reacts accordingly. He picks up the cat and flings it across the room. Alas, the cat lands, claws-first, on the big curtain in front of the picture window. It falls to the floor. When the man scurries to replace it—presumably to avoid the notice of his host—he realizes that he's giving a free lesson in mature male nudity to a group of tittering schoolchildren who happen to be passing by.

To paraphrase Bob Dylan, the moral of this legend, the moral of this song, is simply that men should not be where men do not belong.

Alligators in the Sewers

Even people who know virtually nothing about urban legends seem to know that the widely spread story about albino alligators roaming the sewers of New York has been discredited for some time. Still, the tale has provoked enough discussion to warrant a review of the key points here.

The earliest forms of the story started circulating in the 1920s. Back then, Florida was emerging as a popular spot for New Yorkers to visit on vacation; many of them returned with tiny pet alligators. The skittering critters were lovable as could be when they were tiny, but they somehow seemed to lose that kid-friendly charm when they began to approach their full adult size. What to do with the quickly maturing reptiles? Flush them down the toilet, of course.

Fable Facts

The story of alligators in the sewers of New York may have originated in Robert Daley's 1959 book *The World Beneath the City*. In that volume, a New York superintendent of sewers is quoted as having seen the beasts in the bowels of the city in the mid-1930s. The official in question, however, later described the story as a "fanciful tale" rather than a firsthand experience—which sounds about right.

That, at least, was the story passed on by eager legend-circulators, who typically claimed to have heard of someone who had met someone who had read a story about someone who had seen huge alligators roaming the city's sewers. To make the tale even more memorable—and perhaps, just perhaps, to enforce parental warnings against playing in or around manholes and other sewer openings—the alligators were described as white. (No light would reach the sewers, you see.)

The Real Deal on the Big Apple's White Alligator Epidemic

Here are the facts about this popular story:

➤ Nobody has ever found an alligator, albino or otherwise, in the sewer systems of New York City, although there were legitimate reports in the 1920s and 1930s of alligators showing up elsewhere in the city.

➤ Once Florida made it illegal to remove alligators from the state in 1938, actual sightings, predictably, became quite rare.

➤ Scientists are skeptical that an alligator could survive for long in the Big Apple's sewer system, inasmuch as the gators are (surprise, surprise) accustomed to the warm waters of Florida, not the colder temperatures associated with Gotham's sewers.

Beware of Foreigners Bearing Pets

Animals figure prominently in a whole range of legends involving fear of outsiders. Frequently, the animal is a gift from a foreign land. Heedlessly accepted, the pet becomes an object of horror—and a reminder that unfamiliar people and cultures simply can't be trusted.

For other legends meant to demonstrate the perils of coming into contact with outsiders or their customs, see Chapter 14, "Beware the Outsider."

The most famous of these legends is probably the following.

Legend Lingo

Motherhood nightmares are anxiety dreams involving births of deformed or inhuman progeny.

"Say, You Wouldn't Know What Breed of Dog This Is, Would You?"

An American lady and her husband decide to vacation in Mexico. Shortly after they check into their hotel, they notice a small, odd-looking pooch hanging around their front door. It's not much to look at, but the woman is taken in by its dopey charm and decides to feed it. By the end of the vacation, she and the new animal have made quite a connection, and since no one has claimed the uncollared mutt, she decides to take it home with her. She's in love with the thing.

Strange but True

Some versions of the popular "Mexican Pet" legend take the form of nightmares in which the heroine clasps the new "pet" to her as though it were an infant, cares for it like a baby, or allows the beast to sleep in the bed that she shares with her husband. Compare the image of little Alice clutching the infant/pig in Lewis Carroll's *Through the Looking Glass*, or the horror that Mia Farrow's character feels upon first seeing her son in the film *Rosemary's Baby*.

Foreshadowing alert: Incipient *motherhood nightmare* ahead.

The lady bundles up her new pet in a blanket and takes it with her as she and her husband board the bus that will take them back to the airport. Her new friend is licking her face affectionately when she notices that a man across the aisle is staring at the animal. Thinking that he may know something about dogs, she asks, "Say, you wouldn't know what breed of dog this is, would you?"

The man across the aisle shakes his head grimly and keeps staring at the pet. He explains that the animal she is cradling like an infant is no dog, but a particularly large breed of Mexican rat.

Eeeeew!

Not just a rat, mind you—a particularly large breed of *foreign* rat. Never mind that New York City has huge rats to spare. (Albino alligators, maybe not, but rats, they've got.) This story's not interested in such inconvenient facts, though. In dreamland, you get the really *big, honking, disgusting* rats from a foreign country.

This story—which has many, many variant strains—generally seems to involve a woman who "falls for" the new addition to the family. She often displays maternal care for the rat-that-looks-like-a-dog.

The sequence to bear in mind here is this:

➤ Woman strays from her normal geographic (and cultural) routine by "crossing the border."

➤ Woman bonds with unfamiliar, seemingly cute animal.

➤ Woman realizes she's coddling a monster.

Beware, ladies. That exotic culture you're planning to visit may just seduce you—and may lead you to bring a strange and revolting beast into your family, without your knowledge.

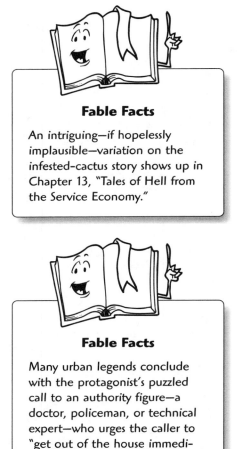

Fable Facts

An intriguing—if hopelessly implausible—variation on the infested-cactus story shows up in Chapter 13, "Tales of Hell from the Service Economy."

Fable Facts

Many urban legends conclude with the protagonist's puzzled call to an authority figure—a doctor, policeman, or technical expert—who urges the caller to "get out of the house immediately."

Beware of Foreigners Bearing Plants

Similar concerns about unfamiliar cultural influences appear to be behind the many stories concerning exotic—and infested—plants brought home from foreign climes. Consider the following memorable example.

A family receives a large imported cactus as a gift; the plant lands in a prominent spot in the dining room. Not long after its entry to the house, however, the folks notice something strange about this plant. It appears to be breathing.

The sides of the huge cactus actually seem to be moving back and forth. The movement isn't obvious at first, but it is perceptible. A few more days go by, and the cactus is *still* breathing. The mother calls the local nursery, describes the plant's "symptoms," and asks what's up.

The reaction that she hears over the phone from the plant expert horrifies her. The panicked voice on the other end of the line orders her to remove the cactus from the house immediately. She does so, and the very moment she gets the expanding/contracting cactus out the door, the strange plant explodes. Thousands of tiny spiders are expelled from the heart of the cactus.

See what happens when you let those untrustworthy foreign plants in the door?

And Now, a Few Words About the Whole Hidden Bug Nests Thing

Urban legends about hidden nests of bug eggs (or scorpion eggs) are so numerous that they deserve discussion as a category all their own.

Many of these strange stories carry the familiar trust-nothing-that-comes-from-a-foreign-country moral, but a few have other points to make. Here's a representative sampling of the genre. People must be really worried about bugs that symbolize disease, bugs that symbolize sexual passion, bugs that represent punishment for excessive vanity, bugs that represent all of the above, and bugs that represent, well, bugs.

Exploding Bugs in the 'Do (Female Version)

This legend tells the unfortunate story of a teenaged girl who loved the attention that she got from having her hair up in one of those sky-high "beehive" hairdos—but hated the work that the 'do entailed. Instead of putting in the daily effort to wash her locks and tease them back into their gravity-defying structure, she came up with a brilliant idea. Soak the locks in sugar, and then use a special pillow so that the whole thing would hold up while she caught 40 winks. Why bother washing your hair every night when you can look great by lacquering your hair into place with an edible substance?

The poor kid should have either put in the long hours associated with actually using conditioner and shampoo, or given the whole "must-have" hairdo idea a rest. Sure, the beehive may be great for attracting the notice of the guys at school, but it does carry certain drawbacks. For instance, if you keep up the sugar-water routine for a couple of weeks, your mom finds you dead as a doornail in your bed, gnawed to death by the hungry bugs that have been patiently building a nest in that sticky cone of hair.

Time out. Long, unnaturally tapered hairdo … torrents of swarming foreign bodies … death in bed—maybe sexual anxieties played a role in the development of this legend? Who can say?

Fable Facts

Interested in upping the yuck factor? The sugar–lacquered hairdo story sometimes features hungry rats instead of hungry bugs, or even a version involving dough that resulted in—no, this is neither the time nor the place. If you're really interested in following that variation through to its sickening conclusion, see Chapter 23, "Too Disgusting for Words."

Exploding Bugs in the 'Do (Male Version)

Those pesky bugs. You've tried scrubbing them out. You've tried soaking them out. And all you get is eggs inside the hairdo.

Ever wonder how those guys with dreadlocks wash their hair? You'll be too disgusted to ask after hearing this legend. According to the myth, a dreadlock fan decided that it was time to change his image. He went to the barbershop, but the barber found that a standard pair of scissors wouldn't do the trick. He tried a bigger pair. No dice. He tried the biggest pair in the shop—and finally cut through one of the dreadlocks. You'll never guess what came crawling out.

Bugs. Redbacked spiders, to be precise. Lots of 'em, biting the poor dude all over. He ran screaming from the shop, and his girlfriend eventually found him bitten to death in his apartment.

So the next time you're considering adopting an extravagant, stand-out-in-the-crowd, multiple-phallic-symbol hairdo, consider the virtues of the humble crew cut.

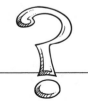

Strange but True

Remember the old Billy Crystal routine on *Saturday Night Live?* Impersonating Fernando Lamas, Crystal opined that it's "more important to look good than to feel good." The bugs-in-the-elaborate-coiffure suggest that, at some level, people actually have had their doubts about this for some time—like, say, seven or eight centuries.

The various "killer hairdo" legends may date all the way back to the thirteenth century. A folk tale from that era tells of a narcissistic woman who spent so much time preparing her hairstyle that the Devil himself placed a spider within her locks.

Predators, Predators Everywhere

Fanciful animals-on-the-attack legends take many forms. Snake attacks are perennially popular subjects; sometimes the slithering beasties are said to have shown up in children's play areas, or in the lining of a (foreign-made!) woman's coat. Just as grisly, and equally lacking in foundation, is the story of the bear that attacked a boy whose parents had covered him in honey, the better to snap a memorable photo. Parental guilt overload! Finally, there's the alligator who wandered onto the links and *swallowed an adult golfer whole.* Right.

What these attack stories "prove" is not that fearsome creatures lurk behind every tree—but that fears about predators, real and imagined, are woven very deeply indeed into our collective psyche.

Here's an example of an animal-attack legend that appeals to our innate desire to protect children. (The heck with the golfers—they can fend for themselves.)

Anacondas Chomp Helpless Kid! (Not)

Planning a trip to South America soon? You might think twice if the following breathless e-mail message, complete with lurid photo attachments, lands in your in-box.

The horror! The horror!

> Apparently, three boys were sleeping in the jungle in South America. When the other two woke up, one was missing and a huge snake was lying next to them, You'll see the snake in the first two photos, with the boy inside; the third one shows the snake cut open to reveal the boy. You have to see this … unbelievable ….

Unbelievable, indeed.

Apparently hoping that the prospect of honest-to-goodness gross-out photos will keep you from noticing this message's lack of supporting references, vague geographical references, and abysmal writing, the creators of this child-in-jeopardy story put all their chips on the visuals. So what, exactly, do you get once you click on the pictures?

Not the stomach-churning mess you were expecting, that's for sure. Photos 1 and 2 are indeed of a big snake in the back of someone's pickup truck, and the snake has certainly had something sizable for dinner. Could be a dog or something. Photo 3 is a suspiciously different-looking image—no truck in sight—featuring a suspiciously different-looking "snake" (or, perhaps, just fake snakeskin) with someone's legs emerging from an opening we're supposed to believe was just made by a knife. Photo 4 is a close-up shot of the same person's legs.

If you feel like throwing up over this sequence of images when they come your way, it's certainly your prerogative under state and federal law to do so. Before you yield to temptation, though, consider that even the biggest snakes are regarded as highly unlikely to gulp down the person whose legs show up in the "evidence." The entrée is too big. It's too much trouble to digest. And there's the potential for a lot of bad press.

Then again, a snake might conclude, you might get the bad press even if you *do* behave yourself, play by the rules, and steer clear of humans and their environs.

Just ask the alligators.

Fable Facts

Reptile Really Gets Around Department: The snake-swallows-helpless-kid story, and its accompanying goofy mock-horror photo sequence, has been placed in Asia, South America, and the South Pacific.

The Least You Need to Know

➤ In considering the popularity of urban legends involving animals, bear in mind that some animals bring strong positive or negative associations to mind, and people love projecting human attributes onto other creatures.

➤ Avoid placing poodles in microwaves. (But you knew that already.)

➤ Remember that some legends involving dangerous or repellent animals heedlessly imported from "exotic" locales are thinly veiled warnings against the influence of foreign cultures or people.

➤ Relax—cats can't suck the breath out of babies, and neither snakes nor alligators are likely to gobble you whole.

➤ Consider, however, that fears about predators, real and imagined, are woven very deeply into our collective psyche.

Chapter 10

Brand-Name Nightmares

> ### In This Chapter
>
> ➤ The hidden fear that brand names we've come to trust are, in fact, deeply nasty
>
> ➤ The great-granddaddy of brand-name urban legends
>
> ➤ Mythical problems with popular soft drinks
>
> ➤ Other strange stories about familiar brands

Advertisers spend untold millions of dollars to get consumers to anchor positive associations such as trust, pride, love, and cleanliness to specific products and services. Their reward: Skeptical consumers who ask, "Are those associations really accurate?"

Let's put it this way: They're a heck of a lot *more* accurate than the stories that appear in this chapter.

In this part of the book, we explore urban legends that take all that carefully cultivated brand awareness as the basis for graphic, impossible stories that share a single urgent point: Things aren't at all what they seem.

(A side note: stories involving familiar companies also appear in Chapter 13, "Tales of Hell from the Service Economy," and Chapter 23, "Too Disgusting for Words.")

Unknown Danger Ahead!

There's an old saying, "Skepticism is a virtue." And maybe a little skepticism once in a while regarding the interests of the corporations that manufacture and distribute popular consumer products *is* a good thing. The following stories, though, do nothing but scare and enrage people about things that aren't worth getting scared or angry about—and they distract attention from genuine consumer safety issues.

Welcome to the topsy-turvy world of *brand-name urban legends* that use the familiarity of established products and services to play cynically on social fears, or to take advantage of our uncertainties about processes that we don't understand (and can't control).

Legend Lingo

Brand-name urban legends usually tell their tales at the expense of brand identities that have taken years or decades to build up. Some of these stories may have arisen from innocent mistakes, but most appear to persist as the result of conscious attempts to tarnish the reputation of the companies involved.

The legends that follow reflect our hidden fear that something we've come to trust over years and years of direct personal experience is in fact deeply nasty; sometimes there are sub-themes involving deeper issues such as diversity and gender roles. The legends all rely on familiar brand names to make their points.

In urban legends, contrast, surprise, and reversal of expectation are often key elements. The idea that something familiar is actually dangerous is a familiar theme in popular folklore. A couple centuries ago, the image might have been that of an apple that looked delicious but was actually poisoned. Nowadays, we may wonder whether that tube of Crest is in league with the Prince of Darkness. (It's not.)

Looking on the Bright Side (Kind Of)

If you work for one of the companies that has been unfairly associated with some unwarranted nastiness as the result of a legend like the one that appears in this chapter, you have one consolation. Some creative individual or group has used your firm's good name to make all the advertising pros on Madison Avenue look like a paragon of honesty.

Granted, that may not be a *huge* consolation. But it's the best anyone has been able to come up with.

The Biggie

Let's dispose of the great-granddaddy legend in this category right away.

Somehow, somewhere, sometime when you least expect it, someone is going to walk up to you and say, "Hey, did you know that Procter & Gamble is a haven for Satanists? Remember that moon-and-stars symbol? That was a clue!"

It seems as if the good folks at P&G have been trying to put out this particular fire for the last couple of millennia. There's not much help to be found in idiotic e-mail messages like this one, which has circulated extensively:

The President of Procter & Gamble appeared on the Sally Jesse Raphael Show on March 1, 1998. He announced that "due to the openness of our society," he was coming out of the closet about his association with the church of Satan. He stated that a large portion of his profits from Procter & Gamble products goes to support this satanic church. When asked by Sally Jesse if stating this on TV would hurt his business, he replied, "THERE ARE NOT ENOUGH CHRISTIANS IN THE UNITED STATES TO MAKE A DIFFERENCE." …

If you are not sure about the product, look for Procter & Gamble written on the products, or the symbol of a ram's horn, which will appear on each product beginning on January 1, 2000. The ram's horn will form the 666, which is known as Satan's number. Christians should remember that if they purchase any of these products, they will be contributing to the church of Satan.

Inform other Christians about this, and STOP buying Procter & Gamble Products. Let's show Procter & Gamble that there are enough Christians to make a difference. On a previous Jenny Jones Show, the owner of Procter & Gamble said that if Satan would prosper, he would give his heart and soul to him. Then he gave Satan credit for his riches.

Anyone interested in seeing this tape should send $3.00 to: SALLY TRANSCRIPTS, 515 WEST 57TH STREET, NEW YORK NY 10019. WE URGE YOU TO MAKE COPIES OF THIS AND PASS IT ON TO AS MANY PEOPLE AS POSSIBLE.

Fable Facts

For years, high school and college students—and a fair number of adults without anything better to do—have subjected tubes of toothpaste and other consumer products to intense analysis. Their fruitless search for satanic markings placed by officials of Procter & Gamble makes obsessed Beatles fans look cautious by comparison.

Gee, *that* all sounds plausible enough, doesn't it?

As the people at P&G could probably recite from a coma by now, none of the imagery on any Procter & Gamble product is a signal of the corporation's ties to Satan. The ram's horn thing is pure fiction, as is the supposed insertion of the numbers 666 on P&G products. The whole message is bogus.

There was no such appearance on Raphael's show (or any of a dozen other talk shows to which the company's president has been falsely linked). No transcript will come your way if you send three bucks to the address given. The whole thing is banana oil.

How Did It All Start?

The legend regarding Procter & Gamble and various dark forces has its roots in a much-discussed symbol, the familiar man-in-the-moon-and-stars emblem. This symbol, a company trademark of long standing, was developed by crate-makers in the nineteenth century. Lummoxes in the *twentieth* century insisted on linking the symbol to any number of implausible practices, so P&G changed its package designs.

That didn't rule out the worldwide circulation of dark stories, though. The long-running delusion appears to be a variation on the ever-popular paranoid fantasy that Unspecified Dark Forces control major companies. It's hard not to conclude, though, that a large part of the story's appeal lies in the simple, perverse joy some people get out of spreading it.

Lately, the good people at Procter & Gamble have had to contend with yet *another* urban legend, this one alleging that its product Febreze can cause house pets to get sick or die. There's nothing to that one, either. Dr. Steve Hansen, of the National Animal Poison Control Center, has been quoted saying that, "based on the information we've got, we would be very surprised if this product presented a problem at all to dogs and cats."

Strange but True

The Procter & Gamble Talk Show Hoax is a baseless rumor alleging that the head of the consumer products company openly admitted, on some nationally televised talk show or other, his company's ties to Satanism. The company has no ties to Satanism. It does have a lot of lawyers, though, and it has started suing people who spread lies about it. So, if you know someone who gets a kick out of circulating this sort of stuff, remind him or her that there may well be a price to pay.

Dirty Bubble-Gum Card Alert!

How could anyone possibly top the Procter & Gamble whopper? Well, how about suggesting that Star Wars bubble-gum cards feature a dirty picture?

It ain't Satanism, but it sure has caught people's attention.

There is a persistent rumor that one of the Star Wars bubble-gum cards from the 1970s features an erotic image of the robot C-3PO, courtesy of a disgruntled artist.

(The disgruntled artist theme is a tip-off that we may be dealing with an urban legend here; there are similar stories about various snatches of animated naughtiness in any number of popular cartoon videos.)

The truth, as usual, is more complicated. The card in question is an *unretouched photograph,* making the disgruntled artist theory a bit of a stretch. And the image is not so much obscene as coincidental.

A lighting oddity and a disconnected bit of the robot costume makes it look as though C-3PO is, um, exposed about the groin area, revealing a small metallic component that one wouldn't expect a robot in a kid's movie to flaunt.

What do you want, a picture? Well, this is a mainstream book, so you're not going to get one. Suffice it to say that the image is one of those Rorschach things. If someone pointed it out to you, you'd notice it. If you noticed it on your own, you might wonder if you've been working a little too hard lately.

And, for the curious: No, the robot is not aroused. He looks rather as though he just got out of a cold android shower of some kind.

Fable Facts

Legends involving familiar brand names may invoke (supposedly) sexually explicit images, tales of revenge, and threats to innocent children. The myth about the obscene Star Wars bubble-gum card does all three.

America Online Is Watching You (Not)

Has America Online tracked down one of those magical e-mail trackers? Is it using this remarkable piece of equipment to find out just how many people really want to keep the company's instant messaging service free? Or have some anonymous troublemakers who failed Business Writing 101 just set up a nasty little scheme to get people worked up for no good reason?

Tough call. See what you think.

> Dear America Online and Instant Message users,
>
> Our America Online staff is planning to take away our Instant Messages by July 14, 1999. If you want to keep your Instant Messages free of charge, send this mail to everyone you know. It will be used as a petition.
>
> Each person you send this to counts as one "signature." If this petition gets 100,000 "signatures," our Instant Messages will still be available at no extra charge. If America Online does not receive 100,000 "signatures," Instant Messages will still be available, but only to those who pay an extra $15.00 a month.

113

If you do not care about not getting any future Instant
Messages, please send this for the sake of those who want to
keep their Instant Messages free of charge. Thank you for your
time and consideration.

Robert McDoggan
America Online
Assistance Director

Hmm. Is this another dark corporate plot to restrict the free flow of public information, or is it a ham-handed attempt to tie up a company's customer service lines?

If you're still on the fence about this one, take a look at Chapter 20, "You've Got Mail (and It's a Scam)," which features a number of equally implausible "petition" appeals. For now, though, let's file the message under "Yeah, right" so that we can move on to something more interesting—like the (nonexistent) perils of carbonated beverages.

The Pop Rocks and Pepsi Crisis, Revisited

As discussed in Chapter 7, "The Family Hour (Not): Twisted Legends About Your Favorite Children's Television Stars," intake of Pop Rocks (the allegedly ominous exploding candy) when combined with carbonated beverages will supposedly cause your teeth to burst loose, your jaws to unhinge, your head to fall off, or your stomach to do a Hindenburg. Everybody knows that's how Mikey, the little kid from the Life cereal commercials, met his untimely end. Actually, not *everyone* knows that, but it seems that everyone knows someone who knows a friend of a friend who "knows" that Pop Rocks were withdrawn from the market because of their lethal consequences.

Anyway, the stuff is apparently still around in some new formulation involving chewing gum. And in case you missed the discussion in Chapter 7, the whole exploding-head story is just as much carbonation. Nobody has ever blown up from mixing Pop Rocks and Pepsi, the soft drink to which it has been unjustly and persistently linked in all those gory schoolyard tales of explosive death.

A New Use for Mountain Dew?

Just as implausible (and almost as widely disseminated) as the Pop Rocks and Pepsi myth is the legend holding that the soft drink Mountain Dew will …

➤ Function as an effective contraceptive when drunk before lovemaking
➤ Cause impotence in males
➤ Cause shrinkage of the testes
➤ Lower sperm counts
➤ And so on

114

This is one of those legends that's not merely false, but also more than a little unsettling. Suppose that teenagers and young adults across the country actually started *believing* that swigging down Mountain Dew made it unlikely or impossible to impregnate one's partner? Well, that's what high school and college kids across the country began telling each other in late 1999.

Will unplanned pregnancies skyrocket in communities with high concentrations of Dew drinkers? We're still monitoring the data. But using soda for birth control is a pretty dumb idea, no matter how you analyze it.

Here's another question: Could fears regarding the onset of adult sexuality, combined with easy Internet access, have some role in the popularity of such stories? It's a theory. The only thing that the people at PepsiCo are sure of is that they didn't mean for the stuff to be used as birth control.

Fable Facts

Commonly circulated tall tales about the Coca-Cola Company include the spurious tales that it created Santa Claus (it didn't) and that it gets youngsters high when they mix the Pause That Refreshes with standard aspirin (it won't).

"The Real Thing" Gets a Turn in the Urban Legend Spotlight

Pepsi, of course, is not the only soft drink outfit with urban legend problems. The following alert incorporates some of the most common misconceptions about Coca-Cola.

> Subject: Say Bye to COKE!!
>
> An interesting piece of information …
>
> Have a look at the wrapper on a Coca-Cola 1.5-liter bottle, and on the ingredients label you will find phosphoric acid in it. Minute quantities of ethylene glycol is also used (which is acknowledged in the soft drink world for making it really "chill").
>
> This is popularly known as antifreeze, which prevents water from freezing at 0 degrees C and instead drops it by 4-5 degrees with minute quantities.
>
> This chemical is a known slow poison in the caliber of arsenic. So, if you manage to drink about 4 liters of Coke within an hour or so, you can die ….

A Minor Correction ...

That message, while touching in its concern for humanity, carries with it some factual problems. To wit, the additive in question is not ethylene glycol, admittedly nasty, but rather propylene glycol, which is a whole different deal and is generally accepted as safe for use in food products.

Other misconceptions about Coke (and any number of other soft drinks) include the notion that drinking cold liquids causes food poisoning, that carbonation can kill you, and that "Coke dissolves bones and teeth." This last notion, a particularly popular legend, misses the point. Many acidic foods and drinks (hot sauce, for instance) *could* cause harm to bones and teeth if directly exposed to them for prolonged periods. But when, exactly, is that going to happen?

Is anyone seriously arguing that Coke or any other soft drink is "good for you"? No. But pointing out that a product is high in sugar and not particularly heavy on nutrients is not the same as branding it a poison.

Is That Really Chicken?

So what have we debunked so far? Corporate tycoons worshipping Satan. Risqué bubble-gum cards. Heartless denial of access to instant-message technology. Explosive mixtures of candy and soda. Lethal chemicals in your next can of pop. Have we hit the high end on the "give me a break" scale yet?

Not by a long shot.

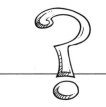

Strange but True

The rumor that KFC has stopped serving chicken appears to be a sophisticated variant on similar rumors involving McDonald's restaurants. For years, the story has circulated that because McDonald's refers to its milkshakes as "shakes," something ominously Not Milk (soybeans, Styrofoam, or who knows what else) is the primary ingredient. Wrong. Another tale has it that apple pies at the Golden Arches are really made from potatoes. Wrong again.

Just when you think you've heard everything there is to hear when it comes to consciously cultivated consumer paranoia, along comes a legend that proves you haven't. If you're ready for a cutting-edge, high-tech piece of malarkey, read on.

> KFC has been a part of our American traditions for many years. Many people, day in and day out, eat at KFC religiously. Do they really know what they are eating?
>
> During a recent study of KFC done at the University of New Hampshire, they found some very upsetting facts. First of all, has anybody noticed that just recently, the company has changed its name? Kentucky Fried Chicken has become KFC. Does anybody know why?
>
> We thought the real reason was because of the "FRIED" food issue. It's not. The reason why they call it KFC is because they cannot use the word *chicken* anymore. Why?
>
> KFC does not use real chickens. They actually use genetically manipulated organisms. These so-called "chickens" are kept alive by tubes inserted into their bodies to pump blood and nutrients throughout their structure. They have no beaks, no feathers, and no feet. Their bone structure is dramatically shrunk to get more meat out of them. This is great for KFC because they do not have to pay so much for their production costs. There is no more plucking of the feathers or the removal of the beaks and feet. The government has told them to change all of their menus so that they do not say "chicken" anywhere. If you look closely, you will notice this. Listen to their commercials—I guarantee that you will not see or hear the word *chicken*.

What, besides exploitation of our fear of new technology and an apparent desire to drop a big company's stock price, is going on here?

Open-ended fantasy, that's what. As fast-food urban legends go, this one has the distinct advantage of being ridiculous—as opposed to vaguely plausible and completely disgusting. (For examples of fast-food legends that *are* vaguely plausible and completely disgusting, see Chapters 13 and 24.) In case you were worried, though, the scenario of the genetically manipulated organism just doesn't hold up.

For the record, nobody has come close to being able to pull off the "genetically manipulated organisms" stunt described here, and if anyone ever does, the technique is not likely to be secretly adopted by the folks at KFC.

Like many of the "big-corporation-is-out-to-get-you" legends, this one seems both outrageously implausible and prohibitively expensive. A similar tale posits the expansion of hamburger meat with earthworms to save money.

Problem: Earthworms cost more per pound than hamburger does. Nobody knows how much a genetically manipulated organism whose flesh resembles that of a chicken costs to develop, but it sounds pretty pricey from here.

117

More Fast-Food Fun

In case you thought the people at KFC were the only targets of lunatic stories, there's the following heartwarming tale, chock-full of official-sounding date-and-place references that, true to form, don't check out.

> Hi, My name is Lauren Archer; my son Kevin and I lived in Sugarland, Texas. On October 2nd, 1994, I took my only son to McDonald's for his 3rd birthday.
>
> After he finished his lunch, I allowed him to play in the ball pit. When he started whining later on, I asked him what was wrong. He pointed to the back of his pull-up and simply said, "Mommy, it hurts," but I couldn't find anything wrong with him at that time. I bathed him when we got home, and it was at that point when I found a welt on his left buttock. Upon investigating, it seems as if there was something like a splinter under the welt.
>
> I made an appointment to have it taken out the next day, but soon he started vomiting and shaking; then his eyes rolled back into his head. From there, we went to the emergency room. He died later that night.
>
> It turned out that the welt on his buttock was the tip of a hypodermic needle that had broken off inside. The autopsy revealed that Kevin had died from a heroine overdose. The next week, the police removed the balls from the ball pit, and lo and behold, there was rotten food, several hypodermic needles (some full, some used), knives, half-eaten candy, diapers, feces, and the stench of urine. If a child is not safe in a child's play area, then where?
>
> You can find the article on Kevin Archer in the October 10, 1994, issue of the *Houston Chronicle*. Please forward this to all loving mothers and fathers!

Don't Believe It!

Stories of ball-pit needle pricks that lead to fatal overdoses among toddlers who visit fast-food restaurants are not factual. (These paranoid fantasies notwithstanding, though, it's a good idea to check play areas and supervise children in public.)

The Sad Tale of Kevin Archer

Little Kevin gets around. The kid always seems to stay 3 years old, he loves fast-food restaurants, and he has an amazing propensity for falling into ball pits featuring hidden heroin needles.

This legend has shown up in a number of heart-rending variations. It shares intriguing similarities with the movie-theater legends discussed in Chapter 17, "Hazardous Amorous Duty," in which crazed AIDS victims have supposedly left virus-infected needles to infect the innocent. In those legends, the subtext is the danger of promiscuity. Here, note that Kevin's mom is a prominent part of the story. Is she perhaps being punished for relinquishing or ignoring her traditional protective maternal role? What terrible risks do we force our children to take when we take them to (insert fast-food chain name here)?

The story, which is *not* confirmed by the *Houston Chronicle,* turns out to be another in the seemingly endless series of cautionary tales about the dangers of the Outside World. This time, though, just for fun, the trust-no-one message is linked specifically to a (supposedly) heartless corporate giant that doesn't much care if kids are subjected to delayed heroin overdoses.

Every Shampoo You've Ever Heard of Is Laden with Carcinogens (Not)

The following chilling message was widely circulated in the spring of 1999. Its intended audience: people with hair.

> Subject: FW: Read this about the shampoo you use
>
> Check the ingredients listed on your shampoo bottle, and see if they have a substance by the name of Sodium Laureth Sulfate, or simply SLS. This substance is found in most shampoos, and the manufacturers use it because it produces a lot of foam and it is cheap. BUT the fact is that SLS is used to scrub garage floors, and it is very strong. It is also proven that it can cause cancer in the long run, and this is no joke. I went home and checked my shampoo (Vidal Sassoon); it doesn't contain it. However, others such as VO5, Palmolive, Paul Mitchell, and the new Hemp Shampoo contain this substance. The first ingredient listed (which means it is the single most prevalent ingredient) in Clairol's Herbal Essences is Sodium Laureth Sulfate.
>
> So, I called one company, and I told them their product contains a substance that will cause people to have cancer. They

said, "Yeah, we knew about it, but there is nothing we can do
about it because we need that substance to produce foam."

By the way, Colgate toothpaste also contains the same substance to produce the "bubbles." They said they are going to
send me some information. Research has shown that in the
1980s, the chance of getting cancer was 1 out of 8,000, and
now, in the 1990s, the chances of getting cancer is 1 out of
3, which is very serious.

So I hope that you will take this seriously and pass this on
to all the people you know, and hopefully we can stop "giving"
ourselves the cancer virus. This is serious—after you have
read this, pass it on to as many people as possible. This is
not a chain letter, but it concerns our health.

Naaah. That's not a chain letter. It concerns our health.

Before you dump all the bottles in your shower stall, you may be interested to learn
that the American Cancer Society looked into the whole SLS-in-shampoo scare and
pronounced it baseless. You might also notice the classic "callous corporate giant" references in this legend that are so common to this genre. The author called the company to complain about a product safety issue. What happens next? Someone within
the organization *instantly acknowledges wrongdoing and says that the company simply
doesn't care.*

That's not good business—and it's not particularly plausible, either. When you hear
something like that, it's a pretty good bet that you've hooked up with an urban
legend.

The Last Word on Brand-Name Urban Legends

Assessing these stories can be tricky because it's easy to be drawn into a lengthy discussion of particular details and lose sight of the most important question. Why on
earth would companies want to engage in any of the activities described in this
chapter?

Does it really make sense for a board of directors of a global consumer products firm
to align itself with the Dark Lord of the Underworld? To launch genetic experiments
likely to win it boatloads of horrible publicity? To mistreat or kill its customers?

These are questions for us all to ponder as we wander the aisles of that huge, tabloid-
heavy supermarket known as life in the less-than-reliable Information Age.

The Least You Need to Know

➤ The folks at Procter & Gamble are not out to turn us into a nation of Satanists.

➤ The folks at Pepsi and Coke do not think that soda pop is health food.

➤ The folks at KFC have had to contend with some *very* weird, totally untrue stories.

➤ Keep an eye on your kids, but don't freak out about needle-laden ball pits at fast-food restaurants.

Chapter 11

The Government Is Out to Get You

Did the U.S. government mount a huge coverup to conceal evidence of a UFO crash in Roswell, New Mexico? Are the feds out to tax your every outgoing e-mail message? Does the FCC want to ban all religious broadcasting? Is martial law imminent? Did the CIA invent AIDS, traffic in cocaine, and launch other modern plagues targeted against people it doesn't like? Is Bill Clinton the antichrist?

Naaaah.

As entertaining as these notions may be, Uncle Sam is not presently in alliance with the Prince of Darkness. That doesn't keep urban legends about high-level government conspiracies from flourishing, though; stories of shadowy power plays—past, current, and forthcoming—are among the most memorable of today's urban legends.

Myths involving shadowy, intricate government conspiracies and coverups are legion. Some of these stories sound vaguely plausible—for a moment. Then you ask yourself, "Can the outfit that mired itself helplessly in Vietnam, botched the Iranian hostage rescue mission, blew up the space shuttle, and shut down the veterans' hospitals *really* be expected to execute an effective conspiracy about anything?"

Strange but True

For an entertaining, if scary, peek at the paranoid mind-set that makes the government-is-out-to-get-you legends possible, check out www.pushhamburger.com. A representative quote: "Watch your butt or the coming global government will get it. Government of, by, and for the people no longer exists. Under the controlling power structure, controlling our elected [sic], we are now being notified how to live our lives. Not too long now ...."

Well, some people certainly think so. In this chapter, we look at a representative sampling of the most interesting urban legends about sinister government plots. There are too many such legends to count, and more are hatched every day. But those examined in this chapter have captured the popular imagination—and have demonstrated their staying power over time.

How to Build Your Own Urban Legend About a Government Conspiracy

Myths about the nefarious plots of the government usually share core elements. They usually incorporate these themes:

➤ The government is not the network of inept, shortsighted bureaucrats that it may seem to be from a distance. It is actually a powerful, many-tentacled monster that's basically out to get you (or keep you from discovering the truth).

➤ This many-tentacled monster is ominously withholding (or is about to withhold) something essential to humanity (access to special knowledge or documents, access to the Internet, access to new technologies, the ability to exercise fundamental rights, and so on).

➤ Thanks to the selfless efforts of those select few who are "in the know" (self-appointed "researchers," activists, persecuted innocents, witnesses of alien autopsies, and so on), this monster can be overcome through a grass-roots informational effort. Such an effort ensures (at some point in the not-too-distant future) ...

➤ ... humanity's eventual inheritance of what it had coming all along.

Try It at Home!

You really can use this handy list to develop your own brand new urban legend! The Supreme Court is secretly out to shut down your local Elks Club. Congress secretly wants to repossess all but officially sanctioned translations of the Bible. Bill Clinton is secretly planning to mount a coup to re-enter government as Dictator of American Samoa. Well? What are you doing wasting your time reading this book? Get the word out! Tell everyone you know what's *really* happening! Fight the power!

This four-point "build-your-own-conspiracy-myth" kit is good for a giggle, until you realize that some folks actually believe quite passionately in the resulting twaddle.

A word to the wise: Did you notice that the all-purpose Government Urban Myth Kit you just read casts the person who circulates the myth into the role of Savior and Redeemer of All Humanity? You did? Good. Did it occur to you that among some— not all, but some—people who pass along these stories, this self-image could lead to behavior that is, shall we say, a trifle unbalanced? It did? Excellent.

You now have all the information you need to handle the next person who wants to talk to you at prosecutorial length about, say, the supposed UFO crash at Roswell, New Mexico. You now know better than to bother trying to convince this person of anything by means of logical reasoning.

Logic isn't always the most popular destination in this part of town.

Roswell, U.S.A.

So let's start with the big one. Let's talk about Roswell.

Guess what? Aliens crash-landed in the New Mexico desert in 1947. And guess what else? The government conducted (and filmed) autopsies on a few of the alien corpses found in the desert. And you know what else happened? Totally neutral bystanders, average tax-paying Americans like you and me, saw scraps of material marked with strange hieroglyphics. The symbols, they swore, were embossed on a strange metallic compound stronger than any ever seen on Earth.

You're never going to guess what happened next. While persecuting UFO enthusiasts trying to bring the truth to light, the federal government simultaneously threw its world-famous cloak of secrecy around all these facts for half a century or so. (A skeptic might point out that the full-court press has not kept a free-spending community obsessed with the "Roswell phenomenon" from blossoming in recent years, but don't listen to skeptics.)

Oh, and there's one final detail you may not have heard about. The author of the book you're now reading has the deed and title from the National Security Agency to the two surviving aliens from the Roswell crash and has bred them in captivity. You can secure two adorable space monkeys of your own right now for the low, low price of $9.99. Leave them in water overnight, and watch as they expand to 40 times their original size. Call now, and you'll receive a free pair of X-Ray Specs. Amaze your friends!

Do you have doubts about any of the foregoing? Then congratulate yourself. You have a functioning central nervous system.

What's Up with That "Spacecraft Debris"?

And now an update from the real world: Weird debris was, in fact, discovered on the New Mexico ranch of Mac Brazel on June 14, 1947. A week and a half later, a flying saucer was reported in the state of Washington. Brazel called the sheriff's office, which alerted the good folks at military intelligence. Possibly influenced by the recent press accounts from the Pacific Northwest, the military intelligence people issued a press release announcing their discovery of the wreckage of a flying saucer.

Did nervous top-level army people swoop in and take over the operation at that point? Yes. Did they invent a coverup story about a weather balloon? Yes. Were they trying to conceal superior Venusian technology, alien corpses, or anything else otherworldly? Nope. They were trying to conceal Project Mogul, a secret project employing high-flying radar-equipped balloons designed to track Russian nuclear tests.

Strange but True

The "Roswell phenomenon" was inadvertently fueled for years by Defense Department officials who were really trying to maintain a coverup—not about aliens, but about Project Mogul, a secret attempt to track Russian atom-bomb tests with radar-equipped balloons. One of the balloons crashed near (but not in) Roswell, New Mexico, in 1947. The debris got lots of people all hot and bothered about UFOs, and eventually secured the town's status as a mecca for people interested in alien sightings.

And that's what crashed on Brazel's ranch: a spy balloon. The "hieroglyphics" were actually a flower pattern printed on ornamental tape produced by a company in New York. It turns out that the technicians had to fix something on the radar device, and the military-issue tape didn't cut it, so Project Mogul ponied up the cash for some private-sector goods. Your tax dollars at work.

The Veil of Secrecy Descends

That's what happened. Really.

Now, it sure would have saved everyone a lot of trouble and agitation if the nation's top generals had assembled shortly after the device in question had crashed on Brazel's ranch and cleared everything up. And they certainly could have confessed about exactly what was up in New Mexico.

For example, they could have livened up 1947's newspapers even further by saying, "Hey, you know those press releases those wacky military intelligence people sent out about flying saucers? Ignore 'em. Those guys had just gone a little too long between vacations. They got caught up in that whole flying-saucer business in Washington State that you may have read about recently. What was *actually* going on with that debris was this: We were trying to figure out just what the Soviets were up to.

"Here. Take a look. No, bring your cameras in a little closer, folks. Here's what the spy balloon looks like when it's fully assembled and ready to be launched. And here's what the farmer found on his ranch. See? It matches. Case closed. By the way, if you wouldn't mind forwarding a copy of everything we've just told you to Josef Stalin, that would be a great help. He should probably be in on this as well."

For some strange reason, though, the top brass didn't say that. They did what any self-respecting bureaucracy would do when some lamebrain points the media at stuff that you don't want to talk about. They stonewalled.

Strange but True

Most government myths center on some form of conspiracy against the interests of its own citizenry. For example, assume that you're a publicity-obsessed cross-dressing head lawman by the name of J. Edgar Hoover. Assume that it's late 1963. Your supposedly all-seeing FBI fails to keep adequate tabs on loudmouthed defector nut Lee Harvey Oswald after he returns to the United States, and he kills President Kennedy. You probably *won't* hand over all your files to the media with a note reading, "Here it is, everybody—evidence of our incompetence, with a few stunning photos of me in a chic black negligee thrown in for good measure. Make of it what you will."

Things Get Interesting in the 1970s

While the rest of the country was learning to do the Hustle and refining its cocaine-snorting technique, a small band of UFO enthusiasts was busy laying the foundation for paranoid excursions later to be made famous by television shows such as *The X Files*. On the assumption that the truth really was out there, these folks combed over the "Roswell incident" with a fine-toothed comb.

Fable Facts

Roswell enthusiasts are fond of pointing out that many "witnesses" to UFO events are not paid cash to pass along their stories. True enough. They sure do get a lot of attention, though, and lots of people are more starved for attention than they are for cash.

Legend Lingo

Area 51, as UFO enthusiasts can attest, is the popular name for the Air Force's supposed secret facility for housing aliens, their corpses, and attendant paraphernalia.

In what can only be explained as a fascinating example of communal psychosis, a number of locals start talking about having seen or heard tell of alien corpses in 1947. UFO buffs tried to sort the wheat from the chaff. Skeptics opined that there was a whole lot of chaff.

But the urban legend ball is now rolling. Ominous tales circulate to this effect:

➤ The government is hiding alien technology discovered during the Roswell incident.

➤ The government is hiding information about messages from alien civilizations uncovered during the Roswell incident.

➤ The government conducted autopsies on aliens that survived the Roswell crash.

➤ The government is still in possession of alien corpses recovered at Roswell.

➤ Much of this stuff is stashed at a secret facility known as *Area 51*.

The main strands of the stories spawn innumerable variations. Try to take on the contradictions and logical flaws in each and every one of them, and you'll come to feel as though you've been assigned the job of giving the cat a bath in a vat of strawberry Jell-O.

Money, Money, Money

As more people bought into the rumors, more sneaky, malevolent entrepreneurs—sorry, purveyors of the Truth—got into the act. Want to buy a book about Roswell? Got it right here. Want to buy a shirt with a Roswell alien logo on it? Come to Middle of Nowhere, New Mexico, and visit the nation's most implausible tourist trap—or use your credit card and order by phone. Want to see pictures of actual Roswell aliens being sliced up during an autopsy? Hmmm ... let's see what we can find for you.

This brings us to the height of the Roswell nonsense, which has to be the circulation of laughably fraudulent "autopsy footage" that was—and remains—hard to watch without laughing. (Or debunking: The footage included a "Danger" sign that was later shown to have been unavailable before 1967.) Nevertheless, the Fox network built a television special around this non-news event in 1995.

The Fox show did prove one thing, though. Roswell was about capitalizing on the paranoia of others. There's nothing inherently wrong with that, of course, as long as what you're producing is clearly labeled as fiction.

The Air Force Comes Clean

Finally, in 1997, the Air Force responded to decades of implausible accusations from the "UFO community" (an interesting concept in itself) and admitted the deception that it had practiced to conceal Project Mogul from the eyes of the world. End of story, right?

Wrong. If you log on to the Internet today, you can *still* find passionate debates about the sinister designs of the government (frequently acting in concert with big business) to cover up the truth about what really happened at Roswell. Lately, the paranoia soup features a medley of Secret Alien Technology Kept Under Wraps by Huge Global Corporation, with a garnish of CIA Plot to Discredit People Trying to Poke Holes in the Official Air Force Account.

The moral to this story? Anyone who is still deeply worried about Roswell likes getting deeply worried or has somehow avoided the most credible explanation of what happened on a Godforsaken stretch of desert half a century ago.

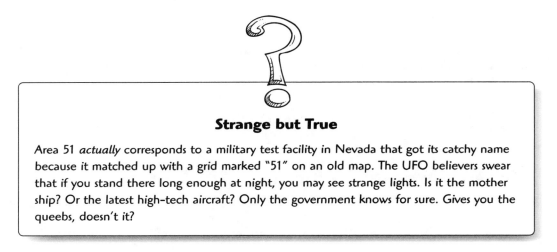

Strange but True

Area 51 *actually* corresponds to a military test facility in Nevada that got its catchy name because it matched up with a grid marked "51" on an old map. The UFO believers swear that if you stand there long enough at night, you may see strange lights. Is it the mother ship? Or the latest high-tech aircraft? Only the government knows for sure. Gives you the queebs, doesn't it?

So, have UFOs visited—or crashed into—our planet? Inquiring minds may want to know, but they're going to have to come up with another theory because this one doesn't hold water. It does make a great myth, though, and it's a classic of the misguided coverup-equals-collusion genre of which self-appointed Redeemers of Humanity are so fond.

The Kennedy Assassination

Admit it. You're tired of this.

You've heard it all. The CIA was linked to the Mafia, which was linked to the Cubans, which were linked to Big Oil, which was linked to Lyndon Johnson, who was linked to the Warren Commission, which was linked to Nelson Rockefeller, who was somehow linked, for all we know, to Jack Ruby camped out near a pay phone at Area 51 clutching a handful of change and a pair of night-vision glasses. Links, links, links. Never proof. Always links. Where are we? A golf course? You don't really want to hear any more of this.

Fable Facts

Oliver Stone's film *JFK,* an irresponsible hodgepodge of existing urban legends surrounding the Kennedy assassination, was nominated for Best Picture in 1991. The film's popularity (like the persistence of the endless, multivaried rumors of conspiracy in the president's death) says more about America's attitude toward government in the post-Vietnam/post-Watergate era than about the case itself.

Except, perhaps, for the following: Someone once opined that if Lee Harvey Oswald had been accused of shooting his brother-in-law rather than the President of the United States, the evidence against him would have been sufficient for an open-and-shut case in any state in the Union. Food for thought, eh?

Debates about the Kennedy case (which nowadays are likely to take on the tone of sober theological discussions), have actually faded in recent years as sources of urban legends. However, their remarkable popularity in the 1970s, 1980s, and early 1990s, and their conformity with the four-step model for government-is-out-to-get-you myths, are worth noting here.

If still more pointless and irresponsible hyperventilation about the tragedy in Dealey Plaza is your cup of tea, check out Oliver Stone's profitable travesty *JFK* at your local video outlet. Better yet, keep it for a couple weeks and don't pay the late fee.

Other intriguing variations on the "government-is-out-to-get-you" format include these:

The Government Wants to Kill You

We're not discussing the excesses of capital punishment here, but the alleged development of sinister man-made diseases and custom-designed drug plagues. Sad but true: Members of minority groups sometimes get taken in by these myths.

For the record, the 1997 claims that the CIA had established an alliance with the Contras to engage in cocaine trafficking were eventually withdrawn by the *San Jose Mercury News,* the paper that originally leveled them. This story, which spread like wildfire through the African-American community and appears to have spawned a number of unfortunate variants, was a major journalistic black eye for the *Mercury News.* (See Chapter 20, "You've Got Mail [and It's a Scam]," for a stubbornly persistent urban myth concerning the supposed expiration of the Voting Rights Act.)

Equally groundless stories hold the U.S. government responsible for the development of the AIDS virus, for the planned perpetuation of a new epidemic of smallpox, and for the corruption of our precious and vital bodily fluids. If you encounter a Redeemer of Humanity circulating one of these stories, ask yourself two questions:

1. Doesn't the government enjoy taxing me?
2. How can the government tax me if I'm dead?

The Government Has Ceded Control ...

You might think that this sort of urban legend has gone completely out of style. You're wrong. Recent allegations include the refreshingly direct one that the Bilderberg Group (which might more accurately be called an annual Bilderberg *meeting* of internationalist business, government, and labor leaders) "could even be the advance team of the antichrist."

Confirming or denying such allegations is trickier than it might at first appear. Suffice it to say that as of this writing, the Trilateral Commission has not hijacked the federal government, and the Amsterdam-based Bilderberg gang continues to engage in ponderous, apparently innocuous discussions of international affairs on a once-a-year basis.

Shadowy really is the right word for these and other groups accused of secretly controlling the world. To continue the metaphor, there's nothing to see under the bed when the lights go out—unless we *want* there to be something to see under the bed when the lights go out.

The Government Is Planning to Institute Martial Law

Sinister plans for a Big Brother-style clampdown are afoot. You haven't heard? You're still in the dark about the imminent collapse of democracy? Let the nearest Redeemer of Humanity set you straight!

Fable Facts

The "signs-in-the-truck" myth is just one of scores of urban myths predicting a government crackdown on civil liberties. Others involve the monitoring of reading materials selected by patrons at public libraries, draconian penalties for smoking, the assumption of (vaguely defined) "emergency powers" to deal with some current event or familiar national problem, and the imposition of one-world government by means of black helicopters.

The news flash that you hear may sound something like this:

> Not long ago, my close friend/churchgoing relative/ spouse/other seemingly unimpeachable source told me something that really disturbed me. He/she told me that he/she got a phone call from a close friend/churchgoing relative/other seemingly unimpeachable source involving an unsettling incident on a public highway. An inspector at a weigh station asked a truck driver what he was transporting; the truck driver said he did not know. The inspector opened one of the boxes held within the cargo area and found, to his shock, a supply of about a hundred big plastic signs reading, "This City Under Martial Law" and citing a legal reference of some kind.

Not one of these "signs-on-the-truck" rumors has ever been verified as an actual event. As with the Roswell avalanche of stories, the many variations (sometimes the truck overturns and spills its cargo, sometimes major corporations employ the driver) should be a tip-off that something funny is up, and it isn't a plot to keep you from voting.

You may well hear one of these stories at the next party you attend. Nod supportively, tell your conversational partner that you find the account fascinating, and change the subject. Again (and this cannot be emphasized enough), be sure not to attempt to employ any form of rigorous logical analysis in discussing the myth. You could be trapped by the punch bowl for hours.

The Government Is Tracking Your Every Move by Means of the New Currency

Some people may try to tell you that the new bills issued by the U.S. Mint have been manufactured with a concealed magnetic strip that allows the government to track your purchases. Sound far-fetched? That's because it is. Why has the rumor spread? Well, if the government's tracking you, you must be important enough to track, right?

What the new bills *really* contain is a tiny *visible* strip that makes it harder for counterfeiters to ply their illicit trade. Hold up the new bill to a bright light, and you can see it yourself. Granted, this is not quite as thrilling as the magnetic-strip story, but it's what we got. To quote the U.S. Treasury's official Web site, "A polymer thread is embedded vertically in the paper and indicates by its unique position the note's denomination .... Additionally, the thread glows red when held under an ultraviolet light."

The Government Is Out to Ban All Religious Broadcasting

Among the longest-running urban legends, this one has accounted for tens of millions of protest letters to the Federal Communications Commission.

The facts: Back in the 1960s and 1970s, two activists named Lorenzo Milam and Jeremy Lansman wanted to make it easier for minorities to launch noncommercial FM radio stations. Ticked off at the ease with which religious broadcasters appeared to be able to secure licenses, they filed a petition with the FCC. Among the requests in the petition was a request for a "'Freeze' on all Applications by Religious 'Bible,' 'Christian,' and other Sectarian School, Colleges, and Institutions for Reserved Educational FM and TV Channels." The petition, designated RM-2493, was rejected in 1975.

But the fun was just beginning. For the past quarter-century or so, anyone interested in really riling up churchgoing folk has had a pretty easy job of it. Just cite RM-2493, pretend that it's still pending, and suggest that the FCC is taking the request very seriously indeed. A fair number of irresponsible demagogues appear to have gone even further, making the most of an old but persistent lie that activist Madalyn Murray O'Hair was securing hundreds of thousands of signatures in support of the petition.

Balderdash. O'Hair had no connection whatsoever with the appeal that Milam and Lansman filed. RM-2493 has been dead for decades. And the only reason this nonsense keeps coming up is that some people need—or find it convenient—to have an imposing enemy to rail against.

The Government Wants to Tax Internet Usage

Cutting off religious broadcasting is one thing, but when people start hearing that they're going to have to pay Uncle Sam to send e-mail, they know that those idiots in Washington have crossed the line.

Well, somebody has crossed something, that's for sure. Submitted for your consideration is the following press release from the Federal Communications Commission:

Don't Believe It!

Atheist Madalyn Murray O'Hair had nothing whatsoever to do with petition RM-2493, an obscure request to deny licenses to religious broadcasters that the FCC rejected in 1975. Despite special funding from Congress to deal with an avalanche of mail from credulous churchgoers, the FCC has been unable to convince certain segments of the country that it has no plans to ban religious broadcasting.

RUMORS REGARDING A COMPUTER MODEM SURCHARGE

The FCC has received letters from a number of computer modem users expressing concern about an alleged "proposal" before the Federal Communications Commission (FCC) that would result in a surcharge for the use of computer modems on the telephone network.

There is *no* proposal pending before the FCC that would result in the application of a surcharge for the use of computer modems on the telephone network …. (Our) staff is continuing to investigate possible sources of the surcharge rumors and to distribute correct information to computer modem users.

Be honest. Aren't you glad you don't have to answer the Federal Communications Commission's mail? What must it be like to handle those phone banks?

A recent variation on the bogus modem surcharge story is the bogus story on a 5¢ tax per e-mail message. An excerpt from a 2000 election-year debate between two New York senatorial candidates sets the story up more eloquently than your humble author ever could. (No kidding—the following exchanges actually took place.)

Excerpt from October 8, 2000, senatorial debate between First Lady Hillary Clinton and Congressman Rick Lazio

WCBS REPORTER MARCIA KRAMER: I'd like to ask you how you stand on Federal Bill 602P. I'm going to actually tell you what it is.

CLINTON: I have no idea. [Laughter.]

KRAMER: I'm going to tell you what it is. Under the bill that's now before Congress, the U.S. Postal Service would be able to bill e-mail users five cents for each e-mail they send, even though the post office provides no service. They want this to help recoup losses of about $230 million a year because of the proliferation of e-mails ….

CLINTON: Well, based on your description, Marcia, I wouldn't vote for that bill. It sounds burdensome and unjustifiable to me. I have been a supporter of the moratorium on taxation on the Internet ….

LAZIO: I am absolutely opposed to this. This is an example of the government's greedy hand in trying to take money from taxpayers that, frankly, it has no right to. We need to keep the government's hands off the Internet ….

Just thinking out loud here, but is it possible that Kramer could have done a *little* more research before posing that particular question? You guessed it: Bill 602P is a hoax. And all three of them bought it—on live television, no less.

The e-mail tax is the sort of proposal that voters seem to *want* to believe exists, the better to be protested against. Among the usual dizzying array of variations is a Canadian version of 602P supposedly pending before the Canadian parliament.

Note that each candidate was willing to tap into the fictitious bill's (genuine) ability to arouse the emotions of potential voters. That's a candidate's job, of course, and you have to admit that it would be a fairly low-percentage shot to question your moderator's intelligence during a televised debate. Still, wouldn't it have been entertaining to hear Hillary ask, "And how exactly did you hear about this legislative initiative, Marcia?"

Speaking of the Clintons ....

Bill Clinton Is the Antichrist

So is Bill Gates, as it turns out. It's some intricate trick involving extremely selective application of ASCII code values to the letters in their names.

You're on your own with this one.

The Least You Need to Know

➤ Some—not all, but some—of the people who circulate ominous urban myths about the government may think of themselves, on some level, as self-appointed Saviors of Humanity and thus may not respond well to logic.

➤ Don't worry—nothing involving an actual alien crash landing took place near Roswell, New Mexico.

➤ Don't be ashamed if you've had it up to here with myths relating to the Kennedy assassination; you are not alone.

➤ The U.S. government is not interested in killing off large segments of its taxpayer base, imposing martial law, tracking your activities by means of magnetic strips within the new currency, banning religious broadcasting, or taxing the Internet out of existence.

➤ Relax—neither Bill Clinton nor Bill Gates is the antichrist (unless you want them to be).

Chapter 12

Total Strangers Are Out to Get Someone You Love

In This Chapter

➤ The Blue Star myth

➤ Child abduction myths

➤ Nonexistent date rape drugs

➤ Why we circulate stories like this

➤ The pros and cons of lone-nut legends

Some of the stories that follow may well have intricate layers of subtle meaning behind them. For the most part, though, we're talking about (literally) fantastic tales designed to prove a simple but compelling contention: Unseen, malevolent weirdos are everywhere.

This, of course, is the lesson to be learned from any number of children's stories. In these updated modern versions, the focus is on subtle, insidious loners who lurk just beyond our peripheral vision to victimize innocent people, typically kids.

Family members share these kinds of stories with the people they love because they want to protect those people. People with odd worldviews *make up* many of these stories and pass them around, presumably because they find it entertaining to do so.

Apparently, it takes all kinds.

Fable Facts

Groundless, cynically circulated stories of abuse, abduction, and neglect by fictional "lone nuts" is likely to detract public credence and attention from legitimate cases of child mistreatment.

To find out how you can help reduce the number of genuine cases of victimization, visit the National Center for Missing and Exploited Children's Web site at www.missingkids.org.

Carlyle Weighs In

These popular stories may be reflections of the insecurities we feel about a society in which neighbor-to-neighbor relationships have been eclipsed by heavy work schedules, massive infusions of television, and round-the-clock Internet access. Or they may be free-floating expressions of parental and other anxieties.

Whatever can be said about them, though, it's a safe bet that blind acceptance of the legends here wouldn't have gone over well with Thomas Carlyle. He opined that the first duty of each human being is "that of subduing fear." That's something to think about the next time you hear about some of these.

The Blue Star Playground Crisis

One of the most extraordinary urban legends of all—at least in its ability to persist in countless variant strains—is the Blue Star legend. When it comes to adaptability, the Blue Star myth is in a league of its own. It has been making the rounds for at least two decades, and it's still going strong. (Not long ago, it reportedly turned up in Abu Dhabi.)

The hardy legend raises a fear that most parents are unwilling to dismiss out of hand—namely, that their children are at risk for exploitation by drug dealers. What's more, the story has enough in common with actual practice to lend it some initial credibility. (Various kinds of acid are, in fact, distributed on small squares of paper, but these are meant to be consumed, not used for tattoos.)

Here's one of the dozens (hundreds?) of variant e-mail messages that circulate the Blue Star myth:

```
This is not a joke. Please read this note and pass the word
around. We have some sick people on this planet!?!?!

WARNING TO PARENTS

A form of tattoo called "BLUE STAR" is being sold to school
children. It is a small piece of paper containing a blue star.
They are the size of a pencil eraser, and each star is soaked
with LSD. The drug is absorbed through the skin simply by han-
dling the paper.
```

There are also brightly colored paper tattoos resembling postage stamps that have the picture of one of the following:

1. Superman
2. Mickey Mouse
3. Clowns
4. Disney characters
5. Bart Simpson
6. Butterflies

This is a new way of selling acid by appealing to young children. These are laced with drugs. If your child gets any of the above, do not handle them. These are known to react quickly, and some are laced with strychnine.

Symptoms: Hallucinations, severe vomiting, uncontrolled laughter, mood changes, change in body temperature.

Please feel free to reproduce this article and distribute it within your community and workplace. Get the word out about this danger to our children!

Different versions of this constantly mutating legend reference acid-laced tattoos bearing the latest popular animated characters. As though that weren't enough to get a parent's heart racing, the listener may also be cautioned about one of these warnings:

➤ Older kids have started distributing the tattoos to younger kids for the sadistic fun of watching the 5-year-olds have bad trips.

➤ The acid takes effect with extraordinary speed and is likely to result in a "fatal" trip, thanks to the presence of strychnine in the tattoo.

➤ Deaths of young kids have already been reported in (insert name of nearby city here).

➤ Children have reported symptoms that include hallucinations, severe vomiting, and (my favorite) sustained laugher. Message: If you hear any children laughing around the playground, they're probably tripping.

Needless to say, it's all bogus, as are the assurances that the crisis has been verified by Beth Israel

Don't Believe It!

The Blue Star myth has spawned dozens of variants and is reported to have appeared in North America, Europe, and the Middle East. Its alarming tale of LSD-laced kiddie tattoos has never been verified.

Medical Center, a spokesman for the White House, a local chapter of the PTA, a representative of the New York City police department, a representative of any number of European police departments, and so on.

Don't Believe It!

Stories of child abductions that feature imprecise or misleading contact information are highly unlikely to check out. A recent bogus plea for help included this emotional appeal: "If anyone anywhere knows anything, sees anything, pleeeeeaaaase contact me if you have my number." Ah, but we don't, do we?

Fable Facts

In a striking parallel with modern weirdo-could-be-anywhere stories, the Brothers Grimm passed along a tale about a little girl who wore a red hood. Her mother urged her not to wander from the path to Grandma's house. Little Red Riding Hood chose to ignore the advice, and for centuries kids and adults have replayed the nearly fatal consequences of her choice.

Children are indeed at risk when illegal drugs surface in playground settings, and our youngsters are not well-served by any attempt to deny that. But this story is about drugs in only a very superficial way. What it's really about is terrifying parents, teachers, and law enforcement authorities.

Abduction Myths

False "alerts" and stories about the abduction of specific children from public places far outnumber the actual events. Unfortunately, there are always new such tales out there, most circulated by bored idiots who think that the best way to entertain themselves is to take advantage of the empathy and concern of others.

The stories often share some common elements:

➤ Geographic locations are usually vague (as in "Southern Minnesota"), the better to trip up people trying to check the story.

➤ The child in question is suspected of having been abducted by a loner, typically an adult male with no family ties. (A recent hoax attributed the abduction of a nonexistent child to an unspecified "mentally handicapped [man] living on his own.")

➤ The circulator of the bogus stories is unwilling to share his or her direct contact information, and may claim that the police have insisted against supplying this information.

The Classic "Close-Call" Abduction Legend

One legend that has been around for years concerns a mother's harrowing separation from her daughter in a grocery, discount, or department store. The (endlessly updated) tale usually begins with the distracted mom noticing that her child is missing. She calls the child's name—and hears no response. At that point, a nightmare unfolds.

The following e-mail version, set in a store called Sam's, hits all the bases of this classic legend, relating it from the point of view of a bystander who supposedly saw the event unfold:

> I asked a man at Sam's to announce it over the loudspeaker for Katie. He did, and then all the store's doors were locked at once. This took all of 3 minutes. They found the little girl 5 minutes later in a bathroom stall. Her head was half-shaved and she was dressed in her underwear with a bag of clothes, a razor, and a wig sitting on the floor beside her (to make her look different). Somebody had taken the little girl, brought her into the bathroom, shaved half her head, and undressed her in a matter of less than 10 minutes. This makes me shake to no end. Please keep a close eye on your kids when in big places where it's easy for you to get separated. It took only a few minutes to do all this. Another five minutes, and she would have been out the door.

Strange but True

Tall tales about victimizing weirdos have a long and storied pedigree; some (but not all) have a clear social objective. For instance, in the early part of the twentieth century, countless books and pamphlets told lurid stories of white slavers who targeted young rural women who had recently moved to the city. The aim of these lowlifes: to kidnap innocent young women and force them into a life of prostitution.

These implausible stories were meant, of course, to remind young ladies of the dangers of moral compromise. They are not all that different from some of today's urban legends. Consider, for instance, the urgent warnings about the (nonexistent) date-rape drug Progesterex, which, we are told, is a sterilization drug originally designed for horses. Sexual predators supposedly pop the pill in a young woman's drink; when she consumes it, she is not only knocked out, but also sterilized for life, thereby ensuring that no evidence of the rapist's crime arises. Message: Don't mess up your family plan—steer clear of guys bearing drinks.

"Stay on the Path! Lone Nuts Are Everywhere!"

The help-find-a-lost-kid appeals, like their abduction and drug-pusher cousins, circulate because we're concerned about the safety of children (especially the children we love), and because we want to do anything we possibly can to help out.

Come to think of it, similar motivations almost certainly explain the popularity of the Little Red Riding Hood story—and its reminder to "stay on the path." These days, both parents *and* kids get the warning: You can't be too careful.

"I Am the Weirdo"

For sustained anxiety—and proof that people will circulate even the most relentlessly unlikely stories—it's hard to match the following account. Copies have landed in the e-mail inboxes of people across the country.

Like other urban legends dealing with solo predatory weirdos, this one appeals to our uncertainties and urges us to take no chances. Unlike most modern legends in this category, however, this story attempts to execute a strange literary back flip. It uses an unwieldy narrative shift to tell the second half of its account from the point of view of the (seeming) weirdo.

```
PLEASE READ AND PASS IT ON TO YOUR KIDS

Something to think about …

Shannon could hear the footsteps behind her as she walked to-
ward home. The thought of being followed made her heart beat
faster. "You're being silly," she told herself, "no one is
following you." To be safe, she began to walk faster, but the
footsteps kept up with her pace. She was afraid to look back,
and she was glad she was almost home. Shannon said a quick
prayer, "God, please get me home safe." She saw the porch
light burning and ran the rest of the way to her house. Once
inside, she leaned against the door for a moment, relieved to
be in the safety of her home. She glanced out the window to
see if anyone was there. The sidewalk was empty.

After tossing her books on the sofa, she decided to grab a
snack and get online. There she could talk to strangers with-
out being afraid. After all, none knew who she really was and
couldn't hurt her.

She logged on under her screen name ByAngel213. Checking her
Buddy List, she saw that GoTo123 was on. She sent him an in-
stant message:
```

ByAngel213: Hi, I'm glad you are on! I thought someone was following me home today. It was really weird!

GoTo123: LOL You watch too much TV. Why would someone be following you? Don't you live in a safe neighborhood?

ByAngel213: Of course I do. LOL I guess it was my imagination 'cause I didn't see anybody when I looked out.

GoTo123: Unless you gave your name out online. You haven't done that, have you?

ByAngel213: Of course not. I'm not stupid, you know.

GoTo123: Did you have a softball game after school today?

ByAngel213: Yes, and we won!!

GoTo123: That's great! Who did you play?

ByAngel213: We played the Hornets. LOL Their uniforms are so gross! They look like bees. LOL

GoTo123: What is your team called?

ByAngel213: We are the Canton Cats. We have tiger paws on our uniforms. They are really kewl.

GoTo123: Do you pitch or what?

ByAngel213: No, I play second base. I've got to go. My homework has to be done before my parents get home. I don't want them mad at me. Bye.

GoTo123: Catch you later. Bye.

GoTo123 decided that it was time to teach Angel a lesson, one she would never forget. He went to the member menu and began to search for her profile. When it came up, he highlighted it and printed it out. He took out a pen and began to write down what he knew about Angel so far.

Her name: Shannon

Birthday: January 3, 1985 / Age: 13

State where she lived: North Carolina

Hobbies: Softball, chorus, skating, and going to the mall

Besides this information, he knew that she lived in Canton. She had just told him, and he knew that she stayed by herself until 6:30 every afternoon until her parents came home from work. He knew that she played softball on Thursday afternoons on the school team and that the team was named the Canton Cats. Her favorite number 7 was printed on her jersey. He knew that she was in the seventh grade at the Canton Junior High School. She had told him all this in the conversations that they had had online. He had enough information to find her now. "She'll be so surprised," he thought. "She doesn't even know what she has done."

Shannon didn't tell her parents about the incident on the way home from the ballpark that day. She didn't want them to make a scene and stop her from walking home from the softball games. Parents were always overreacting, and hers were the worst. It made her wish that she was not an only child. Maybe if she had brothers and sisters, her parents wouldn't be so overprotective.

By Thursday, Shannon had forgotten about the footsteps following her. Her game was in full swing when suddenly she felt someone staring at her.

It was then that the memory came back. She glanced up from her second-base position to see a man watching her closely. He was leaning against the fence behind first base, and he smiled when she looked at him. He didn't look scary, and she quickly dismissed the fear that she had felt. After the game, he sat on a bleacher while she talked to the coach. She noticed his smile once again as she walked past him. He nodded, and she smiled back.

He noticed her name on the back of the shirt. He knew he had found her. Quietly he walked a safe distance behind her. He didn't want to frighten her and have to explain what he was doing to anyone.

It was only a few blocks to Shannon's home, and once he saw where she lived, he quickly returned to the park to get his car. Now he had to wait. He decided to get a bite to eat until the time came to go to Shannon's house.

He drove to a fast food restaurant and sat there until time to make his move. Shannon was in her room later that evening when she heard voices in the living room. "Shannon, come here," her father called. He sounded upset, and she couldn't imagine why. She went into the room to see the man from the ballpark sitting on the sofa. "Sit down," her father began. "This man is a policeman, and he has just told us a most interesting story about you."

Shannon moved cautiously to a chair across from the man. How could he tell her parents anything? She had never seen him before today!

"Do you know who I am, Shannon?" the man asked.

"No," Shannon answered.

"I am your online friend, GoTo123."

Shannon was stunned. "That's impossible! GoTo is a kid my age! He's 14, and he lives in Michigan!"

The man smiled. "I know I told you all that, but it wasn't true. You see, Shannon, there are people online who pretend to be kids; I was one of them. But while others do it to find kids and hurt them, I belong to a group of parents who do it to protect kids from predators. I came here to find you to teach you how dangerous it is to give out too much information to people online. You told me enough about yourself to make it easy for me to find you: your name, the school you go to, the name of your ball team and the position you play. The number and name on your jersey just made finding you a breeze."

Shannon was stunned. "You mean you don't live in Michigan?"

He laughed. "No, I live in Raleigh. It made you feel safe to think I was so far away, didn't it?" She nodded.

"I had a friend whose daughter was like you, only she wasn't as lucky. The guy found her and murdered her while she was home alone. Kids are taught not to tell anyone when they are alone, yet they do it all the time online. The wrong people trick you into giving out information a little here and there online. Before you know it, you have told them enough for them to find you without even realizing that you have done it. I hope you've learned a lesson from this and won't do it again."

"I won't," Shannon promised solemnly.

"Will you tell others about this so they will be safe, too?"

"It's a promise!"

145

That night Shannon and her dad and Mom all knelt down together and prayed. They thanked God for protecting Shannon from what could have been a tragic situation.

Please send this to as many people as you can to teach them not to give any information about themselves. This world we live in today is too dangerous to even give out your age, let alone anything else. Be safe.

PASS THIS ON!

Note that the story is forwarded as "something to think about" but is not clearly labeled as either fictional *or* nonfictional.

Fable Facts

Fixating on whether or not a particular legend is "true" has its disadvantages. Many legends, like the "online buddy" story in this chapter, use "false" story details to reveal "true"—and valid—concerns.

Legend Lingo

Lone-weirdo stories appear to focus on female childhood victims (and potential victims) more often than on young males.

Is it plausible? Let's address that question by posing another: Is plausibility really the most important thing when you've entered Little Red Riding Hood's treacherous terrain?

Why We Circulate Stories Like This

The tale's unlikely denouement and obvious appeal to parental fears allow it to operate on a clumsy but revealing double level. It's as though the anonymous author were saying: "This subject is important enough for you to treat it as though it were true when discussing it with your children. So please do."

That's a powerful motivator.

Certainly, the literal "truth" of the events related in the story could never be in question to someone with a functioning cerebellum. How could the omniscient narrator read the minds of the characters? And how huge of a network of kids would this concerned parent/policeman need to communicate with online in order to be able to find just one close enough to teach "a lesson" like this?

But such concerns are beside the point. For every skeptic who asks, "Is this story 'true'?" there is an instant, instinctive answer from a parent: "Well, if it isn't, *shouldn't* it be?"

Shouldn't Little Red Riding Hood have stayed on the path? Of course she should have. What else about the story matters? If you're a nervous mom or dad, the answer is, of course, "Nothing."

Pros and Cons

As the "online buddy" story illustrates, there are pluses and minuses to *lone-weirdo* stories.

The most extreme legends about lone-nuts-on-the-prowl aim to encourage not just watchful responsibility, but full-scale paranoia. The tales may make people cynical about cases of real abuse or abduction when the anecdotes are finally exposed as fraudulent. And, of course, when accounts like the mythical restroom abduction circulate, specific businesses are needlessly associated with traumas that didn't actually occur.

On the other hand, it's fair to point out that there have always been and probably always will be fresh variants on stories like these. Legends that don't take an unbalanced or exploitative approach, and that aren't circulated for kicks, may well serve a valuable function, such as alerting parents to valid safety concerns, opening up lines of family communication, and (let's face it) shining a welcome spotlight on the less responsible stories of the genre.

On the other hand, if you actually think it's funny to get people worked up about mythical LSD plots or department store kidnappings, you are hereby advised to get a life.

The Least You Need to Know

➤ There is no documented case matching the Blue Star myth.

➤ Many child abduction myths are untrue and are the product of people with sick senses of humor.

➤ Myths about date rape drugs that instantly sterilize the female victims are similarly bogus.

➤ We circulate stories like this for the same reason we tell the story of Little Red Riding Hood—because we care about the people we tell them to.

➤ That having been said, don't forget that people who craft and circulate these stories just to see how many parents they can terrify are in need of a life—or a whack upside the head.

Tales of Hell from the Service Economy

Have you ever stopped for a moment to think about the profound level of trust you are forced to place each and every day in people who work at lousy, low-playing jobs?

No? Good. Then you won't have any problem at all with what follows.

Urban legends of the kind you're about to encounter carry with them a fascinating new kind of uncertainty. But don't worry. This kind of gnawing inner doubt is relevant only to people who occasionally withdraw money from the bank and then interact with other human beings in order to spend it.

Critical Assumptions

What's that, you say? That's you? Then you're about to learn, perhaps for the first time, that when you place an order at a fast-food joint, you're assuming that the person who puts your order together is doing a good (or even a mediocre) job of quality control. Maybe that's not a good assumption. Yikes.

You're about to learn that when you take a vacation, you're assuming that your personal belongings aren't going to be tampered with the moment you step away from your hotel room. Maybe that's not a good assumption, either. Yikes again.

You're about to learn that when you go to the hospital, you're assuming that the service people aren't going to engage in casual acts of gross negligence leading to your instant death. Maybe that's the worst assumption so far. Yikes to the third power!

Should you trust the people who say, "How can I help you?" but don't really seem to mean it?

The Passing of the Milkman

Why have legends involving commercial transactions gone wrong become popular? Perhaps because we live in a world in which we don't really know most of the people whom we have no choice but to trust implicitly.

Consider, for instance, the last humble glass of milk you drank. Does it bother you? Maybe it should.

Eighty years ago, people had milkmen, guys they knew by name and could (or at least did) trust to deliver quality dairy products. Fifty years ago, people popped down to the corner store to buy a gallon of milk from a proprietor they knew by name. Nowadays, you may stop in at a convenience store at 2:00 in the morning to buy your milk.

In other words, you may hand over your cash to somebody you've never met, somebody who doesn't seem to care how, where, or even whether you live. Somebody who sure as heck doesn't seem to be willing, or able, to discuss the provenance of the milk (or anything else in the store, for that matter).

Fable Facts

For better or worse, we have come to count on poorly paid strangers to watch out for our interests. A number of entertainingly paranoid speculations on this intriguing fact have led to urban legends.

Worrying About the Milk

Did the milkman or the owner of the store really *know* any more about weird stuff that might be in the milk than the nose-ringed, teenage counter attendant at the local Kwik-E-Gouge? Probably not. But people had *friendships* with people like milkmen and store owners. And that counted for something.

And lately, it seems, people are more inclined to worry about the milk.

The Killer Cleaning Lady

When you get an e-mail message containing a news story that's sourced to a mainstream newspaper, you should take it seriously, right? Consider the following e-mail, which cites a "story" from a prominent South African paper, the *Cape Times:*

CLEANER POLISHES OFF PATIENT

"For several months, our nurses have been baffled to find a dead patient in the same bed every Friday morning," a spokeswoman for the Pelonomi Hospital (Free State, South Africa) told reporters. "There was no apparent cause for any of the deaths, and extensive checks on the air conditioning system, and a search for possible bacterial infection, failed to reveal any clues.

"However, further inquiries have now revealed the cause of these deaths. It seems that every Friday morning, a cleaner would enter the ward, remove the plug that powered the patient's life support system, plug her floor polisher into the vacant socket, and then go about her business. When she had finished her chores, she would plug the life support machine back in and leave, unaware that the patient was now dead. She could not, after all, hear the screams and eventual death rattle over the whirring of her polisher.

"We are sorry and have sent a strong letter to the cleaner in question. Further, the Free State Health and Welfare Department is arranging for an electrician to fit an extra socket, so there should be no repetition of this incident. The enquiry is now closed."

—*Cape Times*, 6/13/96

At first glance, it sure *seems* like an excerpt from a legitimate news story, doesn't it? It's not, though. It's a carefully concocted chunk of baloney. If the tale gets you into a panic about idiotic service people, about lapses in the level of care delivered by the medical system, about administrative oversights, about lax discipline, about inhuman bureaucracies—well, that's the whole idea.

The Dubious Quote

Here's one tip-off that we're looking at a manufactured story: Look again at the extended quote—more like a soliloquy—from that unnamed "spokeswoman" for the hospital. A mainstream newspaper such as the *Cape Times* would identify its sources in such a story. It would also be most unlikely to allow *any* source to ramble on for three paragraphs and, in so doing, provide the conclusion to a piece.

In other words, no self-respecting reporter is going to file a "story" in which all but 13 words take the form of a direct quotation from an unnamed source.

Things Get Even More Suspicious

Here's another, bigger, problem: This is not how hospitals work.

Life support systems are, surprise, surprise, backed up with alternate power systems and alarms. Referencing this within the e-mail, however, would undercut the purpose of the story, which is not to report facts, but to reinforce anxieties about callous service from anonymous people who just happen to hold our lives in their hands.

So, Was There Ever a Newspaper Story?

Yes. Just not one matching the account "quoted" in that e-mail message.

For the record, a story entitled "Cleaner Polishes Off Patient" *did* run in the *Cape Times* of June 13, 1996. It was based on an account that had run in another paper; both stories were the result of editors who inadvertently helped a fascinating urban legend to creep into the news section undetected.

To give the reporters and editors involved in the *Cape Times* debacle some credit, the "Cleaner Polishes Off Patient" story ran only after it was determined that hospital officials were investigating rumors of a lethally preoccupied cleaning lady. Investigate they did; no one found anything to substantiate the story.

By the time the *Cape Times* story made the rounds, though—unfortunately, without a critical sentence in an initial draft relating that "(h)ospital staff haven't yet confirmed" the rumor—it was too late. Alas, the Killer Cleaning Lady legend gained credence when an unknown South African editor made a common journalistic decision: to cut out "inessential" portions of a story when faced with space constraints.

Citations and unauthorized rewrites of the article were quickly offered as "proof" that some oblivious cleaning lady in South Africa had been inadvertently unplugging life-support systems on Fridays and had received only a light reprimand for doing so.

Don't Believe It!

The editors of the *Cape Times* in South Africa probably wish they had another shot at the decision to run "Cleaner Polishes Off Patient," now generally accepted as an unfortunate story that fueled an existing urban legend. For a detailed review of the genesis of the *Cape Times* story, which has led to worldwide circulation of this legend, see the fine analysis at Arthur Goldstuck's excellent site "Legends from a Small Country" (www.web.co.za/arthur/cleanfaq.htm).

"Get Me a Rewrite!"

So, a rewritten version of the *Cape Times* article, featuring that extensive monologue from that anonymous hospital spokesman, landed in a half a jillion e-mail in-boxes. Anyone who wanted to use a computer database to check whether the *Cape Times* had actually run a story entitled "Cleaner Polishes Off Patient" on June 13, 1996, would find that it had. What they might not have noticed was that the e-mail version had been substantially rewritten.

Most readers, of course, would *not* trace the *Cape Times* story to its root. This appears to have been an account in another paper about someone at a government agency trying (unsuccessfully) to track down anyone, but anyone, who had firsthand knowledge of the events described in the cleaning lady rumor.

If she's still out there, she's awfully good at covering her tracks.

So What's the Last Word on the Killer Cleaning Lady Legend?

There are three last words, actually: *legend, vulnerable,* and *skeptical.*

1. This is a *legend.* Nobody has yet come up with proof that this ever occurred anywhere. Every account that has surfaced is suspiciously (and classically) vague, with details attributed to unspecified sources at two or three removes from the teller.

2. People circulate this story and others like it, at least in part, because they feel *vulnerable.* We feel ourselves to be in an exposed position when we entrust our lives to large, impersonal institutions. That's because we are, and we have a right to be nervous about policies and procedures. Note the e-mail version's inclusion of a "slap-on-the-wrist" disciplinary measure, the issuance of a strongly worded letter. Boy, those healthcare bureaucrats really know how to respond to a crisis, don't they?

3. Do yourself a favor and be *skeptical* if you come across a similar story. It's a good idea to check twice—or three times, or even four or five times—before you take as gospel an e-mail version of a news story attributed to a mainstream source. Crafty urban legend circulators are pretty good at making something bogus look like it has been verified by a credible media institution.

Lethal ATM Encounters—and More Heartless Bureaucrats

If only killer cleaning ladies were the only perils unsuspecting consumers face.

"Some sicko"—perhaps a disillusioned employee—is the villain of the following dire warning. But how much more worthy of our scorn are the soulless captains of industry who refuse to take any effective action against the threat!

```
Very scary! Please read …

Whenever you go to an automatic teller machine to make de-
posits, make sure you don't lick the deposit envelope—spit on
it. A customer died after licking an envelope at a teller ma-
chine at Yonge & Eglinton. According to the police, Dr. Elliot
at the Women's College Hospital found traces of cyanide in the
lady's mouth and digestive system, and police traced the fatal
poison to the glue on the envelope she deposited that day.
They then did an inspection of other envelopes from other
teller machines in the area and found six more. The glue is
described as colorless and odorless. They suspect that some
sicko is targeting this particular bank and has been putting
the envelopes beside machines at different locations. A
spokesperson from the bank said their hands are tied unless
they take away the deposit function from all machines. So
watch out, and please forward this message to the people you
care about.

Thanks

Kimberly Clarkson
Crime Unit, Department for Public Health
```

"Kimberly Clarkson," eh? She certainly sounds like the kind of investigator who would avoid *papering over* anything, doesn't she? (Sorry.)

Like the inert bureaucrats of the killer cleaning lady legend, the bank officials referenced are presented as worthy objects of righteous scorn and rage. Clearly, people have trust issues with big, powerful companies.

Strange but True

The version of the poisoned-envelopes-at-the-ATM legend just cited intones sadly that bank officials "said their hands are tied." Internet-fueled legends often tell tall tales about heartless bureaucrats who ignore the public welfare, but these legends reflect our very real uneasiness about the trust we are forced to place in businesses and government institutions. Real-life news stories have a way of reinforcing this uneasiness. You thought your car was safe? ("Gee, the tires seem to be exploding.") You thought the person who got the most votes won the presidency? ("Gee, it depends on who's counting in Florida.")

The ATM admonition offers a few half-formed specifics ("Dr. Elliott," "the Women's College Hospital"), but nothing much for a real, live law enforcement official to go on. And that, of course, is the idea—tantalizing allegations, shocking "evidence" that a trusted routine is now dangerous, and a great reason to start giving representatives of any and all banks the skunk eye.

No such case has been verified, of course.

Don't Trust That Bellboy

Here's a whopper that has made the rounds for years. Its most interesting version involves a memorable (but predictably impossible to verify) betrayal by a foreign bellboy.

An American family takes a trip to France. When they check into their hotel, they are shown around the facilities by a particularly urbane and obliging bellboy.

The next day, however, the family returns from a day of sightseeing and finds that the hotel room has been burglarized. The chief suspect: the bellboy, who had, it emerges, quit the hotel the very morning he walked the family up to their room.

Fable Facts

Some variations on the bellboy story involve thieves who are unknown to the innocent travelers, rather than larcenous employees of the hotel where they stay.

The unscrupulous antagonists are usually portrayed as members of another culture or citizens of another country. For more urban legends involving dangerous people who aren't from "around here," see Chapter 14, "Beware the Outsider."

155

Fable Facts

The "French bellboy" variation of this popular legend appears to be meant as extravagant (and eminently disgusting) "confirmation" of countless reports that French natives are less-than-hospitable hosts to American travelers. It's also a general comment on the degree to which we feel that we may be vulnerable to "service" people we don't know.

Don't Believe It!

The fried rat legend is one of several strange and completely baseless stories about ominous events at the local KFC. This particular tall tale appears to have been attached to the national chain of chicken emporiums because of a plot requirement: the need to have the grisly morsel concealed by fried batter.

The robbery, however, is an odd one; only a few of the family's possessions are gone. A valuable camera has been moved, not taken, and left in a different place, and the family's toothbrushes have been left in unfamiliar locations.

The family chalks the incident up to the fates and continues the vacation.

There's a surprise waiting for everyone upon the return to America, however. Once the family makes it home and gets the pictures developed, it becomes apparent that something has gone very wrong indeed. Most of one roll of film carries the standard touristy shots that the family members themselves took, but there are also some pictures of the bellboy with ominous and revolting implications.

There he is, smiling for an unseen shutter-snapping accomplice, with all of the family's toothbrushes shoved snugly and simultaneously up his rectum.

Nobody said the stories in this book were going to be pretty, folks.

What's that old saying about whether you can tell a book by its cover? By initially casting the bellboy as a pleasant, sophisticated sort and then turning him into a vengeful gross-out king, this story lodges in the memory of its listeners forever. It turns out that you really *can't* tell who people are by their exteriors. And maybe that nasty old Uncle Harry *was* right about foreigners after all.

The Kentucky Fried Yecch Nightmare

Here's a myth meant to make you at least consider swearing off fast food for a while. The tale—which is, you will not be surprised to learn, untrue—goes as follows:

It seems that an elderly woman decided to take a break from cooking and so placed a takeout order with KFC. When she got home, she opened up the package and started enjoying her dinner. One of the morsels, however, appeared to have teeth!

She peeled back the batter on the remainder of the chunk of "chicken"—only to find out that she had actually been dining on fried rat!

The Kentucky Fried Yecch Nightmare (Version II)

Perhaps more common is the variation in which a young wife—who "didn't have anything ready for supper for her husband"— decided to swing by her local KFC outlet. She turned the lights down low, lit some candles, and tried to pass the fast-food dinner off as home cooking. She regretted her choice, however, when the romantic evening at home was revealed to be a nightmare repast: deep-fried rat.

What's most interesting about these legends is *not* that they always seem to single out KFC (although the good people at KFC must really think that the stories are a hoot and a half). Nor is it the fact that many variations conclude with reports of huge damage suits against the company, a common wrap-up among urban legends.

No, what's really fascinating about this group of legends is what it says about gender-based social roles. The stories almost always involve women—women who make the poor choice of expecting someone else to cook dinner. By forsaking the classic role of kitchen slave, these ladies are apparently courting major risks.

Sooner or later, the moral seems to be, all such uppity womenfolk should expect to pay a similarly steep price. Before any so-called "modern" woman trusts her stomach, or her marriage, to the staff at the local fast-food outlet, she should reacquaint herself with *The Joy of Cooking*.

The Defiling Cup of Slush

Equally harrowing and even more intriguingly dreamlike is the legend involving the gory cup of slush. The plot on this one goes as follows:

Driving home alone late one night after seeing a movie, a young woman stopped at a secluded gas station. She was thirsty, and she wanted to buy a strawberry slush.

At the counter she saw a handsome man who appeared to be the only person working that night. The woman made her way to the rear of the room and poured herself a big cup of the red slush drink. Then she stuck a straw into it.

As she walked back up to the counter where the attendant waited for her, she took a big pull on the drink. Immediately she realized that she was drinking slush flavored not with strawberry syrup, but with blood.

Legend Lingo

Forbidden fruit is the fruit of the Tree of Knowledge forbidden by God to Adam and Eve in the book of Genesis. Many, many urban legends involve people consuming things that they shouldn't—and later wishing that they hadn't.

The man at the counter, it turned out, was a murderer; he had butchered his fellow employees and deposited their blood in the slush machine.

Clearly, what we have here is a failure of the parent company to administer effective training in stress management to its service station attendants.

The legend, which at least in this one form doesn't even bother to discuss the girl's fate, is actually a dream about desire, appetite, and punishment. It even has an interesting variation on *forbidden fruit*. ("You like strawberries, lady? Sure, we've got something flavored with strawberries. Right over there in the back ....")

Look at it again. The young woman is returning alone from what sounds like a date at a movie theater, and she is thirsty for something. (A physical appetite that must be quenched ... hmm.) She drinks without having yet paid for her selection, using—Freudian symbolism alert—a straw to do so. Finally, she realizes that a good-looking but unfamiliar man is actually a monster who has just defiled her.

Think about all *that* the next time you or someone you love pulls into the local Gas-Up late at night after a flick. And watch out for that guy behind the counter if he recommends the strawberry slush.

The Infested Software

In this intriguing Information Age update of the various gross-out bug stories discussed in Chapter 9, "All Creatures, Great and Small," and Chapter 24, "Some Final Thoughts," a woman places a call to the customer service line about a problem she's having with some software she has just installed.

The woman complains that the computer in which she has just installed the software is humming and vibrating noisily, despite the fact that she has turned it off. The voice on the other end of the line warns her to leave the house immediately, but as is so often the case in these stories, the warning comes just a little too late. The screen starts to glow, the machine shakes even more violently, and there's an explosion. Dozens of tarantulas are flung around the room.

Now that's what I call a problem with a computer bug.

Explanation? You want an explanation? What's to explain? Obviously, a pair of tarantulas crept into the software box, escaping the notice of some factory worker, and then, after the woman installed the software, they found their way into her machine and mated.

That seems likely enough, doesn't it? The only *implausible* part of the story: The service person actually knew what was wrong with the computer system after a brief description of the problem. When was the last time *that* happened?

The Lethal Tan

Finally, a story in which the *consumer* is at fault and the *employees* strive earnestly to do the right thing. Alas, disaster still looms.

In this legend, a young bride-to-be wants to get some color so that she'll look great in her wedding dress. A quick trip to the tropics is impractical, so she settles on the next best thing: a trip to the local tanning salon.

After half an hour on the tanning bed, the attendant tells her that it's time to stop. But the young lady complains that she's hardly tanned at all. "Too bad," says the attendant. "Rules are rules, and I'm not supposed to let you stay on for more than half an hour."

Undeterred, the pale young woman makes her way to a second tanning salon, and a third, and a fourth. Each time, she deems the results unsatisfactory; each time, the attendant in question refuses her another session. The fifth tanning salon attendant finds her dead in the tanning bed, with her insides fried from overexposure to the lights.

Let's see. A bride-to-be keeps going back to bed again and again, despite ardent advice (from people who ought to know) that she's overdoing it. She pays a horrible price. She never sees her wedding day.

Could it possibly be related to concerns about premarital sex?

Just a thought.

The Least You Need to Know

➤ Life support systems have backups and alarms.

➤ There is no ATM crisis.

➤ Nobody has ever tracked down verification on the deep–fried rat thing.

➤ The slush drink is fine.

➤ Ignore advice from tanning salon personnel at your own peril.

Chapter 14

Beware the Outsider

In This Chapter

➤ What is the Other?

➤ The care and feeding of outsider legends

➤ Organ theft rings and their exotic representatives

➤ Grisly Satanic cults

The stories examined in this chapter share a simple, if ominous, theme: People who aren't from "around here" are, more than likely, up to no good.

In a world in which traditional local community ties like garden clubs and softball teams are less evident, urban legends about "outsiders are hatching a nefarious plot" carry a frightening corollary. Here it is: Since we don't often have much of an idea of *who's* from "around here" and who isn't, we should probably assume that *everyone* is up to no good.

In support of that unsettling but not at all uncommon idea, consider the next myth.

The Unknown Driver Who Left a Note

You remember the story of the good Samaritan, the outsider who came to the aid of a wounded, abandoned traveler. Well, this legend, a direct refutation of the good Samaritan ethic, cuts in the opposite direction. Its most common version follows:

After slamming his vehicle into an unoccupied car, a driver gets out and inspects the damage. Knowing full well that he is being observed by members of the crowd that has gathered around the accident scene, he pulls out a pen and a piece of paper and scrawls a brief note.

The bystanders assume that the unknown man has written his contact information on the slip of paper, but in fact what he has done is compose a message that taunts the (absent) victim of the accident. The message says something like this:

Legend Lingo

An **outsider legend** is one that involves a threat from a foreign or nonlocal person, or a threat from someone representing such a person.

All these people are watching me, so I have to write something—but you're never going to find out who plowed into your car because I'm out of here. Have a nice day.

The message of this cautionary myth goes deeper than simply "Keep an eye on your car." What this story is really saying is, "People you don't recognize and can't be expected to track down probably have a hidden agenda—one that will, in all likelihood, leave you high and dry."

And that, as it turns out, is a pretty popular theme for urban legends.

The Outsider Wants to Steal Your Organs

One of the grisliest (and hardest to eradicate) urban legends involves the shadowy representatives of an international black market ring specializing in organ theft.

In these *outsider legends,* agents of rich foreigners somehow befriend a trusting victim, get him or her drunk or high, and then remove vital organs while the victim is unconscious. A typical variation on the story might involve the following elements:

➤ Innocent Guy sits at the bar, minding his own business.

➤ Unknown Sharp-Dressed Businessman approaches Innocent Guy and strikes up conversation.

➤ Innocent Guy passes out.

➤ Innocent Guy awakens in unknown and perplexing surroundings—say, a dumpster.

➤ Innocent Guy is discovered to have tiny incisions—and to be missing vital organs.

➤ Unknown Sharp-Dressed Businessman is revealed or suspected of harvesting said organs on behalf of Shadowy International Group.

The legend has been quite persistent in Europe and North America. It also has spun off any number of sickening modifications involving "harvested" adults, children and fetuses; these have been particularly popular in South America and Africa, where the stories may reflect deep resentment and distrust of developed nations.

Reason to Not Party Anymore

Here's a popular American version of the story in which the shadowy outside group has employed a seductress in pursuit of its nefarious aims. This adds a familiar element of anxiety over the perils of sexual experimentation to the story.

> This guy went out last Saturday night to a party. He was having a good time and had a couple of beers. A girl seemed to like him and invited him to go to another party. He quickly agreed, so she took him to a party in some apartment. They continued to drink, and they even got involved with some drugs. The next thing the guy knew, he woke up completely naked in a bathtub filled with ice. He was still feeling the effects of the drugs, but he looked around to see that he was alone.
>
> He looked down at his chest, where he found "CALL 911 OR YOU WILL DIE" written in lipstick. He saw a phone on a stand next to the tub, so he picked it up and dialed. He explained the situation to the EMS operator and said that he didn't know where he was, what he took, or why he was really calling. She advised him to get out of the tub. He did, and she asked him to look himself over in the mirror. When he did and appeared normal, the operator told him to check his back. He did, only to find two 9-inch slits on his lower back. The operator told him to get back into the tub immediately and sent a rescue team over.
>
> Apparently, after being examined, he learned more of what had happened. His kidneys had been stolen; they were worth $10,000 each on the black market. (I was unaware this even existed.) Several guesses are in order: The second party was a sham, the people involved had to be at least medical students, and it was not just recreational drugs he was given. Regardless, the guy is currently in the hospital on life support, awaiting a spare kidney.

Note that the horror of the tale is accentuated by the implication that the operator manning the 911 line is all too familiar with the stolen-kidney problem.

The "harvested kidneys" myth has surfaced in a remarkable variety of forms. Most versions posit a sophisticated plot engineered by people unknown to the victim and coordinated by rich criminals far outside of his or her social sphere. The stories usually involve contact with an appealing, unfamiliar stranger—contact that eventually lands the victim in the hospital (or the morgue).

As you may have guessed, no actual cases matching the legend have been identified.

Why Organ Harvesting?

In their most common American incarnations, the ghoulish stories of kidney theft share certain plot elements with the classic "AIDS Mary" and "AIDS Harry" stories discussed later in this book (see Chapter 17, "Hazardous Amorous Duty"). In all three stories, a sexual adventure with an unknown stranger leads to a harrowing, life-changing message—one that's delivered in writing rather than in person.

There are any number of ways to interpret the organ-theft legends. Fears about abandonment and lack of control, the motives of outsiders, and the grave dangers of promiscuity in the era of AIDS all appear to be prominent candidates as answers to the perplexing question "What do these stories mean?"

The Outsider Wants to Murder Children to Smuggle Drugs

The following legend, like many of the organ-harvesting stories, features a ruthless group of international criminals who will stop at nothing—not even infanticide—to attain their goals. Warning: The following story is not for the faint of heart.

```
I received the following story via e-mail:

Be Ever Watchful of Your Children

My sister's co-worker has a sister in Texas who, with her hus-
band, was planning a weekend trip across the Mexican border
```

for a shopping spree. At the last minute, their baby sitter canceled, so they had to bring along their 2-year-old son with them. They had been across the border for about an hour when the baby got free and ran around the corner. The mother went chasing, but the boy had disappeared. The mother found a police officer who told her to go to a gate; not really understanding the instructions, she did as she was instructed.

About 45 minutes later, a man approached the border carrying the boy. The mother ran to him, grateful that he had been found. When the man realized it was the boy's mother, he dropped the boy and ran. The police were waiting and captured the man. The boy was dead. In the less than 45 minutes that he was missing, he had been cut open, all of his insides had been removed, and his body cavity had been stuffed with cocaine. The man was going to carry him across the border as if he were asleep!

Don't Believe It!

The bogus story of a dead baby stuffed with cocaine, like so many urban legends, usually begins with a disclaimer to the effect that the person circulating the story has received it from a (presumably) reliable source. In fact, no documented case of this kind exists.

Legend Lingo

The **Other** is the archetypal enemy, adversary, or antagonist who, because of a failure to abide by basic societal norms, is seen as less than human.

This never-verified story—which has been around for years and has even been circulated by credulous law-enforcement officials—proves that trips across the border can be perilous.

The actual border being crossed here, though, is psychological. The victim in the story makes an ill-advised trip into the world of the *Other*; this could represent a strange new country or, just as likely, an unfamiliar part of town. Whatever territory is designated as the Other, its residents are ruthless, violent people who reject or ignore all the customary moral standards. It's no surprise, then, that they'd have no problem carving up a baby to complete a drug deal.

The not-so-subtle message: If you don't want to repeat the mother's horrifying experience, learn from it—and avoid the Other at all costs.

The Outsider Wants to Conduct Satanic Rituals with Your Baby

"I guess this is it. I guess this is where I get cut up like those cats. Nooo! Malachi is coming over by me and then he's saying some funny words and some smoky stuff's going up in the air. He's all crouched over me. He's cutting that baby over me! He's rubbing it all over me! Oh, God, there's stuff all over me!"

Talk about crossing psychological boundaries. This harrowing excerpt from a book entitled *Michelle Remembers* (New York, Congdon & Lattes, 1980) warns against the supposed abuses of Satanic cults. Are stories like Michelle's literal statements of fact, or are they reflections of complex therapeutic issues?

Has Someone Launched a Satanist Cult in Your Neighborhood?

If outsiders are the Other—furtive, secretive enemies of society—then the stories of a shadowy conspiracy to perpetrate and cover up gruesome Satanic religious ceremonies have to rank among the most dramatic outsider legends of them all. What sane person would engage in such rituals or recruit others to do so? And who, while we're on the subject, is coordinating all these violent, abusive rituals?

The (suspiciously) elusive monsters said to be masterminding these grim events have haunted well-meaning parents, therapists, and law enforcement officials for years. The details of the ceremonies are certainly enough to capture any parent's attention.

So, *are* mysterious Satanic cultists mounting a vast conspiracy to corrupt childcare facilities, hypnotize adults, and destroy families? Over the years, such questions have led to any number of media reports. The most sensational of these, not surprisingly, have been heavy on the panic and innuendo, but extremely light on independently verifiable facts.

Sad but true: Stories debunking outrageous claims tend to get a lot less media play than stories *spreading* the outrageous claims in the first place. It's not surprising, then, that responsible reporting has not had the same public impact as some of the initial, breathless, verbatim accounts from people (young and old) who "discovered" that they had been swept up in various hideous rituals.

Fable Facts

According to the book *Satanic Panic* by J. Victor (Chicago, Open Court, 1993), Geraldo Rivera began a 1987 ABC News special on "Satanic Cults and Children" with the following dire warning: "Satanic cults! Every hour, every day, their ranks are growing .... From small towns to large cities, they've attracted police and FBI attention to their Satanist ritual abuse, child pornography, and grisly Satanic order. The odds are, this is happening in your town."

The "Recovered Memory" Problem

Today, stories of Satanic abuse based on "recovered memories" from childhood are more likely to be treated as private clinical issues than as hard news stories.

This is fortunate because there is an emerging consensus that the commonly circulated Satanic abuse stories were fantasies. Many researchers now feel that the most sensational stories from the mid-1980s and beyond were strongly influenced by the questions posed by therapists and others. In other words, if you *ask* someone about X, Y, or Z while that person is under hypnosis, you're likely to get a *response* about X, Y, or Z.

Child abuse in all its forms is, of course, extremely serious business—so serious that it deserves to be investigated with the utmost persistence and professionalism. Whatever complex of shared insecurities led to the mass circulation of grisly, sexually explicit stories of a network of child-centered Satanic rituals, the sinister personages behind that network, like the network itself, still resemble nothing so much as a mirage. Those who feel differently about the matter are invited to forward hard physical evidence (as opposed to secondhand reports or "recovered" memories) to the local constabulary.

Don't Believe It!

In his article "Interpreting the Satanic Legend" (*Journal of Religion and Health*, Vol. 37, No. 3, Fall 1998), James Hunter writes, "(O)ver a decade of investigation by competent law enforcement officials has failed to turn up corroborating evidence of Satanic rituals and cults as they are described in the [clinical] literature."

The Outsider Is Part of a Particularly Dangerous and Ruthless New Urban Gang

You thought those Satanist masterminds were insidious? Wait until you hear about the latest, most horrifying incarnation of the Other: those ruthless, casually murderous new urban gangs that you've somehow escaped being dusted by.

Granted, they're not accused of sacrificing newborn babies on the altar of the Dark Lord (yet). But give them time. If the three legends that follow are any indication of what's in store for decent, hardworking Americans, the stuff with smoke and mutilated babies will, in its turn, surely show up somewhere on the mean streets of the inner city.

Fable Facts

Legends falsely attributing infanticide, orgies, and other baleful practices to various groups have been popular for centuries. Roman writers accused the early Christians of such rituals.

The Fiendish Flashing Light Ritual

Every once in a while, alert motorists will show care and concern for fellow drivers by flashing their lights at someone who has forgotten to turn on the headlights after dark. Bad move, according to the following legend; that act of kindness is a tip-off to cold-hearted killers.

Fable Facts

The Flashing Headlight legend serves as an essential plot element in the lowbrow horror film *Urban Legend*. The film came out in 1998, and did well enough at the box office to inspire a sequel, *Urban Legends: The Final Cut (2000)*. Somehow, both blood-drenched films got shut out of the Oscar voting in their respective years. Probably lost ballots or something.

Legends like this often implicitly lament the passing of the era of civility; at the same time, they're successfully frightening strangers out of treating each other with courtesy.

A police officer working with the DARE program has issued this warning: If you are driving after dark and see an oncoming car with no headlights on, DO NOT FLASH YOUR LIGHTS AT THEM! This is a common gang member "initiation game" that goes like this:

The new gang member under initiation drives along with no headlights, and the first car to flash its headlights at him is now his "target." He is now required to turn around and chase that car, and shoot at or into the car in order to complete his initiation requirements. Make sure that you share this information with all the drivers in your family!

Some game, eh?

Don't be fooled by the official-sounding reference to the youth antidrug program DARE. Local police departments are sick of hearing about this.

The story circulates, though, because people are willing to be convinced that the Other is lurking on the next unfamiliar street. Here's further "evidence" of the vast, unbridgeable gap between decent, innocent folks like you and me and those armies of hardened psychopaths who roam the dark recesses of the inner city.

The Fiendish Slashing Ritual

Or, Ladies, Watch Your Body Parts!

```
This is a true story.

It has been a "ritual" of gang members to take one body part
from women as an initiation into gangs. The rule is that it
has to be in a well-lit area and at a gas station, so be
```

careful. They tend to lie under the car, and slash a female's ankles when she goes to get in her car, causing her to fall; then they cut off a body part and roll and run.

They are known to hide behind the gas pumps, too, so be careful. It might sound bizarre and gross, but the bigger the body part, the higher the initiation they receive.

This was communicated by a person who works in law enforcement in the South. She has investigated and been called to a number of these scenes. She has also confirmed the following statement as true and not an Internet "hoax."

Here is an example of a true case: A gas station attendant yelled at a lady to come back and pay for her gas, threatening that if she did not, he would call the cops if she tried to drive away (this was right after she had been in and paid for the gas). She returned into the station upset and angry at the attendant, only to realize that he had called the cops after spotting a man roll under her car. She was about to be a victim of the initiation.

Please pass these on to as many people you know … mothers, sisters, grandparents, daughters, nieces, friends. It seems the world has become a crazy place to live in, but let's be careful out there and make stuff like this known so that we are better protected.

"A person who works in law enforcement in the South." Boy, you don't get much better independent confirmation than that.

The near-disaster described in the second half of the alert follows a formula common in many legends. Somehow, hearing about someone *just barely escaping* the fiendish slasher is more terrifying than simply hearing that someone was actually done in by a crazed gang member out to snag some unspecified but presumably huge body part. And the fit of pique directed at her rescuer adds just the right "Oh-my-God-what-did-I-just-do?" tone to the story.

Law enforcement officials are sick of this one, too.

The Fiendish LSD- or Strychnine-Impregnated Phone Ritual

Or, Reach Out and Kill Someone.

Notice the "I'm not really writing this, I'm just forwarding it" prologue in what follows. This is a classic ruse.

Hello, this is to warn everyone of a new thing happening in communities as a gang initiation and such. If you care about anyone, please forward this to them immediately so they can learn of the possible harm. Even if you don't read this, at least forward it to people.

* * *

Hello, my name is Tina Strongman, and I work at a police station, as a phone operator for 911. Lately we've received many phone calls pertaining to a new sort of problem that has arisen in the inner cities and is now working its way to smaller towns. It seems that a new form of gang initiation is to go find as many pay phones as possible and put a mixture of LSD and strychnine onto the buttons.

This mixture is deadly to the human touch, and apparently this has killed some people on the East Coast. Strychnine is a chemical used in rat poison and is easily separated from the rest of the chemicals. When mixed with LSD, it creates a substance that is easily absorbed into the human flesh and that is highly fatal.

Please be careful if you are using a pay phone anywhere. You may want to wipe it off, or just not use one at all. If you have any questions, you can contact me at the links listed below. Please be very careful. Let your friends and family know about this potential hazard.

Thank you.

SSgt Terence D. Murchison
DSN 425 7203
4E232 Air Force Pentagon
Washington, D.C.
http://www.safaq.hq.af.mil

Geez, Louise! "If you care about anyone"! (Of course I do!) "Working its way into smaller towns"! (Gosh—*I* live in a smaller town!) "Highly fatal"! (Not just fatal, mind you, but *highly* fatal!)

This *is* serious! Ruthless sociopathic gang members *are* on the loose! The Pentagon is even getting in on the act! And, brother, they sound worried!

Just one question: Why on earth can't I find any reference to Staff Sergeant Murchison at the site listed?

Have rabid computer-savvy gang initiates hacked into the Defense Department's computer system and started manipulating the very Web site thoughtfully included as a point of contact at the conclusion of the message?

Or, just as chilling, is it possible that Staff Sergeant Murchison was himself inadvertently exposed to the LSD-and-strychnine-laden-phone curse before completing his message forwarding Ms. Strongman's concerns, leading him to pass along an unfortunate typographical error?

Clearly, the time has come to call 911 and report this matter to the authorities!

Look, here's a pay phone. I'll just pick up the receiver, feed in a few coins, heedlessly punch in a number using my own exposed flesh, and …

GGGGGGGGGgggggggggggghhhhhhhhhhhhhhhhhhhhhhhhmmmmmmmmmmmmmmmmmmmmmmmmmmnnnnnnnnnnnnnnnnnnnnghrgggh!

The Least You Need to Know

➤ Avoid getting too worked up about stories whose motto appears to be, "People who aren't from 'around here' are, more than likely, up to no good."

➤ Specifically, regard stories of sophisticated organ-theft rings and their exotic representatives with skepticism. Be similarly wary about stories of ritual Satanic abuse.

➤ Maintain comparable neutrality with regard to tales of fiendish gang initiation rituals involving flashing headlights.

➤ Take the same intelligent approach to accounts of fiendish gang initiation rituals involving hidden slashers at gas stations.

➤ In considering whether to expose yourself to the risks claimed to be associated with the use of public pay phones, consider a moment of silence in memory of the many sacrifices of Staff Sergeant Terence D. Murchison.

Chapter 15

Authority Figures Lose It

Military technology misused in disastrously ill-conceived ways. Great ideas ignored, stonewalled, suppressed, or simply paved over. Deplorable "practical jokes" that somehow made their way into the world's most popular business software. Epidemics unleashed. The public trust betrayed through negligence, idiocy, or a combination of the two.

Has The Establishment finally lost its marbles? To judge from the urban legends in this chapter, the answer is "Yes." Incompetent or predatory scientists, software engineers, and accounting departments are apparently either asleep at the switch or—deprived of any semblance of reason—gleefully planting grenades beneath the tracks.

"Oops!"

Bill Cosby used to do a routine about a surgeon who said "Oops!"—causing his (locally anesthetized) patient to stare up in alarm from the operating table. "I know what *I* mean when *I* say 'Oops!'" the patient said. "What do *you* mean when *you* say 'Oops?'"

In this chapter, we look at urban legends about people and institutions that aren't supposed to say "Oops." They're supposed to know what they're doing, but they end up illustrating the chilling old warning, "To be ignorant of one's madness is the malady of the mad."

Bill Gates's Overworked Software Engineers Slip the Tether

Everyone would agree that Microsoft, the dominant global software corporation, is huge. Some people would even sign on with the notion that Microsoft is rapacious. But have the folks behind Windows finally slipped off their rocker?

The following legend may make you wonder.

Did Microsoft Allow a Racist Joke to Slip into Millions of Copies of Microsoft Word?

Sometime in 1999, the following e-mail started circulating among users of Microsoft Word, the preeminent word-processing program in the known universe. Its alarming message: Bill Gates and associates had somehow allowed a hateful racial slur, presumably inserted by one of Microsoft's overstressed programmers, to slip past unnoticed.

Plausible? You be the judge.

> Subject: FW: ms word
>
> You will not believe this …. TRY IT FOR YOURSELF!!!!!! I did this on my system, and it's true. I don't believe it! You won't believe your eyes!
>
> 1. Go into MS Word.
> 2. Type: I'd like all Negroes to die.
> 3. Highlight the sentence.
> 4. Go into Tools > Language > Thesaurus.
>
> I know you may not have MS Word, but what happens is you get a message saying, "I'll drink to that."
>
> Lesson learned: Don't be fooled into thinking that racism isn't alive and well—it has just taken different form. I wonder if Bill Gates knows what his programmers have put into the system.
>
> NOW might be the time to let him know! Pass it on!!

Sure enough, if you follow the instructions as laid out in the message, Word's thesaurus will, in fact, respond with the phrase "I'll drink to that." To many folks, the conclusion was obvious: One or more racist programmers had programmed the vile little hate-hiccup into the software, and no one at Microsoft had caught the slur until it had already been released to the planet at large.

But is that what really happened?

The Truth Behind "I'll Drink to That"

Actually, no. What really happened is that some enterprising crank noticed that Word's thesaurus function is not particularly well-designed. As a result, the software will toss up phrases and words that have nothing whatsoever to do with the sentences being analyzed. (Similar carefully wrought chunks of prose involving former President Clinton yielded the same response within the program's thesaurus, and led to similar rumors.)

"I'd like all Negroes to die" seems to have been the most offensive sentence the author of this little hoax could match up with "I'll drink to that." It was certainly offensive enough to get lots of people worked up about Microsoft. Note: This legend applies to Word 97. Word 2000 appears to have been altered, perhaps in an effort to avoid supporting the story.

A side note: Following the same instructions in Word 97, but substituting the sentence "I always double-check foolish rumors about racist programmers" yields the phrase "I appreciate it." This leads to one of three conclusions:

1. The folks at Microsoft are crazy because they planted *this* little clue, too.

2. The folks at Microsoft anticipated the problems they were likely to have with cynical legend-spinners out to prey on peoples' racial tensions.

3. With a little ingenuity, you can make the thesaurus "say" pretty much anything you want.

Option 3 looks pretty good from here, but you can take your pick.

Fable Facts

Many urban legends reflect deeply held societal concerns and misgivings. Tensions about racial relations are a common starting point. It will be interesting to see what new legends surface as our society continues to work through racial issues—and eventually becomes a nation in which no majority race predominates. (This, the statisticians tell us, is supposed to take place by the middle of this century.)

Strange but True

Also playing on racial tensions is a similar legend purporting that someone within the U.S. government had secretly instituted a racial coding system within each and every Social Security number—sounds even more ominous than the Microsoft legend. Did someone really come up with a plan to assign all African-Americans Social Security numbers featuring an even fifth number? Did the same person ensure that all Caucasians received an odd fifth number? Is it possible that someone actually implemented this overtly racist system without attracting the notice of, say, *Newsweek* or the Attorney General's office? Naaah. But the story, like the Microsoft Word myth, does play on legitimate misgivings about racial prejudice and government malfeasance.

Scientists Slip the Tether

John F. Kennedy once opined that the reason life didn't exist on other planets was that the scientists of alien cultures were more advanced than ours. Cynical, maybe, but there's a germ of truth there about the ambitions—and occasional lunacies—of the scientific establishment.

What with Hiroshima, Chernobyl, genetically altered corn, and the abject failure of the scientific community to deliver a cure for the AIDS virus, people have had good reason to be skeptical about the doings of scientists for the last half century or so. That skepticism has found plenty of ways to express itself in popular culture. Remember the Doomsday Machine that ensured global annihilation in Stanley Kubrick's film *Dr. Strangelove?* How about the neutron bomb, which decimates people, not buildings, and prompted one wag to have himself officially declared a building?

Today we live in an era in which anything and everything appears to be possible through science. We suspect, though, that anything and everything can go *wrong* with the stuff science sends our way—and that we may not get the straight scoop when it does. The following legends illustrate our various uncertainties about the folks in the long white coats.

Scientists Cooked Up the AIDS Virus on Purpose

Did mad scientists at the KGB, a U.S. intelligence establishment, a biological research center in Maryland, or any other shadowy facility concoct the lethal AIDS virus to target homosexuals, minorities, and users of illicit drugs?

No. Sometimes we need to find "reasons" for terrifying and seemingly inexplicable events, though. Hence the proliferation of myths about scientists singling out undesirable elements with the AIDS virus. (Actually, from what your humble author has been able to track down, developing a targeted disease in this way would be well beyond the range of most of the sinister groups associated with this legend.)

The equally (il)logical proposition that the ultimate authority figure, God, came up with the AIDS virus as a scourge has been neatly debunked by author Sol Gordon. "If God was angry enough at homosexuals to come up with the AIDS virus," Gordon once said, "then He must also have been angry at the American Legion, because He also came up with Legionnaire's Disease."

Don't Believe It!

Scientists *didn't* invent the AIDS virus as part of an ominous attempt to liquidate specific groups of people. The disease appears to have arisen from a similar virus in certain species of monkeys.

Technology Kills

Part of what terrifies us about science is the possibility that we may just find a way to misuse what it gives us. The *JATO legend*, in this widely circulated e-mail, tells of a horrific amateur experiment gone awry in the Arizona desert, with John Q. Taxpayer footing the bill for the destroyed equipment, of course.

> The Arizona (U.S.) Highway Patrol came upon a pile of smoldering metal embedded into the side of a cliff rising above the road, on the outside of a curve. The wreckage resembled the site of an airplane crash, but it was a car. The type of car was unidentifiable at the scene. The boys in the lab finally figured out what it was and what had happened.
>
> It seems that a guy had somehow gotten hold of a JATO unit (Jet Assisted Take-Off, actually a solid-fuel rocket) that is used to give heavy military transport planes an extra "push" for taking off from short airfields. He had

Legend Lingo

The **JATO legend** involves a supposedly fatal, unauthorized civilian experiment with a Jet Assisted Take-Off unit strapped to an auto. The most popular version of the legend says the guy got the rocket from the Air Force. It sounds more like the Acme Company.

177

> driven his Chevy Impala out into the desert and found a long, straight stretch of road. Then he attached the JATO unit to his car, jumped in, got up some speed, and fired off the JATO!!
>
> Best as they could determine, he was doing somewhere between 250-300 miles per hour (350-420 kilometers per hour) when he came to that curve .... The brakes were completely burned away, apparently from trying to slow the car.

Quite an image, yes? Too bad there's nothing in any local news resource or police report to support the story.

The tale is essentially a moderately amusing revision of an old Road Runner cartoon, with a deft sprinkling of adult-level horror and panic in the final mental image of the poor fellow attempting in vain to jam on the brakes. If *that's* not a metaphor for technology that has spun out of control on us, nothing is.

If only the "boys in the lab" had developed safeguards against the tragic misuse of their little jet-propelled toys!

"Hmm ... Did We Forget to Send a Guy to the Moon?"

> The idea that we went to the Moon—and that we were successful in our Apollo endeavors—is so firmly embedded in the cultural lives of most people on this planet that to voice the opposite opinion that this might be untrue smacks of paranoia.
>
> —*The Fortean Times,* 1994

Good point.

Every once in a while some self-appointed "skeptic" unleashes a book or article purporting to "prove" that the Apollo Program was a shrewd public relations campaign designed to camouflage our nation's manifest failure to conduct a successful manned moon mission. Actually, the "proof" offered typically consists of less-than-persuasive attempts to poke holes in some narrowly chosen segments of the standard account of events related to the space program. But I digress.

The anti–Apollo landing argument takes many forms, but its thesis may sound something like this: The Establishment is covering up for corrupt or incompetent scientists, and no one—not Armstrong, not Aldrin, not anyone else—actually walked on the moon. Despite what the public may believe it has heard, seen, read, watched on TV, or otherwise encountered, it didn't happen. The whole thing was filmed at night somewhere in the Nevada desert. And those twisted gearheads at NASA have been perpetuating a subterfuge for three-plus decades.

In essence, the suggestion appears to be this:

➤ The powers that be *don't* have enough on the ball to send anyone to the moon, and never have.

➤ Yet these powers that be *do* have enough on the ball to mount a coverup of staggering technical and logistical complexity (to wit, faked transcripts, faked command-center computer systems and readouts, a faked moonwalk, a faked ocean landing of the command capsule, faked lunar specimens, faked readings in records from instruments monitoring takeoff and return, and so on).

In fact, according to these folks, each piece of physical evidence advanced in support of the idea that the moon landing occurred is actually an attempt on the part of NASA and the scientific establishment to cover their collective butt.

Like many seriously wacko "theories," this one is pretty much unanswerable. If the persuasiveness of *every* piece of evidence one points to is immediately dismissed as further "proof" of the detailed nature of the coverup, then something's wrong. All that's really happening is that somebody who's deeply worried about *something* (probably people with PhDs) is working on some complex internal issues.

Here's the bottom line: People who don't believe that people landed on the moon hold persistently to this state of mind for their own reasons. Among these reasons is probably a fear of the potential for excess or error on the part of government scientists.

Scientists Are Covering Up the "Secret Challenger Transcript"

Not quite as inventive as the proposition that the Apollo launch was fictional is the proposition that the folks at NASA are concealing from public view a transcript of the last words of the doomed *Challenger* crew. Supposedly, the conversation went as follows (M stands for male voice, F for female voice):

M: What happened? What happened? Oh God, no—no!

M: I told them, I told them .... Dammit! Resnik, don't ....

F: Don't let me die like this. Not now. Not here ....

F: I'm ... passing ... out.

M: If you ever wanted (unintelligible) me a miracle (unintelligible). (Screams.)

M: Can't breathe.

M: God. The water ... we're dead! (Screams.)

F: Goodbye (sobs) ... I love you, I love you ....

M: Our Father (unintelligible) hallowed be thy name (unintelligible) ....

There is, of course, no need for an urban legend to convince people of NASA'S many errors before the catastrophic *Challenger* launch. The reason that this "transcript" legend has proved so popular is that it puts an exclamation mark next to the failure of the authorities to do right by the astronauts (and the nation). The text emphasizes the details of the human suffering of the explosion and leaves us to wonder what *else* those wacky O-ring fans down at Cape Canaveral are trying to keep us from finding out about.

Is the dialogue an actual transcript of a radio transmission from the *Challenger?* NASA says it's bogus, but if you aren't in the mood to take their word for it, consider that the earliest sighting of this particular document appears to have been in the *Weekly World News*—not exactly an unimpeachable source.

Admit it. That oh-so-cruelly-ironic "I told them, I told them" business is just plain fishy.

Predatory Bureaucracies Slip the Tether

Greedy, shortsighted functionaries get deliriously hot and bothered in support of the sacred activity of chasing down a buck. In fact, they get *so* deliriously hot and bothered that they consign the best interests of the general public to the circular file.

No, we're not talking about the working habits of the second Bush Administration. We're talking about the plot outlines of the following urban legends, all of which feature bureaucrats who may well have gone daft Working for the Man every night and day. In an apparent fit of derangement, they make choices with bad repercussions for folks like you and me.

Somehow, we expect the profit motive to cause things to go haywire every once in a while. If the almighty dollar can drive Scrooge McDuck over the edge, why not the accounting department?

Are Oil Companies Hiding a Component That Could Dramatically Enhance Fuel Efficiency?

Could it be? The solution to the world's energy and environmental problems is in our grasp—only to be plucked thence by a few deranged executives who can't see the folly of long-term reliance on fossil fuels?

It's a nice idea: a simple gadget installed on a lazy Saturday afternoon that could boost a car's fuel efficiency up into the range of 200 miles per gallon range, save you bucks at the pump, and slow down the destruction of the planet. Because no such device has ever existed, though, it's hard to pin the blame for its concealment on maniacal bureaucrats at the nation's big oil and auto corporations.

The technology in question is known as a vapor carburetor; its proponents argue that it helps autos burn fuel much more efficiently and with less pollution than a standard carb. Problem 1: The extraordinary improvements in fuel economy promised by the device's supporters have yet to materialize in a real (as opposed to theoretical) automobile. Problem 2: Carburetors themselves are pretty much irrelevant, what with the current preference for fuel injectors.

It turns out that no single doodad is going to turn your car into a 200-miles-per-gallon econocruiser. According to the engineers, big jumps in fuel efficiency mean changing a lot of little things, not just one component.

P.S.: We seem to get awfully worried about nefarious plots by the auto and oil industries to damage the environment, but we never seem to get worried enough to *buy* fuel-efficient automobiles in significant quantities. That makes *us* the real lunatics because consumer demand plays the most important role in determining the kinds of cars Detroit puts on the showroom floor. (No surprise there.)

While we're on the subject of environmental impacts ....

Fable Facts

A similar story involving a man who invented an engine that could run on water and then found himself persecuted by representatives of unidentified business interests inspired David Mamet's play *The Water Engine*. (The designs for the engine, um, evaporate—so does the guy.)

Did Oil Companies Conspire to Obliterate the First Los Angeles Trolley System?

Demented business interests make another environmentally unfriendly appearance.

You still hear this one a lot, in part because the story was adapted into the animated/live-action film *Who Framed Roger Rabbit?* (Hey, if a movie starring an animated bunny says there was a crazy plot to undermine the L.A. trolley system, *that's what happened.*)

Back in the 1930s, Los Angeles had the nation's biggest system of urban trolley cars. A company called Pacific Electric ran the routes; it was bought out by a holding company owned by major auto, tire, and oil companies. Not long thereafter, all the trolleys were gone, and all the tracks were paved over. In place of the trains were (sleuths of crazed money-grubbing schemes, take note) fleets of petroleum-sucking, smoke-belching buses and a steadily increasing number of private automobiles.

Smell a rat? Well, you're not the only one. Before we accept the contention that fiendish gas-burning interests conspired to make sure that the trolleys disappeared, though, we have a couple of pesky details to contend with:

➤ Pacific Electric had already begun to convert from trolleys to buses *before* being bought out by the holding company.

➤ The conversion was endorsed by a state commission, apparently because trolleys were considered slow, expensive, and bothersome in comparison to buses.

➤ In getting out of trolleys and into buses, Pacific Electric was only doing what most other big cities were doing at the time.

None of that turns the auto and oil industries of the 1930s into tree-hugging mass-transit fans, of course. But their executives were not the demented road warriors often depicted by the circulators of the legend.

Did an Unnamed Russian Insurance Company Attempt to Withhold Payment on an Unusual Shipping Accident?

In this story, a poor Russian fisherman gets the skunk eye from his insurance company after his boat is destroyed at sea. His livelihood is at stake, but the folks behind the desks steadfastly refuse to pay up.

The reason? The fisherman claims that his boat was totaled by a *falling cow.* The underwriters think that's a laugh and a half (which is perhaps understandable) and refuse to investigate the merest syllable of his claim (which is, presumably, yet another example of the abject failure of capitalism on all fronts).

The poor man tells his sad story to anyone who will listen, and soon the story of the falling cow reaches the American embassy in Moscow. Some empathetic soul there takes pity on the fisherman, tracks him down, and offers both compensation and an explanation. An Air Force transport on a famine relief sortie had a bit of a midflight crisis: One of the cattle being transported got wacky and started running around in the plane, knocking people over and causing all kinds of chaos. Solution? Toss it out the cargo door, of course.

Fable Facts

The falling cow claim story has a variant version involving the Russian Air Force, which drops a cow on a Japanese ship.

Those heartless underwriters. Why on earth would they be skeptical about something that turned out to have an explanation as simple and logical as that?

Did Company Policy Tick Off One Customer Too Many?

In this legend, the little guy, at long last, gets the last word.

The following tale has made the rounds for years; the version that follows indicts the allegedly snooty, unresponsive representatives of Neiman-Marcus for a shocking example of unresponsive customer service. Truth be told, the angry consumer's fictional act of vengeance has been exacted on dozens of different establishments over the years.

> My daughter and I had just finished a salad at Neiman-Marcus Cafe in Dallas, and we decided to have a small dessert. Because we are such cookie lovers, we decided to try the "Neiman-Marcus Cookie."
>
> It was so excellent that I asked the waitress if she would give me the recipe. She said with a small frown, "I'm afraid not." "Well," I said, "would you let me buy the recipe?" With a cute smile, she said, "Yes." I asked how much, and she responded, "Two fifty." I said with approval, just add it to my tab.
>
> Thirty days later, I received my Visa statement from Neiman-Marcus, and it was $285. I looked again, and I remembered that I had spent only $9.95 for two salads and about $20 for a scarf. As I glanced at the bottom of the statement, it said, "Cookie Recipe—$250." Boy, was I upset!! I called Neiman's accounting department and told them the waitress said it was "two fifty," and I did not realize she had meant $250 for a cookie recipe. I asked them to take back the recipe and reduce my bill, and they said they were sorry, but all the recipes were this expensive.
>
> I waited, thinking of how I could get even or even try to get any of my money back. I just said, "Okay, you folks got my $250, and now I'm going to have $250 worth of fun." I told her that I was going to see to it that every cookie lover would have a $250 cookie recipe from Neiman-Marcus for nothing. She replied, "I wish you wouldn't do this." I said, "I'm sorry, but this is the only way I feel I could get even," and I will. So, here it is, and please pass it to someone else or run a few copies …. I paid for it; now you can have it for free …. Have fun!!!
>
> This is not a joke—this is a true story.

The message concludes with a (not particularly imaginative) oatmeal chocolate chip cookie recipe using quantities apparently designed to yield 112 servings.

If you want a copy, you're going to have to forward a check for $250 to the author. That's what it says right here in my Huge Book of Insane Publishing Regulations. We have *policies* here, do you understand? *Policies!* And they're put in place for a *reason!* No one deviates from them without *prior written permission* from the National Aeronautics and Space Administration's Feverish Subterfuge Division!

Cough up the bucks, bunky. You're not running things around here.

> ## The Least You Need to Know
>
> ➤ Racist software programmers have not overtaken Microsoft.
>
> ➤ Urban legends about the nefarious doings of twisted scientists often reflect our fears about the unknown implications of technological advances.
>
> ➤ Legends about power-tripping representatives of big organizations that stomp all over the little guy reflect a suspicion that the profit motive doesn't always benefit everyone equally.
>
> ➤ If you're out fishing, check the sky from time to time for falling cows, just to be on the safe side.

Part 4
Intimate Entanglements

An old Latin proverb holds that "every animal is sad after intercourse."

Humans are certainly no exception—and we might add "terrified" to the proverb if we focused it exclusively on our own species. Regrets and misgivings about sexuality run rampant through the legends in the following chapters. Why? Maybe we use scary and disturbing stories about sex to instill acceptable patterns of behavior in this dicey area. Maybe humans are profoundly frightened of the force of their own libidos. Or maybe, just maybe, we like talking about situations involving sexual extremes—and riding vicariously the emotional whirlwinds that always seem to accompany those situations.

Humiliation Is a Many-Splendored Thing

In This Chapter

➤ The showering minister

➤ The surprise party for the career woman

➤ The bottomless skier

➤ Various ill-advised "anonymous" sexual encounters

Do you remember the old television show *Candid Camera?* In it, the venerable host, Alan Funt, always argued that his filmed practical jokes showed people "caught in the act of being themselves."

In this chapter, we hear stories about people caught in the act of, well, being people they weren't necessarily planning on introducing to anyone. Hidden desires, careless oversights, and repressed insecurities come to the fore, and the result is big-time humiliation. That makes for rough sledding for the protagonists, of course, but more voyeuristic fun for you and me.

Relax. What follows occurs first and foremost in the deep, dark recesses of our own minds rather than in the real world. In a way, we are *all* the humbled main figures of these embarrassing stories, and we are *all* the shocked, wide-eyed observer of the shame.

In this chapter, we all get a chance to play at Peeping Tom—with our own psyches.

The Minister Gets a Surprise

We'll start with the big stuff: God and the libido. In this legend, a wife's frank sexual expressiveness causes a shocking breach of propriety involving the local minister.

Fable Facts

At least she's married! Many variations on the "humiliated lustful woman" subject their frisky *unwed* heroines to similarly mortifying embarrassment, presumably for failing to color inside the socially mandated lines of matrimony. For a legend that leaves a young *unmarried* woman exposed to the prying eyes of her relatives and warns of the hazards of premarital sex, see Chapter 17, "Hazardous Amorous Duty."

Here's how it goes: A husband pitches in and helps out the local minister by spending the day doing some yard work around the church. The legend usually specifies that the husband and the minister are doing their work on Saturday—an interesting detail, as it confirms that both men are in accordance with God's commandment not to work on Sunday, the Christian Sabbath. The gentlemen, at least, are playing by the rules.

As their workday wraps up, the husband invites the minister home for supper. He agrees, but points out that he's dirty from all the yard work. "No problem," the husband replies. "You can shower at our place." The minister agrees, and the two head to the husband's home. There the minister steps into the shower and begins to wash up.

The lady of the house, unaware that the minister has been invited over for supper, has finished preparing dinner. She hears the shower running and decides to play a sexy joke on her husband. She steps quietly into the bathroom, reaches through the shower curtain, and takes hold of the nearest indisputable evidence of manhood. Giving it a tug, she pronounces, "Ding, dong—dinner bell!"

When she makes her way downstairs and finds her husband parked in front of the TV, she faints. The moral: Aggressive displays of sensuality can backfire, especially if you're a woman. So beware—and remember, The Man Upstairs (if not the minister in the shower) is always privy to your deepest, darkest acts.

The Mechanic Gets a Surprise

An interesting variation involves an unfortunate mechanic rather than a minister. This time the result is not shame before the local representative of the Word of God, but a bloody mess.

The (now-iconic) Wife a Little too Frisky for Her Own Good, hereafter WALTFFHOG, arrives home from a round of grocery shopping to find two male legs sticking out from under her car. Smiling at what she assumes to be yet another example of her husband's obsession with the family automobile, she leans down and unzips his fly, and then saunters into the house.

There (you guessed it) she finds Innocent Husband engrossed in a television program. Alarmed, she asks him who's beneath the car. The husband explains that the mechanic has come by to do some work on the automobile. The poor woman has to explain her mistake—and the two head outside to clarify the strange situation for the mechanic. They find him out cold, lying in a puddle of blood. When WALTFFHOG pulled the zipper stunt, the shocked grease monkey instantly, and instinctively, tried to rise bolt upright. (Make of *that* what you will.) In so doing, he banged his head against the underside of the car.

Fable Facts

Legends and warnings incorporating horrific (and mortifying) fates for their libidinous heroines have been around for centuries. The Bible's Proverbs 2:16 warns the reader against "the loose woman ... (whose) path runs downhill towards death, and her course is set for the land of the dead; no one who resorts to her finds his way back or regains the path to life."

A stranger exposed, fluids spilled, the house in chaos—and all because the WALTFFHOG can't seem to wait for her husband to make the first move. Clearly that's a safer way to go, or so the story suggests.

Being coy never looked so good. At least, when you make it a firm policy to play hard to get, you don't end up making dangerous overtures to anonymous guys who aren't your husband.

This legend's continued popularity in the era of the steamy e-mail message and the adults-only chat room is perhaps understandable.

The Whole Darned Office Gets a Surprise

In the following legend, the perils of remaining *unmarried* are emphasized. Let's face it: You can't win with urban legends. If you get married and express your sexuality, something awful will happen. If you don't get married and you express your sexuality, something equally awful will happen. Like Catherine the Great (see Chapter 6, "Did Catherine the Great Really Do It with a Horse?"), the unfortunate heroine of the following tale pays dearly for the unorthodox expression of her prurient impulses. The story seems to suggest, too, that the working woman's priorities are misplaced and that something is deeply wrong with any lifestyle choice that would force her to live without a man in her life.

Here's the story. A single career woman, surrounded by close friends at work, has a birthday. Her colleagues decide to throw her a surprise party. Unbeknownst to her, they filch the spare key from her purse. All her friends leave work a little bit early on the special day, the better to surprise her for her birthday.

The group makes its way into the career woman's basement and hides out there in the dark, followed by the woman's loyal, if not particularly smart, dog. (Why, you may ask, are the woman's friends hiding out in the *basement* to give the lady a surprise party? Because the plot demands that our heroine have a few moments to herself upstairs in private, that's why.)

After a bit of a wait, the office buddies hear the woman walk in the door, put down her things, and walk around in the kitchen a bit. Then, after a few more unidentified noises, they hear her call the dog. The voice comes nearer … and nearer … and nearer … until finally the woman opens the door to her basement and calls again for her dog.

She takes a step or two down into the basement, and her friends know the moment to reveal themselves has come.

"Surprise!" yell the co-workers as they flip on the lights.

Fable Facts

In urban legends, basements are a popular spot from which to launch disastrous surprise birthday parties. It's tempting to theorize that the basement setting represents our "lowest" selves.

It's a surprise, all right. There on the stairs they see the lonely career woman in search of her dog, stark naked—unless, of course, you count the peanut butter smeared about her breasts and nether regions.

Not quite clear on the point of this one? Just think about it for a minute. There, you've got it.

Talk about your "Wanna get away?" moment.

Hard to forget, eh? Here's one take on the subtext. The poor peanut-butter lady wouldn't have been forced to sink to such depths—or endure such disgrace before her friends—if only she had put as much effort and energy into finding a man as she had into building a career. (It couldn't be a *guy* flirting with bestiality. No, no, it has to be a career woman.)

So, all you female achievers, beware, and let this horrifying story be a lesson to you. The next time you think about asking for a raise or staying late at the office, try to find something else to do. Like, say, locate a guy who'll ask you out on a date. That's where you *ought* to be working. Put the career on hold and snag the man while you can. If you wait too long, you may find yourself on a stairway to the basement with a jar of peanut butter in your hands, surrounded by stunned friends, praying that those expensive obedience lessons pay off when you shout, "Brutus, *freeze!*"

The Pharmacy Customer Gets a Surprise

In this legend, a teen Romeo gets more than just a box of condoms from a trip to the local drugstore. He gets seriously humbled.

Having secured a hot date with a young female classmate renowned for a certain moral adaptability, the young fellow figures that he should head over to the pharmacy to buy some condoms. As he makes the purchase, he even boasts about the forthcoming evening's conquest to the pharmacist: "I'll be scoring tonight—no doubt about it." He smiles and leaves the store, certain that he has made a memorable impression on an envious middle-aged man.

Sure in his prediction, Don Juan bides his time for the rest of the afternoon, fantasizing now and then about the delights to come. When evening rolls around, he saunters over to his date's house, rings the bell, and waits for it to open.

When it does, he realizes that his prediction may have been just a tad off-base. The pharmacist he had talked to earlier in the day turns out to be his hot date's dad.

Make that *former* hot date.

Pride goeth before a fall—and before chastening encounters with all-seeing, all-knowing authority figures. Watch out, guys. They really *are* everywhere.

The Dinner Guest Gets a Surprise

Trying to impress the future in-laws? Check out the following legend for an example of what *not* to do.

A young man is invited to his girlfriend's home for supper. Knowing that he is being given the once-over, he makes a mental note to behave with impeccable manners as the evening unfolds.

The meal is delicious, and the young woman's mother insists that the fellow take helping after helping of her cooking. Knowing that he will score points with his girlfriend's folks if he acquiesces, he agrees to every suggestion that he eat more. He cleans his plate.

All this eating leaves him feeling a bit saturated. The fellow's midsection feels like it's about to burst his trousers (any symbolism *there?*), so he undoes his waist button. As he does so, his zipper accidentally comes undone (any symbolism *there?*). Figuring that no one will be watching him under the table, he quietly zips his fly back up, hoping, as surreptitious fly-zipper-uppers so often do, that no one will notice his unseen indiscretion.

The meal concludes; the mother and her daughter leave the table to give the menfolk time to talk together. In a gesture of gallantry worthy of a bygone age, the young man stands up as the women make to leave the room. When he does so, the tableware

Fable Facts

Legends involving food and eating often incorporate a sexual subtheme. Some of these references, like the tablecloth-in-the-fly myth, are comparatively subtle and understated; some are all too explicit. For a memorable example of the latter, see the homemade cookies story in Chapter 19, "Amatory Comeuppance."

Legend Lingo

The **narrow escape** syndrome is one in which the story's protagonist *nearly* experiences some ultimate horror (mutilation, murder, or public nudity before 700 occupants of a hotel lobby, for example) but barely avoids doing so. Many legends use narrow escapes to emphasize the dire consequences of thoughtless, inappropriate, or morally suspect acts—and to place the listener in essentially the same situation as the protagonist.

and all the food crash to the ground. He had unwittingly zipped the tablecloth into his trousers.

On one level, this is a simple story of a catastrophic etiquette lapse during dinner with prospective in-laws. On another level, it's an admonition to men everywhere: Your appetites, when exposed, may have consequences and can even lead harmonious, carefully prepared social orderings into anarchy and turmoil.

And now, a word from our Gender Roles Department: It's interesting that the woman in, say, the showering minister story seems to be being cautioned against the *direct expression* of sexual impulses—that's apparently quite dangerous for ladies. In this story, the message for men seems to be a very different one: If you're going to do things "under the table," be sure you don't get *caught*. "Eat" all you want, but zip up your fly properly after having done so. If you're heedless of such details, you may just find that your little ruse has become public knowledge.

Various Hotel Guests Get a Surprise

Legends involving nude hotel guests whose room doors slam shut and lock at inopportune moments are legion. Stranded in the hall without a stitch, they search, usually successfully, for something to cover themselves with until they can track down a manager or a bellboy to help them return to the safety (and blessed privacy) of their rented room. Now that's a *narrow escape*.

There are so many actual incidents conforming to the main elements of this endlessly recycled and revised story that one might be tempted to bar the nude hotel guest tales from a discussion of urban legends. The story is worth considering closely, however, because it is usually passed along as an impossible-to-forget example of what can happen to you—yes, you—if you're not careful.

Nudity in public may well be the most humiliating thing most people can imagine. If public speaking is ranked higher than death in the pantheon of experiences to be avoided, how much more onerous is the plight of the hotel guest who must decide whether to knock on the door of a total stranger or take an elevator ride town to a (doubtless crowded) reception area?

This story is a communal nightmare that will probably endure as long as humans persist in covering up their naughty bits.

The Skier Gets a Surprise

A fascinating (and more fanciful) elaboration of the nudity-in-public theme shows up in the story of the novice skier who had to answer nature's call.

According to the story, the poor woman *really* had to go at the top of the slope. Her husband convinced her that because she was dressed in white, she would not draw any attention to herself and could safely and discreetly relieve herself in the woods. (Foreshadowing alert: The previous sentence establishes the woman's modesty.)

Alas, when she got to the part where she dropped her trousers, the unfortunate woman started hurtling down the slope, with her pants to her knees—backward. Observers were treated to a rare spectacle as she hurtled past. The strange journey finally stopped when she crashed into a pylon—but she had, alas, broken her arm, which left her (of course) unable to pull up her pants for an extended period.

Don't Believe It!

If somebody tells you the "bottomless skier" story happened at a local lodge, ask politely for proof. The "bottomless skier" story has yet to be verified; it has, however, been assigned to famous ski slopes around the world.

Finally her husband arrived, pulled up her trousers, and shuttled her off to the emergency room. There, she was placed in a room with a man who had broken his leg. When she asked how the injury came about, he explained that he had fallen out of a ski lift trying to get a better look at a madwoman who had decided to ski backward down a mountain with her pants down. He then asked the woman, "How did you break your arm?"

The story's endurance can be attributed both to its unforgettable central image and to its elaborate but effective structure, which pays off when the poor lady faces the final indignity of encountering a total stranger who had seen her nude. At the end of the day, this is a substantially gussied-up (and completely unverified) version of the nude hotel guest story. Its point is simple: Don't let this happen to you.

Poor Jen Gets a Surprise

Urban legends multiply and reformulate themselves at an astonishing rate. They also tend to focus on fears, insecurities, and taboos. Given these two facts, it was probably only a matter of time before a story like the following bubbled up to the surface, blending age-old proscriptions with Information Age technology.

➤ An anonymous female college student (we'll call her Jen) works hard, holds down an outside job, and (uh-oh) breaks up with her boyfriend.

➤ Jen surfs the Internet for entertainment.

➤ Jen logs on to an adult chat line, using an assumed name.

➤ On this chat line, Jen hooks up with Jeremy, a bright, experienced, libidinous, and inventive fellow who—surprise, surprise—actually likes to talk to Jen about issues that matter to her.

➤ Jen intuits that Jeremy is an older man; accordingly, she omits certain important biographical information in her discussions with him (for instance, the fact that she is a college student).

➤ After becoming close emotionally online, the two engage in various frenzied forms of cybersex.

➤ This goes on for several months.

➤ The two become closer and closer online, until Jeremy finally floats the idea of marriage.

➤ Jen and Jeremy agree to meet face to face at a mutually agreed-upon resort to discuss the matter further and, well, to do anything else that crosses their minds.

➤ Jen arrives early and makes the room as romantic as possible, turns down the lights, strips, and gets into bed.

➤ Jen hears a key in the door and whispers her lover's name. He sits next to her, pulls back the covers, and turns on the light.

➤ Jen's eyes widen as she stares in horror at the face before her.

➤ A single horrified word escapes her lips: "Dad?"

Now *there's* a story to liven up the next family reunion.

Such a sequence of events sounds horrible—it *is* horrible—but it is, of course, completely imaginary. There are a number of competing versions of this story floating around. In the raunchiest, the two actually wear each other out in bed before discovering the incestuous nature of their attraction. The moral—beware of cyberspace, don't sleep with strangers—is carried out in a number of stories attaching Jen or her equivalent to a partner other than her dad.

Strange but True

Legends in which a sexually adventurous person is punished for (knowingly or unknowingly) sleeping with the wrong partner are quite common and have been around for centuries. In many of these stories, the "price" for succumbing to temptation is the shared knowledge that one has crossed a shameful boundary and brought ruin to one's family. Stories with such themes were common at the time of the ancient Greeks, such as Sophocles' classic play *Oedipus the King*, in which the proud ruler learns that he himself is responsible for defiling his own kingdom because he has, as was foretold at his birth, killed his father and married his mother. Freud's later discussion of the "Oedipus Complex" brought the primal incest taboo into the spotlight in the twentieth century.

Variations on Jen's Disgrace

Here are some of the more interesting variations on the story of a bad choice of lover leading to violation of the *incest taboo*.

"Hello, Room Service? There's a Problem with My Order ..."

A businessman travels to an unfamiliar region. Presumably thinking himself free from the restraints of his normal social environment, he has a discreet chat with the fellow at the front desk of the hotel. The discussion culminates in an arrangement for a prostitute to visit the businessman's room that evening.

Hmm. Another visit to a new place. Another break from established routine. Another sense of impending doom. Sure hope he doesn't pick up any stray "dogs" or bring any plants home (see Chapter 9, "All Creatures, Great and Small"). Has it occurred to you by now that the best way to avoid disaster may be to avoid doing *anything*

Legend Lingo

The **incest taboo** is the prohibition of sex between partners who share kinship ties. Historically, most cultures have proscribed sexual relationships between close relatives (father/daughter, mother/son, brother/sister). Incest stories, which are usually heavy on horror and self-loathing, are important elements of cultural mythology worldwide; the very act of encountering such stories may play an important role in an individual's social and psychosexual development.

once you've landed in a foreign land, psychological or otherwise? Good. Now, back to our story.

Our restless executive has settled upstairs in his room when he hears a knock on his door. Ready for action, he opens the door of love—and wishes for all the world that he could close it again. There, made up and ready to conduct business, is his daughter. Turns out she's been earning some money on the side while studying at a local institution of higher learning.

This "prostitution" version of the near-miss father-daughter coupling is a reformulation of a couple of centuries' worth of cautionary myth-making. (Something very similar happens, for instance, in Luigi Pirandello's play *Six Characters in Search of an Author*.) Most of the tales freeze-frame the action at the awful moment of realization, leaving the reader to fill in the horrific details of the—doubtless fascinating—conversation that follows.

In this legend, the punishment for straying from the straight and narrow—consorting with loose women, betraying the trust of parents when far from home—is severe: sexual humiliation shared with a member of the immediate family.

The stakes are similarly high in this next story.

Fable Facts

In the dream language of urban legends, enrollment at college often serves as a metaphor for exposure to the moral consequences of adult life. It makes sense—for many of us, college life constitutes our first opportunity to live alone and make choices independent of the influence of our parents (see Chapter 22, "Maniacs, Unlimited").

The Fateful Frat Party

During a loud, alcohol-sodden party, a frat boy is urged by his companions to take part in an exercise in serial debauchery. A willing, if drunk, girl has been secreted away in an upstairs room, and the young men plan to service her one at a time.

Our hero agrees and takes his place as the last in line. When he finally makes his way upstairs, he finds himself greeted by the southerly end of a young woman whose northerly end extends out of the open frat-house window. Not bothering with such niceties as a face-to-face introduction, he does his business. Then, gentleman that he is, he decides to pull the young lady in rather than leave her exposed to the elements for the evening.

You guessed it: His conjugal companion was his sister.

Fable Facts

Some modern myths involve sexual choices that lead the protagonists of the stories unwittingly to incest. Like many compelling dreams, these urban legends often conclude by placing their heroes in a humiliating situation that is impossible to explain, justify, or escape. The notion that the participants must forever be held accountable for their (ill-advised) actions pervades the stories.

A variant on the Fateful Frat Party story features a fraternity brother who is too drunk to perform the act of love with his latest conquest. He leaves the bedroom, returns to the party, pulls one of his comrades aside, and asks *him* to attend to the young lady. The second fellow, who also has had a few drinks, enters the darkened room and does so. He then falls asleep. The cold light of morning, however, reveals the truth: Brother and sister are in the same (polluted) bed, and *somebody's* got some explaining to do.

Fable Facts

The novelist Vladimir Nabokov, no stranger to scandal and controversy, used a brother/sister incest theme in his masterful 1969 novel *Ada*. Some people thought he was an unrepentant degenerate. People with functioning minds realized he was a genius.

Don't Cross the Borderline, Children

Most of these stories carry a simple but chilling message: There's far more at risk when we cross moral borderlines than we may imagine. Anonymous sex? Seems like an interesting idea, especially if you've had a few drinks. A discreet pee at the top of the ski slope? What's the big deal?

But if you're not careful, your whole world can turn upside down. If you don't want to cross the *big* boundaries, think twice before crossing *any* of them. So the stories seem to be saying, at any rate.

The Least You Need to Know

➤ Avoid tugging the body parts of people occupying your shower whom you have not positively identified.

➤ Never forget that the sexual double standard is alive and well; it's exemplified in urban legends that counsel women to avoid overt sexual expression, and parallel legends that counsel men simply to conceal their indiscretions.

➤ Keep your mouth shut around the pharmacist.

➤ Beware the whole sex-with-anonymous-people thing, if only to avoid the horror of learning that you've just mated with a member of your immediate family.

Chapter 17

Hazardous Amorous Duty

In This Chapter

➤ Sex and death, sex and disease, sex and physical danger

➤ The perils of premarital experimentation

➤ Untoward things ticked-off women may do to a sleeping mate's manhood

➤ Various urban legends about the AIDS virus

The most memorable urban legends are often darkly funny, cautionary tales that correspond to some commonly held fear or doubt. Frequently, they lodge in the mind because they mete out punishment to some person in the story who ignores societal norms.

Are these stories a hoot to talk about at parties? Sure. But they are also often a great deal more: gaudily clad metaphors for lessons we'd prefer not to have to face directly. We assume that the details are true—perhaps because, deep down, we think they *ought* to be true.

To put it another way, the most striking urban legends take shared bits of social paranoia and spin them into entertaining dreams (or nightmares). And is there any paranoia more gripping that that which combines sex, violence, and death?

In this chapter, we focus on those widely circulated urban legends that don't just subject their amorous victims to public humiliation, but move into the realm of fatality, injury, disease, and—perhaps worst of all—superglue. (Gentlemen, you may cross your legs.)

Fable Facts

Stories linking sex and physical danger are as old as the Bible. (See, for instance, the account of God's wrath against Sodom and Gomorrah.)

Let's face it, doing the nasty in the modern era can be a dangerous undertaking. And, at some level or other, we all usually want to hear exactly *how* dangerous—hence the stories in this chapter.

If you're interested in hearing urban legends that emphasize the dire (and often fatal) physical consequences of actual lovemaking, read on. (Other chapters deal with such fun-filled topics as humiliation, revenge, and mere proximity to danger; in this chapter, the perils are considerably more direct, and they're all experienced firsthand by the principals in the story.)

Here we go. And by the way, if you choose to go out on a hot date with someone once you've finished this chapter, don't say you weren't warned.

The Prehoneymoon Surprise

Jan Harold Brunvand, author of the landmark book *The Vanishing Hitchhiker* (W.W. Norton, 1981), is one of several who have encountered a variation on this fascinating "friend-of-a-friend-told-me" story. It carries many elements common to the sex-related urban legend (for instance, the abandonment or betrayal of the woman in the story, and some element of humiliation before a group or an authority figure).

Fable Facts

Many urban legends having nothing to do with sex use themes of violence, illness, and death to reinforce their messages. Why? Because human beings find these themes impossible to ignore, and good storytelling has always been about holding the attention of your audience. For a sampling of some of the most outrageous legends, see Chapter 23, "Too Disgusting for Words."

This legend, however, incorporates a stay in the hospital for one of the protagonists. The moral: You'll pay a steep and literally painful price for expressing sexuality in a way that runs afoul of social norms. Brunvand's source ambiguously cites "a local minister," but it's hard to tell whether this is meant to refer to the minister/narrator within the story.

The sad tale unfolds as follows. Two young lovers miss a premarital counseling meeting with the local minister. (Note the foreshadowing. Clearly, the pair has a hard time playing by the rules; they can't manage to keep an appointment with the local representative of God.)

Curious, the minister makes a call to the home of the young bridesmaid. Her mother answers and will reveal only that the young girl is in the hospital. She advises the minister to visit the girl there himself if he wants to find out why she missed the appointment.

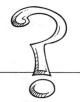

Strange but True

Ministers and other religious representatives often serve as emblems for society as a whole in urban legends. Actual members of the clergy, however, may find their life stories twisted in a surreal way when their names and roles are appropriated for dramatic effect in these stories. See Chapter 7, "The Family Hour (Not): Twisted Legends About Your Favorite Children's Television Stars," for an example of a fallacious urban legend defamatory to television's Fred Rogers (of *Mr. Rogers' Neighborhood*), an ordained minister.

Off the minister goes to the hospital, where he finds the bride-to-be in traction. She relates the events that landed her in the ward, and the following sequence of events emerges. (This could also be called, "How Not to Prepare for a Wedding: An Urban Legend in the Form of a 12-step Nightmare.")

1. The bride-to-be's parents announce plans to leave town for the weekend.

2. The bride-to-be is asked to watch the house for those few days.

3. The bride-to-be invites her fiancé to her parents' home so that the two of them can (in the bride-to-be's charming phrase) "practice for their honeymoon."

4. Practice sessions are undertaken with abandon in the parents' bedroom.

5. While the two spent lovers are gathering energy for another round of practicing for the honeymoon, the phone rings.

6. The bride-to-be answers the phone and hears her mother's agitated voice. Can she run down quickly to the basement and turn off the iron?

7. The husband-to-be picks up the bride-to-be and carries her down to the doorway of the basement. (Key fact to retain: They are both nude.)

8. The nude bride-to-be, still held in the arms of the nude husband-to-be at the top of the staircase, reaches out her nude arm and switches on the light switch by the door. (Did we mention that both the bride and the bridegroom are nude?)

9. The lights illuminate the bride's parents and relatives, all of whom joyously shout "Surprise!" (It's the famous fake-trip-out-of-town-to-set-up-the-basement-wedding-shower trick.)

10. The startled nude husband-to-be drops his fiancée down the stairs and then bolts.

11. The horrified family stares at the nude bride-to-be, who has just broken her collarbone and a leg. So profound is the shock that no one makes any attempt to cover her.

12. No one ever hears from the prospective groom again. The poor girl loses her mind. The wedding is called off.

As cautionary sex-based legends go, this is certainly a classic of the genre. Notice the not-so-subtle moral: "Practice" for your honeymoon, and disaster awaits—you'll get hurt, and (even worse) your man will hit the road.

Could it have really happened? Brunvand seems skeptical. Your humble correspondent is skeptical as well because a close review of the legend indicates that the details of the story raise some puzzling issues.

Fable Facts

Sometimes a story is "about" more than its plot. Urban legends that subject their female characters to injury or humiliation after a sexual encounter may be "about" insecurities regarding the open expression of eroticism by women.

A Few Pesky Questions About the Prehoneymoon Surprise

Among the problems and ambiguities left unaddressed in the prehoneymoon surprise story are the following questions:

➤ With the entire house to themselves, why would the pair choose to make love in the parents' bedroom? (One possible answer: The better to take advantage of a plot device with ominous Freudian overtones.)

➤ Why include the prurient—but not entirely plausible—detail that the entire family stared at the nude young woman rather than help her? (Possible answer: Doing so plants an indelible image in the hearer's mind.)

➤ Finally, and most importantly from the standpoint of credibility, how in the world does the young woman manage to recount the story in such lucid detail? She has, we are told, been driven insane by the trauma of this episode! Think of it this way: If you visited a hospital ward and asked an injured, insane patient for the details of a recent life crisis, would you really expect to hear a reasoned, step-by-step summary of each key event? (Possible answer: No. If, however, you were trying to put together an interesting narrative, you might hope that your listener would overlook the fact that the bulk of the story is supposedly being repeated from a hospital bed by a mentally unbalanced patient.)

The Superglued Husband

A wronged spouse's obsession with revenge after the discovery of adultery is a perennial theme in urban legends. (See Chapter 19, "Amatory Comeuppance," for a sampling of these stories.) Here's a variation of the genre that incorporates a trip to the emergency room and plays to one of the most deeply held fears men hold—namely, someone messing with your, um, equipment while you sleep.

In one of the most commonly circulated versions, the married mayor of a small town has embarked on an affair. His wife discovers his indiscretions and sets about finding a way to take her revenge.

The wife waited until the husband was sleeping—and physically aroused. Then she pulled back the covers, undid his pajamas, and superglued his penis to his stomach. The cheating town official had to drive to the local emergency room to get himself disconnected.

Strange but True

In the summer of 2000, news reports told of a teenage girl who pulled the "superglue trick" on her boyfriend, whom she apparently believed to be unfaithful. The man was told to soak in a tub until the adhesive became inert. It's tempting to conclude that the revenge via superglue urban legend, which arose at least a decade and a half earlier, played some role in the young lady's choice of method.

This rumor, which has been circulating since at least the mid-1980s, has, like most of the gaudier accounts of domestic revenge appearing in this volume, proved quite difficult to trace down to a reliable source. The only documented case of superglued genitals appears to have arisen well after the legend entered popular discussion. (See the accompanying sidebar.) Indeed, the superglue story may well have inspired the actual event.

Five Fasten-ating Issues About the Superglued Husband Story

The punishment theme in this legend is obvious enough not to require discussion. Five more particularly interesting points stick, as it were, in the mind when considering revenge via superglue:

➤ The husband is not just *any* cheating husband, but a mayor or town official of some kind. In other words, he has political and social power within the (small!) town that we must assume the wife lacks. The implication is that she has no option and no redress for the wrong that has been done to her. This "unjust judge" or "unjust mayor" theme runs through many ancient myths involving sexual opportunism and is central, to give just one example, to Shakespeare's *Measure for Measure.*

➤ Note that the husband is forced to drive *himself* to the emergency room. Message: As a result of his misdeed, he alone must explain his condition to the staff there, thus subjecting himself to the public humiliation that is a central element of so many urban legends (particularly those involving sex).

➤ Many versions of this urban legend strive for "believability" by inserting a particular city or state for the incident and the emergency room. They always seem to omit the names of the two participants in the story, however.

Strange but True

The Red Ribbon story is a variation on the superglued husband story. Each addresses female revenge for male infidelity, and each employs a castration theme. In the 1990s, the infamous Lorena Bobbitt case made physical (as opposed to metaphorical) emasculation an acceptable topic for water-cooler discussion. Shortly after the Bobbitt case swept the nation, a new urban legend began making the rounds: A philandering man returns home after one of his assignations with his illicit lover, and gets into bed with his wife. He awakens the next morning with a bright red ribbon tied around his (insert euphemism for manhood here).

The unspoken threat: "I didn't do anything nasty, but I sure could have. So watch yourself—and quit running around with that bimbo."

➤ The husband, for all his power, is vulnerable while he sleeps. This element plays to a universal male castration anxiety. (Compare the symbolic elements of the Samson and Delilah story, in which the great warrior is undone while he sleeps by a woman who cuts away the part of his body that is his source of strength.)

➤ Finally, notice the overt physical strategy that the woman takes as her method for revenge. This is actually quite rare in urban legends involving adultery; wronged wives in these stories typically think up ingenious strategies for simply humiliating their husbands or circumventing their instructions. As the stories in Chapter 19 demonstrate, these women destroy or deface property or cause financial distress. Sending the guy to the emergency room is generally not on the agenda.

"AIDS Mary"

Looking for an urban legend that reflects the fears of an era? Look no further than the "AIDS Mary" story.

This ubiquitous tale goes like this: A young male swinger picks up a beautiful young woman (or secures the services of a prostitute for the evening). For the purposes of simplicity, and to do homage to the real-life case of *Typhoid Mary*, whose legend looms large in stories like these, let's call the young man's female companion Mary. The fellow has a wonderful evening with his new friend. The next morning, he wakes up and discovers that he's alone. Inasmuch as he had not really been looking for a long-term relationship, he's more than a little relieved at this turn of events. But then he walks into his bathroom.

There, written in lipstick on his mirror, is a message guaranteed to make him remember his night of pleasure for the rest of his life. Depending on which version of the story you read, the mirror either says "Welcome to the AIDS club" or "Welcome to the world of AIDS."

The message: Sex with total strangers may not be the great idea it seems to be at the time.

Legend Lingo

Typhoid Mary was a notorious carrier of typhoid fever, though she did not have the disease itself. Her insistence on working in and around food helped fuel the typhoid epidemic. Authorities finally tracked her down and kept her from exacerbating a serious health crisis.

Legend Lingo

AIDS is an acronym for Acquired Immune Deficiency Syndrome, a fatal disease produced by two linked retroviruses known as human immunodeficiency viruses, or **HIV,** that severely compromise the human immune system.

So much for the most popular account. Before addressing the issue of whether there's any truth to the story (or to other stories about intentional infection of people with the AIDS virus), let's look at a few stories that share important similarities with "AIDS Mary."

The "AIDS Harry" Variation

This is a companion legend in which a *woman* is intentionally infected by a man with AIDS.

Fable Facts

Many AIDS–related urban legends conclude with the discovery of an ominous message along the lines of "Welcome to the AIDS club" or "Welcome to the world of AIDS."

No one-night stands this time—the lady is swept away to an exotic location by a suave, sweet-talking beau. After a weekend, a week, a month, or some other relatively short period of time (during which the two make beautiful music together), the woman catches a flight home.

She has been given a gift-wrapped box. Her partner has made her swear a solemn oath that she won't open it until she makes it onto the plane. As if *that's* not a sign of trouble in the relationship.

When the woman settles into her seat and opens up the package, she realizes that she's in trouble. The gift—which may be a coffee mug, a tiny coffin, or some other tchotchke—bears the same sinister message as the mirror in the "AIDS Mary" story.

The moral: Sexual escapades with a charming stranger may be fun for a few weeks or days, but it's way too easy to pick the wrong stranger. Eventually, you'll have to pay for the fun.

Target: Half the Human Race

An intriguing feature of some variants on the "AIDS Mary" and "AIDS Harry" stories is the twisted infector's motivation.

Often the dastardly deed was perpetrated by someone who unknowingly contracted the disease from a callous sexual partner. As a result, he or she is now obsessively committed to the goal of making everyone who shares the former lover's gender suffer accordingly.

The Hidden Needles Variation

Pinpricks and piercings have served as potent sexual metaphors for centuries. (Think of the story of Sleeping Beauty or the arrows in Cupid's quiver). Is it at all surprising, then, that in recent years, the Internet has given rise to a wave of stories reflecting our fear of AIDS by subjecting "innocent" people to infection by means of hidden phalluses—er, needles—in public places?

In the late 1990s, stories began to circulate on the Internet that HIV-infected needles had been hidden by secret and nefarious forces in all manner of locales. A brief summary of the supposed primary hiding places follows.

Urban legends have claimed that needles capable of transmitting the virus that causes AIDS have been placed in these locations:

➤ Pay phone change slots

➤ Pay phone headpieces

➤ Movie theatre seats

➤ Gas pump handles

➤ And so on

There's also a version involving automatic teller machines; see Chapter 13, "Tales of Hell from the Service Economy."

A major round of warnings about needles concerned the Jacksonville Police Department, which was supposedly issuing alerts that an unidentified person had been sabotaging the handles of gas pumps with infected needles.

The story, however, is completely fictitious. Jacksonville has no Police Department. It does, however, have a Sheriff's Department, and one gets the sense that when it comes to stories about needles and gas pump handles, it's probably a very weary Sheriff's Department indeed.

Law enforcement officials in Jacksonville have issued public statements refuting the story and calling the whole thing a hoax.

The CDC Makes a Sharp Observation

As entertaining as the stories are, they are not based in fact. The Centers for Disease Control (CDC) issued a public statement pointing out that the organization is "not aware of any cases where HIV has been transmitted by a needle-stick injury outside a healthcare setting."

By the way, moviegoers in the infected-needle legends eventually somehow encounter a note that reads (you guessed it), "Welcome to the AIDS club."

An interesting side note: The use of those morally suspect movie theater seats as one of the public places supposedly spiked with HIV-infected needles provides a tantalizing connection to a much older urban legend.

In the South in the 1930s, young women were cautioned to avoid the Needle Men at all costs. The Needle Men supposedly frequented movie theaters—then, as now, popular makeout venues—and snuck up on unsuspecting ingénues (two at a time) seated, foolishly, in something other than an aisle seat. If a Needle Man assumed a seat next to his intended victim, he could inject her with morphine and whisk her off to a grim future of sexual slavery. All in all, this is a compelling group hallucination about the risks of sexuality—and a great way to get your daughter not to sit in the middle of the theater, where she and her boyfriend might start doing, well, who knows what.

Did Any of This Happen?

Clearly, the AIDS epidemic has spawned a wave of popular accounts purporting to demonstrate that someone nasty is out to get you where you live. Depending on the story, the "someone nasty" might be a crazed AIDS patient, a theater stalker, or a psychopath who spends a lot of time hanging out at gas stations. How much truth is there to all this? Not enough to get worked up about.

Where there is paranoia, there will be urban legends. The lesson of the AIDS-related urban legends is not that needle-wielding wackos are out to get you, but that the simple act of thinking about AIDS causes people to lose their mental equilibrium. Being intentionally infected with HIV is a fantasy that has about as much reality behind it as the notion that Communist brainwashing experts are behind the nation's water-fluoridation projects.

As far as anyone has been able to ascertain, there is not a single case in which chance contact in a public setting has led to HIV or AIDS. So you can continue to make those trips to the multiplex—and even take a seat in the middle, far away from the aisle, if you're so inclined.

What About the Message on the Mirror?

"Yeah," you say, "but what about chance *sexual* encounters? Are there really armies of people out there who try to set up one-night stands—or weekend getaways—in order to infect others with the virus and write notes on bathroom mirrors?"

Naah. The most pertinent advice on sex and HIV and AIDS (and most other sexually transmitted diseases) is well known. Use a condom. Then you probably won't have to worry about anybody using your bathroom mirror to give you a heart attack.

Still uneasy? The truth is that, despite the many stories suggesting that a single unprotected encounter is a common way of contracting the disease, that's not the profile with which the disease is usually associated.

Let's get to the big question: Has *anyone* with HIV had unprotected sex without telling his or her partner all of the salient facts? Sure. But the "I'm out to destroy your gender" fantasy is just that—a fantasy. If it bothers you (or even if it doesn't), then play it safe. When in doubt, follow the simple rule: No glove, no love.

What Does It All Mean?

AIDS has captured the popular attention and imagination—and has become a metaphor for a whole host of sexual insecurities. For some, the disease may well have become a kind of short-hand for the proposition that "God's out to get you for having fun *that way*." If enough people believe, at some level, that they deserve to be punished for their sexual instincts, then they will accept, embroider, and circulate stories that re-inforce that belief.

Here's the bottom line: Most of the AIDS legends aren't so much about AIDS as they are about the guilt and fear we may feel now and again with re-gard to our own sexuality. What does that say about us? It says that we know sex carries poten-tially dangerous implications—and we're not al-ways impressed with our own ability to manage the situation.

Don't Believe It!

People who have AIDS are much more likely to get sick from casual contact with others than healthy people are to contract AIDS or HIV from casual contact. While we're on the subject, you can't get HIV or AIDS simply by riding next to someone on a bus, reading someone's newspaper, or swapping CDs with someone.

Batman Gets His Comeuppance

This story has resurfaced often enough to make one wonder whether it should be en-shrined in the Urban Legend Hall of Fame. Here are the relevant details:

➤ Police are called to assist a couple who have called in with an undisclosed emer-gency.

➤ As they approach the door, they hear the sound of a woman screaming.

➤ The officers make their way into the bedroom and find a nude woman tied to a bed.

➤ On the floor is a man dressed in a Batman costume.

➤ The woman is forced to explain that she and her husband were engaging in a little role-play to liven up their sex lives. When "Batman" attempted to leap to-ward her from the top of a dresser (or jump enthusiastically on their bed, or try out a martial arts maneuver), he smacked his head against a switched-off ceiling fan and knocked himself out cold.

As usual, the account has many variations, some centering on the costume worn by the husband. It is interesting, however, that the version that has surfaced most often has him dressing as Batman. Right or wrong, bats are associated with biting and with vampires. (Note the familiar "piercing" motif.)

The Batman costume, like the hidden needles in the movie-theater legends, leads to a whole range of evocative erotic associations. Did the husband hope to penetrate his wife in the guise of an animal? (Remember, he is often described as swooping down on her, like a bat.) If so, his taboo animal play met with unforeseen obstacles.

The different variants of the legend offer a number of explanations to the obvious technical problem: If he's unconscious and she's tied up, how did she call the police? In one version, she shouts until the neighbors place the emergency call. In another, she manages to use her free foot to punch out 911 on the keypad.

Conduct Those Bedroom Experiments at Your Own Risk!

The popular Batman legend features a number of familiar elements:

1. First and foremost, ill-advised sexual adventurism leads to the woman in the relationship having to cope with a horrible situation on her own.

2. Second, it leads to humiliation before authority figures.

3. Third, we've got interesting symbolism. Note, for instance, that banging your head against a switched-off ceiling fan means banging your head against a cross.

Is It True?

Who knows? Something like this may have happened once somewhere. But nobody seems to have tracked down anything conclusive yet.

The story's subsequent retellings and revisions suggest that, like the most engaging urban legends, it took on a life of its own. Why? Because it played on a fear shared by many of us—namely, our suspicion that unorthodox sexual practices and experimentation may well carry painful consequences.

Some Final Thoughts

What do these urban legends that link sex with violence, death, or disease prove? Some possibilities follow.

First, many aspects of human sexuality are inherently frightening and can lead people into some pretty dark and surreal mental landscapes. This has been the case for a really long time, but the mental landscapes may be even darker and more surreal in the AIDS era.

Second, sometimes people make up (or revise) bizarre sex-and-death or sex-and-injury stories. These stories, as we have seen, may have more to do with fears and insecurities regarding sexual issues than they do about the obvious surface "plot points" of the story.

To this, of course, we can add a final point: These stories stop you cold and make you listen, which is, of course, what a good story is supposed to do.

The Least You Need to Know

➤ Don't bother trying to track down the "real event" behind these intense sexually oriented urban legends because there usually isn't one.

➤ Do bear in mind, though, that each is likely to be a reflection of alarm and doubt relating to some aspect of human sexuality.

➤ Avoid getting bent out of shape over the various legends involving intentional infection with the AIDS virus as a means of punishing an entire gender. They're fantasies.

➤ If you're planning a leap in a Batman costume in the near future, do yourself a favor and check the placement of the ceiling fan first.

Chapter 18

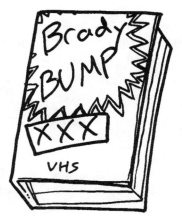

Private Parts in the Public Eye

In This Chapter

➤ Our enduring fascination with the libidos of famous people

➤ Twentieth-century stories about the sex lives of famous people

➤ Feverish dreams of the Brady girls

➤ Speculation about an international conspiracy to provide sex slaves to the international power elite

And you thought the Clinton/Lewinsky phenomenon was over the top. Wait until you hear about the mind-control experiments and the sex slaves ministering to a coterie of world leaders. Inquiring minds, as the saying goes, want to know.

Do they ever.

The habit that the unkempt and ever-curious masses have of speculating on the intimate affairs of notables has a long and storied (if not exactly glorious) pedigree. The occupant of the Oval Office was actually fair game well before the Clinton era. Attacks from political rivals pilloried President Thomas Jefferson for his long-running liaison with his slave Sally Hemings and included the following vicious snatch of doggerel:

> And thou, the scorn of every patriot's name,
> Thy country's ruin and thy country's shame!
> Go wretch! Resign the Presidential chair.
> Disclose thy secret measures, foul and fair.
> Go scan, philosophist, thy Sally's charms,
> And sink supinely in her sable arms.

Under a Watchful Eye

Hey, at least it *rhymed*. That's more than you could say about William Safire's op-ed pieces during the long year the nation decided to fritter away hyperventilating about unauthorized conjugal activity in the White House. Once again, the love life of the biggest celebrity in the land was under the microscope.

Now, then, *who* still wants to be famous?

Strange but True

Contemporary accounts of Jefferson's intimate relationship with Hemings are discussed here to show that the current taste for assailing the high and mighty by means of sexual allegations is nothing new. The story itself, however, can no longer be categorized as a tall tale, given the seemingly conclusive results of modern DNA tests conducted to analyze the long-debated question.

(Hmm ... if memory serves, Clinton faced a similar problem with DNA evidence ....)

"Gee, When I Said I Wanted to Be a Household Name, I Didn't Mean *This!*"

The attacks on Jefferson, like those on Clinton, are part of a never-ending series of rumors about the libidos of well-known people—rumors whose truth or falsehood is, at the time, less important than their capacity to distract. In recent years, this syndrome has received a new level of notoriety and exposure, thanks to the appetites of a supercharged mass media with a continuous news cycle. But it's the same old pattern that people have been following for years: Say something noxious about the habits, anatomy, or long-repented peccadilloes of someone who's a household name, and see whether the story sticks.

True? False? Who cares? To paraphrase Don Henley, it's simply *interesting* when famous people are caught with their pants down, whether literally or figuratively. Thus, people spread the word and bring the high and mighty (or the just plain familiar) down a notch or two. The temptation to do so makes these legends among the hardest to avoid circulating.

In this chapter, we examine sensational stories about the private lives of a cross-section of prominent people from the past century. The veracity of these tales may be questionable, but their repeatability—and their capacity to prey on our suspicion that the high and the mighty have foibles just like the rest of us—is beyond debate.

Did Bing Crosby Boast About Mowing the Lawn in Exchange for Sex?

That depends on how much credence you choose to give an age-old story about the crooner.

Supposedly, Crosby was out mowing his lawn one day when a stranger walked up to him and asked, "So, how much does she pay you for keeping the lawn mowed?"

Crosby thought for a moment and then said, "Nothing—she just lets me go to bed with her every night." At that moment, the inquisitor realized that he was talking to one of Hollywood's biggest stars.

True? Maybe. But the celebrity has been so variously identified—and the punch line has been replaced with so many colorful expressions—that it's hard to avoid concluding that this one is a joke that has taken on new life as an urban legend.

Fable Facts

The story about Crosby mowing his lawn has survived in versions starring other celebrities (for instance, Groucho Marx and Bill Cosby) whom a passerby fails to identify correctly. The moral: Don't automatically assume that you outrank a stranger. For comparison's sake, see the elevator story that appears in Chapter 8, "Other Celebrity Legends That Sound Too Weird to Be True (and Are)."

The Hitler Thing

There has probably been more speculation about Adolf Hitler's sex life than about that of any other world leader of the twentieth century. Why do we keep coming back to stories and questions about this man's libido? Because we want an answer. We want to know if something—anything—could explain the depth of his crimes against humanity. And sex seems as good a place as any to start hunting for explanations.

There are basically two big questions here, one of which is relatively easy to dispatch. The other is uncertain and is likely to remain so.

The First Question: Was He Missing a Testicle?

Yep.

Does that mean we understand what drove the demented fellow to genocide?

Nope.

In his book *The Death of Adolf Hitler: Unknown Documents from Soviet Archives* (New York, Harcourt, Brace, and World, Inc., 1968), author Lev Bezymenski cites Hitler's missing testicle as one of the tests used to confirm the identity of the charred corpse found in a Berlin garden near the end of World War II.

The following facts are now generally accepted:

➤ The bodies of Hitler and his long-time mistress Eva Braun, (whom he married shortly before they both committed suicide) were observed as they were moved from a Berlin bunker to a nearby garden.

➤ The bodies were later discovered by the Russian Army (and eventually were relocated, but that's another story).

➤ The male corpse in question featured teeth that matched Hitler's dental records, thus providing positive identification.

➤ This corpse was missing a testicle.

How did this deficiency affect the Führer's erotic life, if at all? And what *was* his erotic life like, anyway? These puzzling queries bring us face to face with the next question.

The Second Question: Was He into Various Strange Sexual Practices?

Nobody knows for sure.

Over the years, countless rumors about Hitler's amatory routine, or lack thereof, have circulated. Maybe he lit candles, swung from chandeliers, and had himself tied down while fantasizing about receiving a spanking from Ginger Rogers. Maybe he didn't. The record is (predictably) fuzzy hereabouts.

What we do know, though, is this:

1. Hitler wouldn't submit to medical examinations (presumably because this had something to do with the missing-equipment issue).

2. Whatever he did in bed, he did it deficient in the testicle department, to the tune of one.

3. The world would have been a lot better off if he'd somehow managed to dust himself during an adventurous erotic episode or in any other setting before he became prominent in German politics.

Did John Barrymore Once Make a Risqué Film Short Featuring John Carradine?

According to *M*A*S*H* alumni Jamie Farr, the "movie" in question was a screen test. The veracity of the story surrounding this episode is less than airtight. For the sake of thoroughness, we'll place it in the "indeterminate" category until someone comes up with more details.

The pertinent details are as follows:

➤ Carradine, a noted Broadway actor, was trying to gain employment in Hollywood.

➤ Barrymore, his buddy and a major screen star at the time, supposedly arranged for a screen test at Twentieth-Century Fox.

➤ On the set, Barrymore instructed Carradine to enter a room as though he had just finished eating the most sumptuous meal of his life. As the cameras rolled, Carradine entered and followed his friend's instructions by rubbing his stomach, smiling, licking his chops, and so on.

➤ The next day, Carradine showed up with the studio bigwigs to take a look at the test.

➤ What they saw, though, wasn't exactly Oscar material, but more like a party gag. Carradine enters, does his silent "what-a-delicious-meal" routine, and strolls across the room. Then there's a bit of bonus footage. The camera cuts back to the same door Carradine entered through—and out walks Barrymore with a big grin on his face. He winks at the audience—and zips up his fly.

Did Hugh Hefner Use the Cover of *Playboy* to Signify the Number of Playmates (or Playmates-in-Waiting) He Had Bedded That Month?

No.

The story that Hef snuck small stars onto the cover to signify his monthly conquest total reflects only the imagination (and the envy) of the many men who admired his active social life. The stars actually served a much more prosaic function: They had something to do with the various regional editions of the magazines and their circulation plans. They did not constitute a secret diary into the intimate life of the publisher.

The covers of today's *Playboy* may have lacked stars for years now, but it's not because the man at the head of the empire ever lacked material for his memoirs. They've just figured out a more effective way to handle distribution issues.

Did the Actor Who Played Eddie Haskell Star in a Series of Pornographic Films?

No. (He didn't go on to become Alice Cooper, either; see Chapter 7, "The Family Hour [Not]: Twisted Legends About Your Favorite Children's Television Stars.") Ken Osmond, who played the oily Haskell character on TV's *Leave It to Beaver* in the 1950s, ended up in law enforcement. He served on the Los Angeles Police Department for the better part of two decades.

Rumors about Osmond's alleged return to a decidedly less wholesome segment of the entertainment industry peaked in the 1970s. He appears to have tried to ignore them, but when people at his church started giving the stories about X-rated films some level of credence, Osmond seems to have decided that the stories could no longer be laughed off.

The problem appears to have arisen with a porno distributor who began promoting the films of one of its stars by incorporating the words "Eddie Haskell" into ad copy. The actor bore a passing resemblance to Osmond.

Legend Lingo

The **inverted image syndrome** in urban legends assumes the highest possible level of (for instance) sexual looseness among figures associated with propriety and innocence. Thus, legends cast people associated with super-wholesome television shows in (nonexistent) X-rated films—the better to play on our curiosity about the "real truth" relating to the sexual lives of people associated with those shows. The bigger the image, the harder it inverts. Once *Leave It to Beaver* or *The Brady Bunch* becomes shorthand for "that perfect, asexual television family," people become more receptive to legends falsely implying that the principals are somehow associated with the adult film industry.

The former child actor tried to use the legal system to stop the distributor's campaign but failed to win his suit. (One suspects that this had something to do with the fact that his legal name was Ken Osmond rather than Eddie Haskell.) Even if he had won the case, it seems unlikely that he'd have been able to overturn the *inverted image syndrome* so common to urban legends about public figures. (See the bit about Mr. Rogers not being a ruthless former sniper, in Chapter 7.)

The point to remember, though, is that Osmond never had anything to do with X-rated films—beyond, of course, taking part in a popular television show that attracted legends that reversed its image. But you can hardly blame him for that.

Did Any of the Brady Girls Go on to Star in Pornographic Movies?

No. This endlessly recycled rumor has proved to be immune to generous applications of fact. (So, apparently, are the equally stubborn complex of rumors involving death and nude photo layouts that have been associated with the show; these are discussed in Chapter 7.)

Mendacious stories about the supposed excesses of Maureen McCormick (Marcia), Eve Plumb (Jan), and Susan Olsen (Cindy) may constitute the highest (or lowest?) embodiment of the various defilement-of-the-virgin myths. These stories may have been inspired by the following facts:

1. Susan Olsen once portrayed an actress in the adult film industry on an episode of another television show.

2. Eve Plumb once portrayed a teen prostitute on an episode of another television show.

3. Numerous lurid photos featuring the faces of the "Brady Girls" pasted onto other peoples' bodies have circulated on the Internet.

Then again, the stories may have sprung to life without any prompting from actual events in the outside world. It's entirely possible that this myth has more to do with the vagaries of the male psyche than with any happening involving a cast member of the archetypal white-bread 1970s television series.

Strange but True

Why fixate on a (mythical) hyperpromiscuous Cindy, Jan, or Marcia? Maybe because a whole lot of guys have much more than a hunch that virgins are best deflowered. Legends circulating at a number of institutions of higher learning tell of some prominent tower on campus grounds that will cave in, begin to fall apart, or otherwise start to show signs of imminent collapse should a virgin female graduate. After recounting the legend, the fellow telling it invariably points to the (phallic) structure and admires its enduring solidity.

While We're on the Subject, Did the Actress Who Played Carol Brady Date the Actor Who Played Greg Brady?

Date, maybe. (If you're feeling particularly generous about the definition of the word *date*.) Sleep with—naaah.

The actor in question, Barry Williams, referenced in his book *Growing Up Brady* a single night out with Florence Henderson, who played Carol. *Nothing happened.* (Whew.) The fact remains, though, that serious Oedipal implications may nevertheless be spun out of an innocent outing involving two cast members of a TV show. At least, that's the case when one of the cast members plays the ultimate 1970s suburban mom and the other plays her rapidly maturing son.

That Oedipal twist was apparently what the people who handled the P.R. campaign for Williams's book were hoping to use to hook the media, and they weren't disappointed. They got a lot of media bang out of the carefully cultivated innuendo associated with the "date"—and with the oh-so-shocking title of one of the book's chapters, *Dating Your Mom.*

Not surprisingly, Henderson has had to contend with a fair number of inquiries about this matter. To give her credit, she seems to be handling the issue with style, grace, and good humor. Here's what shows up on her Web site, flohome.com:

> That whole thing with Barry got blown way out of proportion. I guess in a sense it was a date, because Barry thought it was. But, of course, I had no idea that his intentions were to "date" me. It has made for a good story, though!

Did a "Government Sex Slave" Minister to the Whims of Four U.S. Presidents?

Did you catch this one? Call me a skeptic, but somehow the claim that a Michigan woman was brainwashed and forced to cater to the carnal whims of four recent U.S. presidents seems lacking in credibility.

The story, which surfaces in an intriguing volume entitled *Trance Formation of America* (Cathy O'Brien, Reality Marketing Incorporated, 1995), is also considered in detail—and discussed as though it were Gospel truth—on a severely strange Web site (www. davidicke.com). The site purports to be "prepared to go where others fear to tread."

One of the places others may fear to tread is the book's sweeping contention that its author was subjected to "the mind-control operation known as Project Monarch" and was "used as a sex slave to pander to the bizarre sexual desires of big-name politicians." The roster of politicos supposedly involved in this dastardly scheme is, admittedly, quite impressive. It includes these men:

➤ Gerald Ford

➤ Ronald Reagan

➤ George Bush, Sr.

➤ Bill Clinton (you had to suspect that *he* was mixed up in all this, didn't you?)

➤ Dick Cheney

➤ Pierre Trudeau (the late Canadian prime minister)

➤ Brian Mulroney (the former Canadian prime minister)

➤ Miguel de la Madrid (the former President of Mexico)

➤ King Fahd of Saudi Arabia

And that's not to mention "the long list of other United States politicians and famous entertainers" highlighted elsewhere in the book.

The story's harmless enough, as long as it's not mistaken for Pulitzer-level investigative reporting (fat chance) and instead is understood as a cry of rage against the civil/social authority whose various representatives stand indicted of crimes against the mind and soul.

Don't Believe It!

In *Annie Hall*, Alvy Singer (Woody Allen) makes a joke at an Adlai Stevenson fund-raiser to the effect that he had been dating an Eisenhower staffer. The punch line: Alvy was trying to do to *her* what he suspected Ike had been trying to do to the *country* for the past couple of years. A similar worldview seems to support the mind-control/sex slave legend involving U.S. presidents—which is ridiculous.

In other words, this legend is simply a useful metaphor for someone who believes that the folks who are running the joint are up to no damn good. It's not a vitally important national story, pursued by the mainstream media in the grandest example of its First Amendment role as guardians of the republic. It's not, for instance, that *other* sex story that held the country (and the world) in its sway throughout 1998.

Now *that* was news. This sex-slave thing, though, is purely a waste of your valuable time.

The Least You Need to Know

➤ Don't worry—Bing Crosby's honor is safe.

➤ So, one assumes, is the honor of the casts of the television shows *Leave It to Beaver* and *The Brady Bunch*.

➤ The cover of *Playboy* never served as a barometer of Hugh Hefner's libidinous activities during the preceding month.

➤ You should probably temper your enthusiasm for becoming President of the United States if your political ambition is fueled solely by a desire to maintain a coterie of mind-controlled sex slaves.

Chapter 19

Amatory Comeuppance

In This Chapter

➤ Abandonment and retribution

➤ Domestic discord aplenty

➤ Revenge against property

➤ Revenge against people

As you've seen in earlier chapters, insecurity about the potential for misplaced trust lies at the heart of many an urban legend. In the stories that follow, the fear of misplaced trust is (yikes!) sexual. What had appeared to be a solid, monogamous relationship suddenly seems not to be so solid after all.

In urban legends involving amatory comeuppance, pain, distress, and heartache have a way of translating themselves into the kind of anger that leads to action. This action is often of the nasty variety.

Let's get right to the heart of the matter.

Scheming Adulterers Get What They've Got Coming

Revenge, the old saying has it, is a dish best served cold. If that's true, then the entrées that follow are downright frosty.

The Bargain-Basement Porsche

In this legend, a car enthusiast is browsing the classified ads in his morning paper when he comes across a startling ad. It claims to offer a nearly new Porsche for the low, low price of $50. The fellow is a huge Porsche fan, so he heads over to the address listed in the ad. There he meets a pleasant woman who confirms that the ad was hers, that the price is in fact fifty bucks, and that the Porsche in question is in the garage.

Don't Believe It!

The bargain-Porsche story showed up in a 1979 Ann Landers column; it was submitted by a reader who claimed to have seen a news account of the event in the *Chicago Tribune*. No such article has ever been located.

When he sees the car, he nearly keels over. It's an exquisite machine. He takes it on a test drive, accompanied by the woman of the house. The automobile is in perfect working order. Upon returning to the woman's house, the fellow hands over the $50. In return, he receives all the paperwork. He is the proud owner of a bargain-basement Porsche.

Before he leaves, his curiosity gets the better of him. He asks the woman to explain why in the world she would sell an automobile like this for such a ridiculously low price. Her answer: "My husband ran off with his secretary a few days ago and left a note telling me to sell the car and the house—and send him the money."

The jilted wife gets the last laugh by outsmarting her husband and following his "orders" to the letter. The message: Men may be beasts at times and may assume power to which they aren't entitled, but bright, wronged women know how to put the gentlemen in their place.

Crisis at the Altar

Suppose that you came across incontrovertible proof that your fiancée had been having an affair. Would the prospect of an intricate payback scheme involving public humiliation cross your mind? Sure it would. That's why stories like the following continue to circulate. The possibility of betrayal is pretty scary—scary enough to make us ponder at least the possibility of an equally unsettling retribution.

This is a true story that just happened at a wedding at Clemson. A buddy of mine from my baseball team knows a guy that was at the wedding.

This was a huge wedding with about 300 guests. After the wedding at the reception, the groom got up on stage at the microphone to talk to the crowd. He said that he wanted to thank everyone for coming, many from long distances, to support them at their wedding. He especially wanted to thank the families of the bride and groom for coming.

To thank everyone for coming and bringing gifts and everything, he said he wanted to give everyone a gift from him. So, taped to the bottom of everyone's chair, was a manila envelope. He said that was his gift to everyone, and he told them to open it.

Inside the manila envelope was an 8-by-10 picture of his best man having sex with the bride. (He must have gotten suspicious of the two of them and hired a private detective to trail them.) After he stood there and watched people's reactions for a couple of minutes, he turned to the best man and said, "[Expletive deleted] you." He turned to the bride and said, "[Expletive deleted] you," and then said, "I'm outta here."

He got the marriage annulled the next day.

While most of us would have broken it off immediately after we found out about the affair, this guy goes through with it anyway. His revenge: making the bride's parents pay for a 300-guest wedding and reception, letting everyone know exactly what did happen, and trashing the bride and the best man's reputations in front of friends, family, and grandparents.

This is his world; we just live in it.

Interesting, isn't it, that the groom first rebukes his best friend and *then* tells off the bride?

Another version, in which the bride discovers that her maid of honor has been having an affair with the groom, features a similar thanks-for-everything wind-up, but with the bride delivering the speech. The talk culminates with the wronged bride simply thanking the husband for his liaison with her best friend the night before and then storming out of the church. Photos would presumably be too lurid when the *bride* is getting *her* last digs in.

Both stories shine a spotlight on the deeply held human fear that the Beloved will not simply betray us, but also will betray us with someone whom we trust implicitly. Suddenly, those nice people you built your life around are revealed to be loathsome subinsect types. Gives you the shivers just thinking about it.

Maybe that's why the groom's behavior is singled out for explicit praise: This is what a *real* man should do in such a situation. No such cheerleading accompanies most accounts of the bride's pronouncement, perhaps because women who deliver stinging public indictments are seen as having crossed a boundary of decorum (though with "justification," in this case).

Surprise! You've Been Dumped!

Sudden abandonment by the person who is supposed to love us is, alas, no myth. It's a painful and persistent reality of modern life that haunts many of us. No wonder, then, that we listen with bated breath when we hear legends involving dramatic separations.

Here are just a few of the most popular.

The Amazing Home Video

"Do you promise to love, honor, and support one another, so long as you both shall live ... unless one of you gets shipped overseas?"

In the 1940s, GIs fighting the Axis on the battlefields of Europe, Africa, and Asia lived in fear of getting a "Dear John" letter from their beloved honey. By the time the Persian Gulf War rolled around, American fighting men apparently started getting nervous about receiving videotapes from their partners.

> Two years ago, a soldier from my unit in Germany told me that he witnessed the following story. When he was deployed for the Gulf War, another guy received a videotape from home. The first part contained greetings from his parents and brothers and sisters. The second part had his favorite TV shows from the United States. The third part was a pornographic scene involving two men and a woman wearing a mask. At the end of that scene, the woman turned to the camera, took off her mask, and said, "I told you I wanted a divorce!"

Fable Facts

In other, raunchier versions of the story, the husband watches with his buddies the video all the way through to its conclusion. Anybody ever heard of an off switch?

A man who is forced to leave his woman behind can never be *absolutely* sure that the lady's not playing the field—unless the fellow resorts to medieval measures such as chastity belts, which are, let's face it, out of fashion nowadays.

This story lends credence to one of the worst male nightmares in this respect. The missus not only wants out, but she is willing to violate the marriage bonds (and offer graphic evidence of said violation that humiliates her husband) to *get* out. What did the poor guy do to deserve such treatment? We're never told. That makes the moral all the more unnerving for men: This could happen to you for no good reason.

A considerably more explicit—and disgusting—version appears in Chapter 23, "Too Disgusting for Words." It's probably not a great passage to read at the dinner hour with the kids gathered in assembly.

Something's Fishy in This Relationship

A similar twist appears in this story: The woman announces her departure from the relationship in a manner that the man will never forget. Note that she does so by attacking his property, the car that he ("typically") treasures above all else. Perhaps there's a message being sent here about valuing earthly goods above the people in our lives?

> Back in 1992, a friend of my fiancé had a major disagreement with her boyfriend, so [she] decided to get back at him. He had bought himself a new car (around $30,000 worth), which was, typically, his pride and joy. She had two other friends remove the passenger seat from the car. Then she cut open the lining along the edge and inserted a fresh fish, neatly restitching along the seam.

> It was fine for the first few days, until the flesh started to rot.

> The boyfriend vacuumed, deodorized, pulled out the seats, and washed everything down, but he didn't find the fish.

> When the two split up, he had no luck picking up a new bird because no woman would set foot in the car.

Fable Facts

The "divorce announcement" video story makes clever use of the inevitable friend-of-a-friend mechanism associated with urban legends. We hear the story from someone who claims to know of some third party who saw the video. That third party is not the cuckolded husband. Therefore, the wife's shameful display has somehow become public knowledge.

This one's priceless. Not only does the wronged woman announce her exit by befouling the boyfriend's car, but she also makes it impossible for him to get new dates!

The legend is also interesting in that, like the story of the amazing home video, it doesn't attribute any specific loathsome activity to the boyfriend; the two were simply having a big fight. Apparently, being the wrong gender was his mistake.

An alternate version of this legend features a woman who *does* have a specific complaint against the man in question. She finds her husband in bed with another woman. The wronged wife sews shrimp into the lining of the house's curtains before leaving for good.

The Mammoth Phone Bill

And you thought *you* had communication problems. According to this story, a young husband and wife fight interminably, causing serious strains on their marriage. The husband has a foul temper; the wife has a habit of calling him on it.

Before he leaves on a long business trip, the husband decides that he has had enough. He sits his wife down and announces that he's finished with the relationship: Apparently she doesn't like him the way he is, and he's not the kind of guy to try to change his ways. So, the marriage is over. And by the way, the house is his. Everything, in fact, is his. While he's away on his trip, she is to collect her things and make her exit. He doesn't want to see her in his dwelling when he returns. End of story.

Actually, that's not quite the end of the story. When the brusque rat returns from his trip, he finds the house in chaos. His wife, however, is gone, which is exactly what he ordered. As he's tidying up, he notices that the telephone is off the hook. He puts it back on the cradle and goes about his business.

A few weeks down the line, though, he gets a phone bill for several *thousand* dollars. He attempts to contest the bill, but the charge is genuine. Someone in the house was apparently checking the weather in Tokyo for three straight weeks.

Fable Facts

Like the bargain-Porsche legend, the mammoth phone bill story features a mistreated woman who follows her unjust husband's orders to the syllable—and turns the tables on him to exact her revenge. This crafty, literal-minded requital calls to mind another Portia, namely the heroine of *The Merchant of Venice,* who outdoes the bloodthirsty moneylender Shylock by reading the law even more narrowly than he and bringing about his financial and social ruin. (Later in the play, she even captures her husband in a lie.)

Portia, a representative of justice, avoids recourse to violence, just as the wronged women in these two legends do. They take their revenge in financial terms rather than by injuring people or destroying possessions.

Revenge Gone Horribly, Horribly Wrong

The people in these stories decide that their mates are due for punishment, only to learn that the fates have decreed that the plans for retribution must somehow go haywire.

It's all beginning to feel a little like a Greek tragedy, complete with *tragic reversal,* isn't it?

More Revenge Involving Automobiles

Here's yet another story of revenge involving the neutralization of a sacred car. This time it's the guy who decides to take matters into his own hands. Too bad his jealous suspicions don't have any correlation with reality.

> [A] favorite [story] is the one about the woman whose husband drives a cement truck. She has saved for years to buy him a Cadillac convertible for their anniversary. The Cadillac is in the driveway, and she is negotiating with the salesman when her husband comes home. Seeing the flashy car, and seeing his wife talking with a strange man, he dumps his load of cement in the convertible.

The moral: Don't go off half-cocked. You could be destroying your own Caddy (and your own chance for domestic peace).

The Inadvertent Adulteress

A wife sees her husband flirting shamelessly at a party—or does she? No time to check the facts—better swing into action and teach the cad a "lesson" right away!

Legend Lingo

Tragic reversal is what happens when a plot or scheme comes back to haunt the hero who launched it. In many legends, heroes who seek revenge for their wrongs often find themselves messed up because the gods themselves seem to prefer administering this kind of justice. See, for instance, the cycle of plays in the *Oresteia* by Aeschylus.

Fable Facts

The Readymix legend may have gotten started when a similar event was reported in the Denver area in 1960. A car was filled with cement—not by a jealous husband, but by a driver who supposedly got tired of waiting to make his delivery. It is possible that the Denver incident was actually staged to win publicity for the driver's employer.

A couple was invited to a swanky masked Halloween party. The wife got a terrible headache and told her husband to go to the party alone. He, being a devoted husband, protested, but she argued and said she was going to take some aspirin and go to bed; there was no need for his good time to be spoiled by not going. So he took his costume and away he went.

After sleeping soundly for one hour, the wife awakened without pain. Because it was still early, she decided to go to the party. Her husband did not know what her costume was, so she thought she would have some fun by watching him to see how he acted when she was not with him. She joined the party and soon spotted her husband cavorting around on the dance floor, dancing with every nice chick he could, copping a little feel here and a little kiss there.

His wife went up to him; being a rather seductive babe herself, he left his partner high and dry and devoted his time to the new stuff that had just arrived. She let him go as far as he wished—naturally, since he was her husband. Finally he whispered a little proposition in her ear, and she agreed; off they went to one of the cars and had a little bang.

Just before unmasking at midnight, she slipped away and went home. She put the costume away and got into bed, wondering what kind of explanation he would make for his behavior.

She was sitting up reading when he came in and asked what kind of a time he had had. He said, "Oh, the same old thing. You know I never have a good time when you're not there."

Then she asked, "Did you dance much?"

He replied, "I'll tell you, I never even danced one dance. When I got there, I met Pete, Bill Brown, and some other guys, so we went into the den and played poker all evening. But I'll tell you … the guy I loaned my costume to sure had a real good time!"

Unjustly suspecting her husband of inappropriate behavior with other women, the wife in this story keeps her own mask on and ends up crossing the line herself. Thus, she finds herself face to face with someone she wasn't aware she was.

The story wraps up with one of the "Oh my God, what have I done?" moments with which urban legends involving deep transgressions of the moral order often conclude. It also suggests that, deep down, we may be as concerned about our own behavior as we are about that of our spouse. If a stranger whispered a "little proposition" in *our* ear, are we certain that we wouldn't find ways to convince ourselves that nothing untoward could possibly follow if we entertained the suggestion?

Masks, it seems, can be dangerous things.

Strange but True

A few awkward logistical questions about the Halloween party story indicate that it takes place in our communal dreamland rather than at an actual social gathering. How, exactly, does it escape the wife's notice that the masked body of the man she is allowing to seduce her is not the familiar one belonging to her husband? And to whom did the wife eventually reveal the details of her "inadvertent" promiscuity—and why?

The Least You Need to Know

➤ Urban legends involving amatory comeuppance, pain, distress, and heartache have a way of translating themselves into the kind of anger that leads to action, often of the nasty variety.

➤ Some of these stories shine a spotlight on the deeply held human fear that the Beloved will not simply betray us, but will betray us with someone whom we trust implicitly.

➤ In considering tales involving sudden abandonment, fear of being left alone is deep and widespread.

➤ Legends involving people who engage in revenge plots against their spouses or lovers often feature plot twists that ensure that the plots come back to haunt their inventors.

Part 5

Nasty Business

Death, lies, manipulation, violence, and gross-out stories aplenty: If this part of the book doesn't make you feel a little bit queasy now and then, there's probably something wrong with you.

From bogus "charitable" e-mail campaigns for sick kids to microwaved poodles, from dead coeds to hook-wielding weirdos stalking Lover's Lane, the dark side of human nature is on grisly display here. Proceed at your own risk.

Chapter 20

You've Got Mail (and It's a Scam)

Why do people perpetuate e-mail scams? Probably for the same reason people use dinner parties to pass along gossip they know to be false, tell pollsters they plan to vote for political candidates they know they can't support, and claim to weigh less than they really do. It can be strangely exhilarating to tell a lie that someone else takes to be the gospel truth.

In the free-wheeling, ever-expanding culture of the Internet, you can make something up as you go along, hit Send, and wake up the next morning to learn that thousands of people have taken you very seriously indeed. Evidently, some people get a huge kick out of crafting and circulating false messages that people *want* to believe.

The scale of this phenomenon defies belief. Honest. There are more e-mail hoaxes out there than any mere mortal could possibly track, although a few responsible Web sites take it upon themselves to try to catalogue the most successful cyber-lies, some of which are pretty entertaining.

You'll learn more about those "scam-buster" sites a little later. For right now, sit back and get ready to learn exactly what kinds of stories people are willing to weave to tug at your heartstrings, make sweat break out on your brow, or get you to believe that your lucky day has finally rolled around. And remember: The people who mount these strange campaigns to launch and perpetuate urban legends from your e-mail in-box don't want your money. They just want you to hit the Forward button.

The Mother of All "Forward This E-Mail" Urban Legends

Have you ever received an e-mail appeal on behalf of a terminally ill boy our girl? Have tears ever come to your eyes upon hearing the tale of the bedridden young cancer victim hoping to collect more business cards than anyone else? Have you ever been tempted to pop a card into the mail in order to help the cause?

If so, you were being duped. As with so many e-mail hoaxes, however, the lie begins with a dash of truth.

Fable Facts

The granddaddy of the "please-forward-this-to-as-many-people-as-you-can" urban legend is probably the Craig Shergold hoax, the origins of which can be traced to an actual news event in 1989. As an Internet prank, the Shergold appeals and their variations have proved nearly impossible to eradicate and have caused expense, effort, and frustration for many organizations, notably the Phoenix-based Make-A-Wish Foundation, which had nothing to do with the original story.

Who Is Craig Shergold?

This much is true: In 1989, an organization known as Children's Wish Foundation International launched a campaign on behalf of a young British cancer patient by the name of Craig Shergold. Young Craig really did want to win a spot in the *Guinness Book of World Records* by collecting more *get-well* cards (not business cards) than anyone else in recorded history. The British media began to circulate his appeal, and the response from the public—both in England and elsewhere—was overwhelming.

Shergold broke the record in a matter of months. His story even had what should have been its happy ending: In 1991, doctors removed most of a cancerous brain tumor, and Craig's prognosis after the operation was good. That *should* have been the happy ending of the story.

Strange but True

The "Shergold hoax" refers to the avalanche of letters and e-mail messages supposedly aiding a young cancer patient in his effort to win a spot in the *Guinness Book of World Records*. The real Craig Shergold (who did not launch any hoax) is now a healthy college student. His true story spawned a host of false appeals that have no doubt made people skeptical of legitimate charitable appeals, thus perpetuating the cynicism already rampant in this jaded world we live in.

A few mean-spirited pranksters, armed with that revolutionary communications tool known as the Send button, had other ideas. Over the years, countless chain letters and e-mail messages continued to circulate Craig's request, often in garbled or deliberately altered form. Eventually, the request specified business cards rather than get-well cards. Bogus addresses and organization names began appearing in the place of Children's Wish Foundation International; other messages included contact information for the Make-A-Wish Foundation (based in Phoenix, Arizona), which had nothing to do with the original Shergold story.

Ominous stories of bad luck that befell those who broke the chain even accompanied some of the heartfelt requests for help in breaking the record. A concerned public continued to respond. The volume of mail showed no sign of letting up, even after the record was broken and Craig was released from the hospital.

Shergold's family, the Make-A-Wish Foundation, the BBC, and Ann Landers, among many others, have appealed to the public to stop sending cards. But the mail has continued to pour in.

Fable Facts

Two years after Craig's initial request, an official at the Children's Wish Foundation International estimated that the total volume of mail received on behalf of the Guinness record effort had exceeded 100 *million* pieces.

The rise of the Internet has given a new generation of point-and-click jokers the chance to circulate earnest-sounding but false appeals on behalf of sick children—instantly and across the globe. If you get one, you may rest assured that your leg is being pulled—and that the appeal of urban legends that take advantage of our protective instincts toward ill or endangered children is still strong.

Clearly, some people don't mind making some serious withdrawals from the karma bank.

And now, a word from our sponsor: Your author would like to take this opportunity to paraphrase the comedian Dennis Miller. If you're low enough to craft and broadcast anonymous, manipulative e-mail messages designed to exploit young cancer victims "for a laugh," you ought to lean in over the plate, stare at the approaching fastball, and take one for the team.

Strange but True

The Make-A-Wish Foundation Web site points out that "most people who forward chain letters really do wish to help the children the Make-A-Wish Foundation serves." Sadly, very few of the millions who have received bogus letters of the "forward this immediately" variety have received any legitimate information about how to contribute to this worthwhile cause. If you want to make a tax-deductible donation to help make a sick child's dream come true, you can do so by mailing a check to Make-A-Wish Foundation, P.O. Box 29119, Phoenix, AZ 85038.

Don't Believe It!

The flood of business cards from well-intentioned (but misinformed) correspondents was so overwhelming that the people at the *Guinness Book of World Records* **retired** Craig Shergold's record in an effort to halt the avalanches of mail. So, if anyone tries to convince you that you can make a sick kid feel better by mailing a card or sending an e-mail message, don't.

Variations on the Shergold Myth

More from the Sad but True Department: Many, many similar Internet chain letters, obviously patterned on the Shergold appeals, continue to make the rounds. A message may garble the original name (for example, "Craig Sherford" or "Craig Sherwood"), change the name entirely, or substitute a new disease before concluding with the usual impassioned request that the reader forward e-mail. It all sounds very convincing the first time around.

Some of these appeals suggest that a huge corporation (or an anonymous donor, or a well-known philanthropist) will supply the funds necessary to complete treatment for the child in question—*if* enough people circulate the e-mail message you've just received. One particularly heartless variation falsely informs recipients that the Make-A-Wish Foundation itself will ensure that a young cancer patient will receive 7¢ every time a message is forwarded.

Now please take a moment to think about this. If *you* wanted to help a child with a terminal disease, would you make your gift rely on the total number of (impossible-to-track) e-mail messages that people forwarded to their friends through the vast echo chamber that is the Internet? Or would you simply pull out your checkbook and make a donation?

Right. You'd fork over the cash. And that's the very best thing to do when you get something like this in your mailbox and then feel that you should really do *something* to help some ill child somewhere.

So, if you get a Shergold letter or anything like it and suddenly feel altruistic, follow this simple three-step plan:

Legend Lingo

The "7¢ ruse" refers to false e-mail messages that claim 7¢ will somehow be forwarded to a sick child every time an e-mail message is forwarded.

1. Delete the message.
2. Pull out your checkbook.
3. Write a check to one or more exemplary organizations.

Strange but True

These are some great places to send money (or to contact about volunteering your time) if you're eager to help kids with cancer:

➤ **American Cancer Society.** Call 1–800–227–2345, visit www.cancer.org, or mail a check to American Cancer Society, 19 West 56th St., New York, NY 10019.

➤ **St. Jude Children's Research Hospital.** Call 1–800–877–5833, visit www. stjude.org, or mail a check to St. Jude Children's Research Hospital, 501 St. Jude Place, Memphis, TN 38105.

➤ **M.D. Anderson Cancer Center.** Call 1–800–392–1611, visit www.mdanderson.org/care_centers/children, or mail a check to University of Texas/MDACC, 1515 Holcombe Blvd., Houston, TX 77030.

The Pull-Tab Myth

No one is quite sure how this one started. Whatever its origins, the pull-tab obsession may just give the Shergold myth a run for its money in the Most Resilient Health-Related Urban Legend sweepstakes.

This myth is also a testament to how far people will go in the name of a good cause, even after they've been informed that they are laboring under a serious misconception. People have been known to become addicted to collecting pull-tabs—and to *keep* collecting pull-tabs, even after the facts of the matter have been patiently explained to them.

To summarize the key points relating to this remarkably hardy myth: Someday, somehow, when you least expect it, someone will approach you in person, via e-mail, or via some other modern communication medium, to try to convince you to save the pull-tabs from soft drink cans. This earnest and (probably) innocent person is likely to maintain that, by saving these small scraps of metal, you will somehow be helping people who are undergoing kidney dialysis treatment.

In support of this notion, your (probably) innocent friend may put forward the idea that the tabs can be forwarded to Reynolds Aluminum or Alcoa, whose management will then make a charitable donation benefiting kidney dialysis patients; exchanged at a special location for a rate higher than that currently prevailing for recycled aluminum, with the proceeds accruing to kidney dialysis patients; or exchanged for treatment at a medical institution, presumably at the cashier's desk.

When this exchange occurs, inform your (probably) innocent friend that all three of these assumptions are simply false. Refer him or her to reporter Katherine Kromer's fine article "Myth in a Can: Earnest Collectors of Pull-Tabs Find They've Been Misinformed," in the May 13, 1997, edition of the *Kansas City Star.*

If your copy of Kromer's article has been mislaid for some reason, refer your (probably) innocent friend to this page of this book, where the following brief extract will serve to reinforce your point:

> (The rumor) popped up years ago and resurfaces every few months, to the annoyance of those in the recycling industry and medical fields .... Students at Sycamore Hills Elementary School have gathered more than 1 million pull-tabs ....

Don't Believe It!

As of this writing, no campaign subsidizing kidney dialysis treatments relies on collections of pull-tabs from soft drink cans. No record of such a campaign has ever surfaced. You can, of course, recycle the tabs and give whatever money you receive to whatever worthy charity you feel deserves it. You'll get more money to contribute, though, if you recycle the entire can rather than just the pull-tab.

One million. Jeez, Louise! Okay, okay—Kromer goes on to explain that the Sycamore Hills collection was part of a math project and that the students eventually recycled the tabs and donated the proceeds to the local Ronald McDonald House.

Forward This Message to Keep Terrible Things from Happening

Long, long ago, in the covered wagon days, your parents had no Internet access. They did, however, have access to chain letters.

These were primitive messages written or typed on pieces of—get this—paper. These letters promised good things to recipients who kept the "chain" alive by forwarding money or something else of value to the person at the top of a list, of names and addresses appearing within the text of the letter. The letters also forecast various intricate forms of doom for those who "broke the chain" by doing the smart thing and tossing the letter into the wastebasket. ("Melvin W. of Head Injury, North Dakota, ignored this letter; six days later, he was found dead beneath his father-in-law's truss.")

Although chain letters involving the exchange of money have been illegal for years, many intriguing variations have made the transition into the Information Age. But, you ask, isn't this a book about fascinating (and false) stories that refuse to die—and not a book about con games?

Right you are. The reason any reference to chain letters appears here at all is that these letters are the ancestors of a distinctive modern variety of urban legend. This kind springs from e-mail messages that predict (or imply) some kind of horrible outcome if the recipient fails to alert others—and "keep the chain alive"—by forwarding the message to everyone imaginable. The payoff is not financial. It's the visceral thrill of seeing your very own e-mail message freak out a significant portion of the world's population.

Fable Facts

The Ronald McDonald House does sponsor various "pull-tab partner" campaigns encouraging people to collect the pull-tabs from soft drink cans. These campaigns, however, do not subsidize treatment for kidney dialysis patients. Instead, income from the recycled tabs is "used to assist the House with operational expenses such as food, household supplies, and utilities."

Fable Facts

There are too many Internet hoaxes involving e-mail forwarding to list in this chapter, but a great site for keeping track of the latest and most outrageous scams can be found at www.netsquirrel.com/combatkit.

Don't Believe It!

Most horrible things foretold by the modern descendants of yesterday's chain letters are in no danger of happening.

In these messages, the terrible stuff that may happen in the future is usually stripped of the ominous pseudomystical doubletalk common in the final paragraphs of chain letters. Instead, the reader is warned of dire changes in his or her own life or in society as a whole, and is urged to spread the word to friends and loved ones—by the quickest means possible.

Here's a brief sampling:

Ignore any e-mail message asking you to spread the word that … because the Voting Rights Act of 1965 will expire in 2007, African-Americans will be deprived of their voting privileges. (This is patently false; voting rights are guaranteed under the fifteenth amendment to the Constitution, and the Voting Rights Act can be extended in 2007 by a majority vote of Congress and the President's signature.)

Ignore any e-mail message asking you to spread the word that … dialing "9-0-#" on a standard residential phone line will allow bad guys to charge any call they want to your line. (There is a germ, but only a germ, of truth to this one. *Business* lines—or other lines that require you to dial 9 to place standard calls—may be subject to a scam in which callers fraudulently identifying themselves as service personnel can gain access to the line after you press the keys in question. The vast majority of residential customers, however, are *not* affected.)

Ignore any e-mail message asking you to spread the word that … certain brands of crayons contain dangerously high levels of asbestos. (Talk about making a mountain out of a molehill. The Consumer Product Safety Commission decided to get to the bottom of this story—originally reported in the *Seattle Post-Intelligencer*—and determined that the amount of asbestos detectable in the crayons in question was so minute as to be "scientifically insignificant." That didn't stop the doomsday patrol from alerting parents to the imminent poisoning of their children via thousands of e-mails, though.)

Virus Hoax Messages

You should definitely *not* ignore e-mail messages warning you about a new computer virus. You should, however, be aware that false warnings in this area are legion and that a certain segment of the Internet community delights in sending such false messages. So, how do you know which warnings are real and which are bogus?

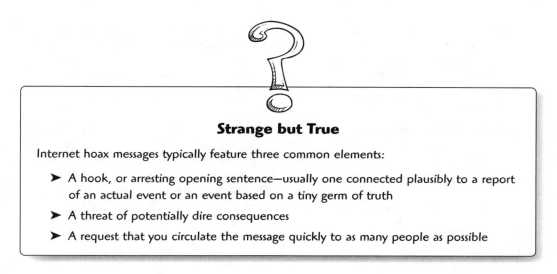

Strange but True

Internet hoax messages typically feature three common elements:

➤ A hook, or arresting opening sentence—usually one connected plausibly to a report of an actual event or an event based on a tiny germ of truth

➤ A threat of potentially dire consequences

➤ A request that you circulate the message quickly to as many people as possible

You don't. Not unless you check out www.Vmyths.com or the Antivirus Research Center, at www.symantec.com/avcenter/hoax.html, two of the best sites out there for sorting out which "alerts" about computer viruses are bogus and which are the real thing. Before you tell everyone in your address book about that strange Turkish hard drive crash warning you just received, check the most recent postings on these two sites. (Oh, and don't download any files you weren't expecting, especially ones with .exe or .vbs extensions. But you knew that.)

Is Microsoft Out to Get You?

Naaah. Bill Gates only wants what's best for the world's computer users. But some eager folks spread the word via e-mail that the Install Disk #2 for Windows 95 had somehow been infected with a sinister virus. Actually, these reports all turned out to be traceable to computers that *were already infected* with a virus that found a way to transmit itself onto the install disk. So, Bill's off the hook. Other dire virus nonevents have included these:

➤ The National Security Agency's deliberate insertion of a virus into Iraqi printers during the Gulf War.

➤ The FCC's decision to release a special warning about a lethal virus known as "GOOD TIMES"—reputedly "unparalleled in its destructive capacity" because of its capacity to place a computer's processor in "an nth-complexity infinite binary loop." ("GOOD TIMES" was the first widely successful computer virus hoax.)

➤ The presence of a particularly devastating virus in a screen saver promoting the Walt Disney movie *A Bug's Life*.

Virus hoaxes are not always easy to spot. Experts in the field opine that one possible tip-off is that the bogus warnings often feature warnings that the virus in question is so new that "not many people know about it." Just in case, though, when you get a warning, check the two sites previously referenced to find out exactly what kind of jive is being passed around about the latest, most terrifying, and completely fictional computer viruses.

If you were charitable enough to overlook the occasional clogged corporate e-mail system, you might conclude that virus hoaxes have a fairly amusing history. One wag responded to the hysteria surrounding the nonexistent "GOOD TIMES" virus by circulating a message of his own. (Note: The screen reproduced here has been posted and reposted so many times without a "From" line that definitive attribution is now, despite the best efforts of your humble author, pretty much impossible.)

```
December 1996

READ THIS:

Good Times will rewrite your hard drive—not only that, but it
will scramble any disks that are even close to your computer.
It will recalibrate your refrigerator's coolness setting so
all your ice cream melts. It will demagnetize the strips on
all your credit cards, screw up the tracking on your televi-
sion, and use subspace field harmonics to scratch any CDs you
try to play.

It will give your ex-girlfriend your new phone number. It will
mix Kool-Aid into your fish tank. It will drink all your beer
and leave its socks out on the coffee table when there's com-
pany coming over. It will put a dead kitten in the back
pocket of your good suit pants and hide your car keys when
you are late for work.

Good Times will make you fall in love with a penguin. It will
give you nightmares about circus midgets. It will pour sugar
in your gas tank and shave off both your eyebrows while dating
your girlfriend behind your back and billing the dinner and
hotel room to your Discover card.

It will seduce your grandmother. It does not matter if she is
dead; such is the power of Good Times—it reaches out beyond
the grave to sully those things we hold most dear.
```

It moves your car randomly around parking lots so you can't find it. It will kick your dog. It will leave libidinous messages on your boss's voice mail in your voice! It is insidious and subtle. It is dangerous and terrifying to behold. It is also a rather interesting shade of mauve.

Good Times will give you Dutch Elm disease. It will leave the toilet seat up. It will make a batch of Methamphetamine in your bathtub and then leave bacon cooking on the stove while it goes out to chase grade-schoolers with your new snowblower.

Listen to me. Good Times does not exist. It cannot do anything to you. But I can. I am sending this message to everyone in the world. Tell your friends, tell your family. If anyone else sends me another e-mail about this fake Good Times virus, I will turn hating them into a religion. I will do things to them that would make a horse head in your bed look like Easter Sunday brunch.

So there. Take that, Good Times.

Forward This Message and All Your Dreams Will Come True

What's the flip side of the e-mail message you get that forecasts certain doom if you fail to forward it to everyone you know? Why, the one that promises cash, prizes, and Turtle Wax to spare—if only you hit that Forward key.

The sheer volume of "send-this-message-and-win-valuable-prizes" messages is impossible to express within the covers of this book. The following table, though, will give you some sense of the (empty) promises currently hurtling through cyberspace.

Do not believe any e-mail promising the following:

➤ You will be paid a fee for the number of times you forward the message.

➤ You will receive a gift certificate for free lingerie from Victoria's Secret if you forward the message to everyone you know.

➤ You will receive a check from Bill Gates for $1,000 if you forward the message to everyone you know.

➤ A first-run Hollywood movie will suddenly start playing on your computer if you forward the message to everyone you know.

➤ Disney will send you on a free trip to Orlando, Florida, if you send the message to everyone you know.

➤ You will win a spot in the *Guinness Book of World Records* if you send the message to everyone you know.

➤ Miller will send you a complimentary six-pack of beer if you send the message to everyone you know.

➤ ... and so on.

A Guiding Principle

So what have we learned in this chapter? Besides the fact that some extremely strange people with easy access to the Internet have a little too much time on their hands ....

Well, we've learned that you can't help sick children by forwarding e-mail. We've learned that most of the dire warnings you get in "forward-this-to-everyone-you-know" e-mail messages are bogus. And we've learned that you can't win valuable prizes by cluttering up other people's e-mail in-boxes.

You probably knew all that already. Just in case you run into someone who needs reminding, though, feel free to pass along this guiding principle: *A fair percentage of the "forward-me" e-mail we receive is good to read for a chuckle but bad to forward.*

Here's the bottom line: If someone you don't know composes a message that promises that something really good will happen (or something really bad won't happen) if you forward it to all humanity, do us all a favor. Read it. Laugh at it. But don't forward it. It only encourages them.

The Least You Need to Know

➤ Some extremely strange people with easy access to the Internet have a little too much time on their hands. They love to craft e-mail messages that are false but that recipients want to believe.

➤ Be skeptical of any e-mail suggesting that you can help a sick kid, keep some awful event from happening, or get cash or anything else simply by circulating the message.

➤ When you get a virus alert, check it against one of the sites referenced in this chapter dedicated to keeping track of bogus warnings, of which there are plenty.

➤ Read these messages if you want. Laugh at them. But please don't send them on.

Chapter 21

The Hazards of the Big, Bad World: Urban Legends About College and College Students

Ah, the perils of leaving home! Transcending that awkward adolescent phase to begin life as a young adult means accepting personal responsibility for a lot of the stuff Mom and Dad used to do for you. It means settling on an independent sense of self. And if you're going to college, it also means (gasp!) being tested on a regular basis.

Fear is what we imagine, in our worst moments, to be true about the unknown. That time span between, say, 15 and 20 years of age features *lots* of unknown things to imagine. No surprise, then, that this can be a pretty scary period.

Not surprisingly, a whole host of urban legends deal with the challenges and fears associated with growing up. Many of them feature bizarre events in a college setting. Why college? Probably because, nowadays, this is the first place where many of us establish social identities separate from our role as a daughter or son of someone else. It's where we're sent to pass all *kinds* of interesting tests.

The following legends—a sampling of the many involving college students—reflect a world that's creepy, surrealistic, and vulnerable to the arbitrary actions of unfamiliar people and institutions. That is to say, they're fairly accurate reflections of the hallowed halls we all enter when we embark on life on our own for the first time.

The Dead Roommate

There are a number of variations on the dead roommate legend; all follow the *brush with death* pattern. In this case, the story features an exceptionally close call that takes the form of a quick trip back to one's dorm room late at night.

Legend Lingo

The **brush with death** syndrome in urban legends describes a seemingly normal sequence of events that actually involves a close encounter with a potentially lethal situation. The structure is a potent metaphor for fears associated with, among other things, the onset of young adulthood.

Fable Facts

The "Aren't you glad you didn't turn on the light?" legend—which has a number of variations—is featured prominently in the horror film *Urban Legend*.

A young lady returns to her dorm room very late in the evening to retrieve some books; she is planning to study and spend the night in her boyfriend's room. Not wanting to awaken her sleeping roommate, she leaves the lights off. She fumbles around for a few moments but finally locates the books and toiletries she's looking for. She makes her exit and shuts the door silently behind her.

Morning comes. When she returns to her dorm room, she's shocked to see that it has been set upon by the representatives of the local police department. One of the policemen takes her aside and asks whether she lives in the dorm room. Our heroine says "Yes." The policeman ushers her into the dorm's bathroom and shows her a heart-stopping sight. There, scrawled on the mirror in her roommate's blood, is the following message: "Aren't you glad you didn't turn on the light?"

Clearly, there's dangerous stuff going on in the dark—dangerous stuff that could happen to you.

The main point would seem to be that this whole sexual autonomy thing is a good deal more complicated than it might at first appear. Remember, the heroine of the story is returning to her dorm room *before* heading back to her boyfriend's room, presumably for a night of lovemaking once she has dutifully completed her reading.

The legend is probably best understood as one anxious, nightmarish answer to some timeless questions: What are the possible consequences of yielding to one's own sexual awakening? What's really waiting for us there in the dark? And, perhaps most important, what untoward reality is likely to emerge in the cold light of morning?

More on Dead Roommates

A strange, persistent rumor has taken hold at college campuses around the country. It is this: If your distraught roommate commits suicide, you are instantly entitled to a 4.0 average for the semester in question.

The story continues to circulate, despite the best efforts of teachers and academic administrators to refute it. From a student's point of view, the legend makes a certain intuitive sense: How can one be expected to study while mourning the passing of one's roommate?

Although that's certainly a valid question, the sad fact remains that no institution of higher learning is on record as having adopted the straight-A policy for surviving roommates. There are, however, any number of extensions, counseling sessions, and other special arrangements likely to be extended to the roommate who finds himself or herself in such a situation. Policies vary, of course, but on one point the colleges and universities appear to be unanimous: Nobody makes the Dean's List simply for outliving a roommate who decides to shuffle off this mortal coil.

Why has the story refused to go away? Just a guess, but the "horrible-things-happening-to-roommates" stories appear to serve as a kind of psychological shorthand for "horrible things could very well happen to *me.*"

Kids choose to believe that there is institutional compassion for those who *lived* with students who couldn't handle the transition from adolescence to adulthood. In so doing, college students may be addressing the fear that they themselves may have trouble making that transition.

The legend appears to send a comforting message to students ill at ease in a new, competitive environment. Stressed out? Worried that you, too,

Fable Facts

The plots of two recent movies, *Dead Man on Campus* (1998) and *Dead Man's Curve* (1998), incorporate the suicidal-roommate-equals-A-average myth.

Fable Facts

The creation of a (totally imaginary) policy rewarding surviving roommates of suicidal college students may be a "defense response" to the seemingly arbitrary exercise of authority by campus authorities whose decisions and policies seem inscrutable compared to Mom and Dad's. Wait until you get a load of the questions they ask you at job interviews, guys.

might crack under the pressure? No problem: There's a loophole. You probably won't *need* it, and it's applied only in extremely *rare* circumstances—but it's there for you.

The Scratching Sound

The moral of this legend is both clear and familiar: Sexual experimentation has its hazards. This version of the tale is specifically targeted at college students. (Equally gruesome warnings about the perils of unauthorized erotic expression among youngsters who *aren't* enrolled at institutions of higher learning may be found in the following chapter.)

The story goes like this:

➤ A male college student and a female college student fall in love.

➤ Lacking a private place to make out, they head for the local Seemingly Abandoned Wooded Area.

➤ Upon arrival, the male college student suddenly realizes that he has to pee.

➤ He announces this to the female college student and steps out of the car to find a spot to relieve himself. (Note symbolic abandonment: Female is now alone and in jeopardy, thanks to the male heading elsewhere to satisfy a biological urge.)

➤ Time passes.

➤ The female college student gets worried, gets out of the car, and hollers her boyfriend's name. She hears no response.

➤ The female college student re-enters the car and hears a strange scratching sound on the roof—and then sees the local Maniac Who Frequents Seemingly Abandoned Wooded Areas.

➤ The female college student gets into the driver's seat and tries to get away, but the car gets stuck.

➤ When she puts the vehicle into reverse and guns the accelerator, her boyfriend, covered in blood, plunges through the front windshield. (Where would the moment of horrific realization be if he plunged through the *back* windshield?)

➤ The scratching sound was her very boyfriend, cunningly gagged and suspended from a tree by the local maniac. When she hit the accelerator, she dusted her main squeeze.

Stay out of the woods, kids. You may end up destroying the thing you love—or being abandoned by it—or both.

Don't Trust the Library of Congress

Why not? Because they're out to reveal your secrets, silly.

A myth that the Library of Congress began collecting the details of secret fraternity rituals during the McCarthy era has proved immune to earnest assurances from the government that such is not the case. What follows is an example of one of the many "updates" on this mock-urgent topic. The story seems to reflect a fear of being subjected to public scrutiny—and censure—for private conduct engaged in as part of one's new identity as a young adult.

> Regarding the rituals being located in the Library of Congress …
>
> Okay, here's the bottom line. In the early 1950s during the Red Scare, several of the movers and shakers of the era felt that some college organizations could possibly harbor pro-Commie sentiments. An act of Congress required all … Greek letter organizations [to] submit final copies of their secret rituals and other proceedings to the Library of Congress for examination.
>
> It's hard to be partial. But Lambda Chi Alpha *never* had its ritual examined nor deposited in the LOC at any time. (The then-)president and newly honorarily initiated brother Harry S Truman from Missouri assured Congress that LCA was not pro-Russkie, thus they did not see our ritual.
>
> At this time it is true that several politicians over the years have "borrowed" their rituals from the LOC on an extended basis.
>
> LCA's was never submitted, ever.

That's the form the classic legend takes—someone solemnly assuring his frat brothers that, despite a decades-old instance of unwarranted intrusion from federal authorities, *this* fraternity has never yielded its secrets to the Man. A number of the variations outline elaborate plots and schemes supposedly undertaken to comply with the letter of the law, without actually revealing the fraternity's rituals. Translation: There's pressure from the outside, but your tribe (unlike others) has successfully preserved your zone of privacy.

The Library of Congress has denied maintaining any collection of secret fraternity rituals and has assured nervous frat brothers from a bewildering array of Greek-lettered denominations that no government plot to collect or circulate said rituals exists. (By the way: Guys seem to be the only ones who fixate on this legend—a fact that may say something about the importance of rites of passage in the male psyche.)

Don't Trust the Academic Establishment

Like there was any danger of *that*. Have you ever had a nightmare in which you're expected to pass a test for which you haven't studied at all? It's a common anxiety dream. Here's an urban legend with a similar theme, only the anxiety centers around one's ability to recover from a wild weekend.

In the legend, the guys are (supposedly) ready to take the test—they're just not in the best state of mind after a long weekend of Pabst Blue Ribbon-sodden revelry.

"Introductory Chemistry" at Duke has been taught for about a zillion years by Professor Bonk (really), and his course is semiaffectionately known as "Bonk-istry." He has been around forever, so I wouldn't put it past him to come up with something like this.

Anyway, one year there were these two guys who were taking chemistry and who did pretty well on all of the quizzes and the midterms and labs so that going into the final they had a solid A. These friends were so confident going into the final that the weekend before finals week (even though the chem final was on Monday), they decided to go up to the University of Virginia and party with some friends up there.

They did this and had a great time. However, with their hangovers and everything, they overslept all day Sunday and didn't make it back to Duke until early Monday morning.

Rather than take the final then, they found Professor Bonk after the final and explained to him why they missed the final.

They told him that they gone up to UVA for the weekend and had planned to come back in time to study, but they had a flat tire on the way back and didn't have a spare. They couldn't get help for a long time and so were late getting back to campus.

Bonk thought this over and then agreed that they could make up the final on the following day. The two guys were elated, relieved, and very proud of their story.

So, they studied that night and went in the next day at the time Bonk had told them. He placed them in separate rooms and handed each of them a test booklet and told them to begin.

They looked at the first problem, which was something simple about molarity and solutions and was worth 5 points. "Cool," they thought, "this is going to be easy."

They did that problem and then turned the page. They were unprepared, however, for what they saw on the next page …

"Which tire?" (95 points)

No, kids, it's not your imagination. The grown-up world really is out to keep you from having fun and getting away with it.

Get used to it.

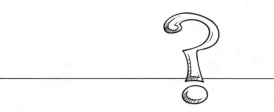

Strange but True

College-test legends are common—and generally full of anxiety about the outcome of the never-ending conflict between the Establishment and the College Kid Who Deserves a Break.

One such myth tells the story of a student who exceeds his allotted time in responding to an essay question. The professor gets tired of watching the guy scribble despite the fact that time has been called. He gathers up the tests and starts to leave. The late scribbler concludes his sentence and rushes to place his exam in the pile. Told that he has violated the rules and will be treated accordingly, the student asks, "Do you know who I am?" The professor explains that he will—once he flunks him. That's when the student lunges at the tests in the professor's hand and sends them falling to the floor. He quickly mixes his own test into the pile and then splits. He passed, of course.

Not *all* forms of intelligence can be measured on college tests.

The Least You Need to Know

➤ Over 21? Remember your own college days, and keep in mind that the passage from adolescence to adulthood can be pretty frightening.

➤ Under 21? Don't count on an automatic "A" average if your roommate commits suicide.

➤ Whatever your age, remember that urban legends that deal with college life expose deep uncertainties about mortality, sexuality, tests (actual and metaphorical), and other daunting facts of adult life.

➤ Whatever your age, beware of meddling authority figures bent on exposing your most sensitive secrets.

Chapter 22

Maniacs, Unlimited

In This Chapter

➤ The infamous "hook" legend

➤ Skinned Tom

➤ Help with a flat tire that you definitely don't need

➤ Baby sitters on the receiving end of menacing phone calls

➤ "Humans can lick, too"

"That way madness lies," King Lear said famously—lecturing himself, and no other character on Shakespeare's stage, about the danger of loosening his grasp on the thread of lucidity and reason. He lost hold of it anyway.

We all seem to fear the existence of a "that way" in which insanity waits for unfortunate folks who relinquish union with their "right" minds. At any rate, we all seem to respond viscerally to urban legends involving mad folk run amok. Is it the resident of the local loony bin we truly fear? Is it the prospect that we, too, could lose our way in the maze?

Or—to get a little more specific—is it just that we guys have a sneaking suspicion that we might come unhinged at any moment?

Maniacs on Lover's Lane

When Elvis Costello once asked the musical question, "Who's making Lover's Lane safe again for lovers?" he didn't offer the difficult answer: nobody.

At least, that's the conclusion waiting to be drawn from the following grisly urban legends. Perhaps you're wondering: Why on earth do lunatics make such a habit of picking on kids who are busy applying stethoscopes to each other's combination locks in the front seats of borrowed cars?

Here's one explanation: Most of the shadows, lurking intruders, and ungodly mayhem that follows would appear to be a means of working through fears and anxieties about (surprise!) emerging sexuality. Apparently, both parents and teenagers are pretty darned nervous about the complications and consequences of early sexual activity. And they're willing to tell some interesting stories about those complications and consequences.

Consider the dire implications of the first myth we'll be examining ....

Fable Facts

Many of the slashing-maniac urban legends appear to fulfill a purpose similar to that of the Needle Man rumor that shows up in Chapter 17, "Hazardous Amorous Duty": They put a scare into teenage girls who may be contemplating "going all the way."

The Hook

This is one of the most widely circulated urban myths of them all; it has shown up in every medium imaginable and has even become a kind of shorthand for "cautionary—but fabricated—story about sex." Say "date gone wrong" to an urban legend enthusiast, and you're likely to hear *hook myth* in response within 30 seconds or so.

There are two major versions of this classic (and much-revised) tale to consider.

Legend Lingo

The **hook myth** is an endlessly recirculated legend involving an unseen weirdo with a hook who hangs out at night around the local Lover's Lane.

The Hook (Classic Version)

➤ On a dark night, two young lovers foolishly stop their car on a seemingly isolated stretch of Lover's Lane. (Wouldn't they just?)

➤ The young lady in the car is skittish; there's a report of an escaped maniac on the radio.

➤ The weirdo on the loose is known as "The Hook" because of the gleaming metal hook he sports in place of his missing right hand.

➤ The young man starts to get angry; he thinks the girl's nervousness about the report on the radio is mere pretense to avoid other activities he's got in mind. He presses his suit.

➤ His companion rebuffs him, insisting that she has an eerie intuition that something is about to go desperately wrong.

➤ Furious, and perhaps just a little restless beneath the waistband, the guy hits the gas pedal and roars out of the Wilds of the Outlands, pointing the car, at long last, in the direction of civilization and its clear moral standards.

➤ The two exchange nary a word on the drive back.

➤ When he pulls up in front of the girl's house, he's still enough of a gentleman to get out and open the door for her.

➤ Before he can do so, however, he's confronted by a sickening sight: a metal hook hanging from the door-handle.

Fable Facts

The "hook myth" was offered as much-needed reinforcement to the moral fabric of American womanhood in the *Dear Abby* column of November 8, 1960. Somehow, the sexual revolution unfolded anyway a few years later.

Talk about your close call. Is there any possibility, do you suppose, that the pointed, invasive instrument of evil intent appended to the madman could carry a symbolic meaning?

The Hook (Oft-Revised Version)

➤ Dark night, Lover's Lane, hopeful young man, radio report of hook-armed maniac, skittish young lady ....

➤ Hopeful young man locks all the doors in the car, in a misguided attempt to assure the skittish young lady of her safety.

➤ This strategy, however, only succeeds in turning his date into a weeping, hysterical mess. Her prescient, eerie sensation that something deeply wrong is afoot gives way to a full-scale crying fit.

➤ The mood is effectively shattered.

Fable Facts

Close Call Department: The "hook" story is the most famous urban legend involving a life-threatening episode narrowly avoided.

➤ Furious and restless beneath the waistband, he stomps on the accelerator and gives her the silent treatment on the way home ....

➤ The cad of a boyfriend *refuses* to do the gallant thing and open the door for his date.

➤ Forced to exit the vehicle herself, the girl steps out of the car—and sees a hook hanging from some part of the exterior. (The hook is on the door handle in some versions, and hanging from a window that has not been completely rolled up in others.)

Concerned fathers of teenaged girls across the land think to themselves, "Let's hear it for intuitions and crying fits!"

The unforgettable story maps out some fascinating psychological terrain. In essence, the "hook" story is telling teenagers, particularly young women, not to dismiss that still, small voice telling them to postpone sexual activity—not to yield to the many pressures that may be brought to bear upon them.

If the young lady in the story *hadn't* stood her ground, who can say what horrible fate would have awaited her?

Meet Skinned Tom

Ready for another nightmare? How about getting sent to the underworld for cheating, when you didn't even know you were cheating? It happened to poor, libidinous Skinned Tom.

Back when he was still alive, the guy who would eventually win fame throughout the South as Skinned Tom was a handsome dude with a history of romantic conquests involving beautiful women. In fact, he "used up" *all* the beautiful women in his own hometown and decided to see what kind of pickings were available in the next town over.

How doomed is *this* guy?

Ahem. Back to our story. Tom, you probably won't be surprised to learn, sealed his grisly fate when he decided to move on to greener pastures. In the next town over, he met a comely young lady who caught his fancy. Unfortunately, she was married. Even more unfortunately, she neglected to inform Tom of this fact.

Fable Facts

The Skinned Tom story, which originated in the American South, appears to predate the "hook" myth and may have influenced it.

Fable Facts

The faithless wife in the Skinned Tom story actually survives her brushes with the handsome stranger from out of town and her own jealous husband. The grave physical injury she sustains may be symbolic of her ruined reputation.

The deceitful vixen embarked on a torrid affair with the virile out-of-towner. One night, the two drove in Tom's car and parked on a seemingly isolated stretch of Lover's Lane. (Sound familiar?) The two were successfully redefining the term "automotive acceleration" when suddenly, someone jerked open the car door.

It was—oops—the deceitful vixen's husband. And he wasn't happy.

Talk about your awkward social situation. Is there anything in Miss Manners that covers what you say when you find yourself face-to-face with the guy you suddenly realize is married to the woman you're presently ravishing?

The jealous husband produced a knife and went to work on his faithless wife, dealing a vicious blow to her abdomen. (Yuck.) Then it was Tom's turn.

Poor Tom pleaded for his life, but the husband was not to be reasoned with. He pulled Tom from the vehicle and proceeded to remove just about every square inch of skin from the libidinous fellow's body. (You were wondering where that catchy nickname came in, weren't you?)

Legend Lingo

A **phallic symbol** is an object whose shape or function broadly coincides with or calls to mind a penis—especially an object associated with power or force, such as the knife in the Skinned Tom story.

Once he had made certain that Tom wouldn't be impressing any more young ladies with his good looks, the husband fled the scene, leaving his *phallic symbol*—er, knife—behind. Later that night, consumed by guilt over his bloody deeds, the husband turned himself in to the authorities and told them what had happened. When the cops hit the scene, they found that the wife was, against all odds, still alive. She survived the attack, but Tom was never seen again.

Unless, of course, you count those strange reports of a knife-wielding, skinless ghost who wanders Lover's Lane in search of couples about to accelerate in an unsafe manner.

Two morals (at least) are available for inspection here. First, for the gentlemen, stick to the local girls—if only because it's easier to determine with accuracy whether they're attached to violent, jealous males. Second, for the ladies, watch out for those good-looking, fast-talking out-of-towners because they're probably a lot more dangerous than they appear.

Fable Facts

Skinned Tom's terrifying adventure, like the "hook" story, may owe its popularity to the fact that it encourages kids to avoid engaging in promiscuous behavior when they step outside of their parents' sphere of influence.

Strange but True

Like many other urban legends dealing with sexual morality, the Skinned Tom story appears to operate on a double moral standard. The story suggests that Tom's flaw is heedlessness and lack of caution rather than a failure to remain chaste in the first place. (If only he had kept on despoiling the honor of local girls!) The woman in the story, on the other hand, should simply have stayed home with her husband.

Maniacs at the Shopping Mall

You were whining recently about having trouble finding a parking place at the local supermall? Count your blessings. At least you weren't approached by a lunatic trying to pull a Norman Bates on you by "helping" you with an unexpected flat tire.

Strange but True

Norman Bates, the front-desk man at the Bates Motel, is a severely unbalanced character in Alfred Hitchcock's horror classic *Psycho;* the part was originally portrayed by Anthony Perkins. After bringing food to his guest Marian Crane (Janet Leigh), Bates sneaks up on Crane in the shower, pulls out a wicked-looking knife, and does her in—all while sporting a fetching outfit he borrowed from his mom.

Urban legends involving loonies who find ways to seclude themselves with pretty young women—so they can butcher them—are common. Interestingly, the nightmarish, surreal tone of the first 30 minutes or so of Hitchcock's masterpiece is strongly reminiscent of many urban legends involving murderous sociopaths.

"Can I Help with That Flat Tire?"

Apparently, these are words to fear if you encounter them in a mall parking lot. Consider the following breathless warning:

A woman was shopping at the Tuttle Mall in Columbus. She came out to her car and saw she had a flat. She got her jack and spare out of the trunk. A man in a business suit came up and started to help her. When the tire had been replaced, he asked for a ride to his car on the opposite side of the mall. Feeling uncomfortable about doing this, she stalled for a while, but he kept pressing her. She finally asked why he was on this side of the mall if his car was on the other. He had been talking to friends, he claimed. Still uncomfortable, she told him that she had just remembered something she had forgotten to pick up at the mall, and she left him and went back inside the mall. She reported the incident to the mall security, and they went out to her car.

The man was nowhere in sight. Opening her trunk, she discovered a brief case the man had set inside her trunk while helping her with the tire. Inside were rope and a butcher knife! When she took the tire to be fixed, the mechanic informed her that there was nothing wrong with her tire, that it was flat because the air had been let out of it!

The moral of this story: Learn to change your own tire, call someone you know and trust to help you, or call mall security in the first place to assist you. Please be safe and not sorry. Although this happened in Columbus, it could happen anywhere there are NUTS around. Just a warning to always be alert.

Fable Facts

Equally fictional stories about close calls at shopping malls involve women who are *almost* tricked into smelling "perfume"— actually ether—that would render them unconscious and vulnerable to abduction to points unknown or other sinister abuse. Fear of being compromised while asleep or intoxicated may be a factor here. See, for comparison, the Progesterex myth that appears in Chapter 12, "Total Strangers Are Out to Get Someone You Love."

> Pass this along to every woman you have access to. Never
> let your guard down. Good story for women to know about—
> although with the NUTS in today's world, everyone needs to
> be careful (not just women).

Tires. Okay. The moral is about learning to change tires. Actually, though, the moral of the story *may* also be that male sexuality often features a streak of violent, anti-social insanity hidden beneath a veneer of respectability.

Is there, perhaps, a knife lurking within a seemingly exemplary citizen's briefcase near you?

Maniacs Stalk the Babysitter

Every morning, some Hollywood film executive wakes up and thanks his lucky stars for stories about lunatics and baby sitters. Where, after all, would the slasher movie genre be without innocent baby sitters for madmen to terrorize?

There are enough baby sitter myths circulating to make one suspect there may not be enough actual lunatics to account for them all. Here's a classic example.

➤ A pretty female baby sitter (is there any other kind?) has just gotten the kids to go to sleep. With the house to herself, she switches on the TV and prepares to relax for a while.

➤ Wacko calls her up and starts breathing heavily into the phone.

➤ The baby sitter hangs up and tries to forget the call.

➤ A couple of minutes later, the wacko calls again. More heavy breathing.

➤ The baby sitter hangs up for a second time.

➤ The phone rings again. Guess who? No heavy breathing this time, though.

➤ Instead, the wacko asks in a menacing voice, "Aren't you going to check on the kids?"

➤ This really rattles the baby sitter's cage; she calls 911 and explains the calls she has been receiving. The 911 guy urges her to keep the caller on the line for as long as possible next time so they can trace the call.

➤ Sure enough, the wacko calls again. The baby sitter follows the 911 operator's instructions. More ominous babble. The call concludes, despite her best efforts to keep him on the line longer.

➤ Instantly, the phone rings again. It's the 911 guy.

➤ He's beside himself. "Get the kids out of the house—and get out yourself—*right now!* The call is coming from another line *inside the house you're calling from!*"

The kids, alas, have all had their throats slit. But the baby sitter escapes—and lives to be terrorized another day.

Are you young? Female? Virginal? Dutiful? If so, there may well be a nameless, face-less, bloodthirsty lunatic out to put an unhappy end to childhood—lurking right there in your midst. And you may not even realize it.

Odd, is it not, that there don't seem to be any stories about helpless teenaged *boys* terrorized by insane *female* predators late at night? Maybe we're just a little afraid that *every* man has a bit of the lunatic inside him.

Maniacs Sneak Under Your Bed

The following legend, which continues the theme of a madman lurking in your very midst, has a long and storied history. Here's a recent e-mail incarnation.

> Once there was a beautiful young girl who lived in a small town just south of Farmersburg. Her parents had to go to town for a while, so they left their daughter home alone, but pro-tected by her dog, which was a very large Collie. The parents told the girl to lock all the windows and doors after they had left. And at about 8:00 P.M. the parents went to town. Doing what she was told, the girl shut and locked every window and every door. But there was one window in the basement that would not close completely.
>
> Trying as best as she could, she finally got the window shut, but it would not lock. So she left the window and went back upstairs. But just to make sure that no one could get in, she put the deadbolt lock on the basement door.
>
> Then she sat down, had some dinner, and decided to go to sleep for the night. Settling down to sleep at about 12:00 A.M., she snuggled up with the dog and fell asleep.
>
> But at one point, she suddenly woke up. She turned and looked at the clock—it was 2:30. She snuggled down again wondering what had woken her, when she heard a noise. It was a dripping sound. She thought that she had left the water running, and now it was dripping into the drain of her sink. So, thinking it was no big deal, she decided to go back to sleep.
>
> But she felt nervous, so she reached her hand over the edge of her bed and let the dog lick her hand for reassurance that he would protect her. Again at about 3:45, she woke up hearing

dripping. She was slightly angry now but went back to sleep anyway. Again she reached down and let the dog lick her hand. Then she fell back to sleep.

At 6:52 the girl decided that she had had enough. She got up just in time to see her parents pulling up to the house. "Good," she thought. "Now somebody can fix the sink, 'cause I know I didn't leave it running." She walked to the bathroom, and there was the Collie dog, skinned and hung up on the curtain rod. The noise she heard was its blood dripping into a puddle on the floor. The girl screamed and ran to her bedroom to get a weapon, in case someone was still in the house—and there, on the floor next to her bed, she saw a small note, written in blood, saying: "HUMANS CAN LICK TOO, MY BEAUTIFUL."

Yet another beautiful young woman in jeopardy. Yet another hairsbreadth 'scape in the imminent deadly breach. Yet another spine-chilling reminder of the passing of the period of life when adult protections (like a big, loveable Collie) can be counted on.

Somewhere, deep in the heart of Farmersburg, USA, a very quiet man indeed lurks under a bed. He may be a recent escapee from the local asylum for the criminally insane. Then again, he may be the harsh truths of life in the adult world, where beautiful things die, Mom and Dad aren't around, people aren't what they seem to be, and the door to the hall of madness is always left slightly ajar.

The Least You Need to Know

➤ In compiling your list of famous urban legends about sex (or anything else, for that matter), consider putting the infamous "hook" story at or near the top.

➤ Pity poor Skinned Tom, stick to the local girls, and recall that gender-based double standards are alive and well in the dreamlike world of urban legends.

➤ Although stories about nicely dressed, briefcase-wielding madmen who prowl shopping malls are exaggerated, to say the least, evidence of uneasiness about the dark side of male sexuality is not.

➤ Check for the presence of a second line in the house before you accept your next baby-sitting job—just to be on the safe side. While you're at it, check under the bed.

Chapter 23

Too Disgusting for Words

In This Chapter

➤ The E.G. problem (or, why a chapter like this in the first place?)

➤ Infested tacos

➤ Nauseating bug dilemmas

➤ Deadly bananas

➤ Warehouse nightmares

➤ A really, really bad rebound relationship

➤ An unusual cookie recipe

Okay. You're working on this book about urban legends, and, every once in a while, you come across stories that make you say, right out loud, "Eeeeew, gross" (hereafter, "E.G.").

You put the stories aside because, deep down, you don't really want people who are reading your book to have to say "E.G." any more than is absolutely necessary.

Then it occurs to you that many of the most enduring myths and legends of all—the story of Little Red Riding Hood, say—feature story elements intended to make the hearer say "E.G." We've just gotten used to them over the centuries. (Come on: Wolf eats little old lady? Wolf eats little girl? Woodsman hacks wolf apart?)

You also ponder the possibility that the very act of saying "E.G." may well be a necessary part of coming to terms with unsavory but illuminating lessons. You consider, too, that this "E.G." process is, in varying degrees, probably an important element of the whole urban legend experience.

So you begin to wonder whether there might not be some legitimate, if queasiness-inducing, function served by stories that occupy what might be considered the far end of the E.G. spectrum.

A Service to One's Readers

You decide you really ought to put at least some of the high "E.G." quotient stories in the book, if only because they often provide some interesting variants on legends that have arisen elsewhere in the book.

And yet, as a service to your readers, you feel these stories should be segregated somehow. Why? So people who don't feel like combating nausea on a regular basis won't be asked to do so every chapter or two.

Thus, you devote an entire chapter near the end of the book to stories that are (usually) interesting and illuminating but (always) undeniably raw. You do this because you figure people who have already had enough of the excesses of our modern media culture will appreciate the opportunity to skip this stuff if they want to.

So, what's the point? The point is that if you continue reading, you are welcome to do so. You stand forewarned, however. If you find yourself repeating a certain phrase that starts with the word "Eeeeew" and concludes with the word "Gross," that's because you have chosen to continue through the slime in search of the occasional shred of meaning.

A final note: What follows definitely ain't for the younger set. To paraphrase George Carlin, only the very old should take it on.

Pass the Tacos, Please

We'll begin at the local fast-food taco outlet.

If you've made it this far in the book and taken every story literally, you already know that every major corporation in America is out to get you. You already know that crawling vermin and their progeny are everywhere. And you may well suspect that any food other than that which you yourself grow and process is not to be trusted.

What you may *not* know is that *all three* of these disturbing trends are capable of converging in a single, nauseating urban legend. Here's the proof. (Don't eat while you read this.)

```
TRUE STORY:

HEY! HOW ABOUT TACO BELL?

This girl was really in a hurry one day, so she just stopped
off at a Taco Bell and got a chicken soft taco and ate it on
the way home. That night, she noticed her jaw was kind of
```

tight and swollen. The next day it was a little worse, so she went to her doctor. He said she just had an allergic reaction to something and gave her some cream to rub on her jaw to help. After a couple of days, the swelling had just gotten worse, and she could hardly move her jaw. She went back to her doctor to see what was wrong. Her doctor had no idea, so he started to run some tests. They scrubbed out the inside of her mouth to get tissue samples, and they also took some saliva samples. Well, they found out what was wrong. Apparently her chicken soft taco had a pregnant roach in it. When she ate it, the eggs then somehow got into her saliva glands and, well, she was incubating them. They had to remove a couple of layers of her inner mouth to get all the eggs out.

If they hadn't figured out what was going on, the eggs would have hatched inside the lining of her mouth!!!!!!!!!!

She's suing Taco Bell! Of course.

If you need to find out more about this, it's in the November 19 New York Times. If you still want Taco Bell after this one, you're really brave. PASS THE WORD AND BE VERY CAREFUL!

If that's not a 10-exclamation-point story, I don't know what is.

What's that, you say? "E.G."? Oh, we're much too early on in the game for you to throw in the towel. There's loads more material ahead.

Ready for a shocker? No account matching the details of the Taco Bell story has appeared in the *New York Times*. What's more, as far as anyone has been able to determine, no such event has taken place as the result of a visit to Taco Bell or at any other fast-food restaurant.

Well, at least the post office is safe.

Wait a minute ....

And More of Those Adorable Roaches

Here, apparently, is the formula for urban-legend notoriety: Take something everyone now does without incident (in the following stories, it's licking envelopes in the local post office), and link it up with something unutterably disgusting. That way you can be sure that your story will circulate.

Every time somebody thinks about performing that common act, that person will have to stop and think about the horrible thing you've associated with the innocuous act.

Roll the tape, please.

> If you lick your envelopes, you won't anymore!
>
> A woman was working in a post office in California. One day she licked the envelopes and postage stamps instead of using a sponge. That very day the lady cut her tongue on the envelope.
>
> A week later, she noticed an abnormal swelling of her tongue. She went to the doctor, and they found nothing wrong. Her tongue was not sore or anything.
>
> A couple of days later, her tongue started to swell more, and it began to get really sore—so sore that she could not eat. She went back to the hospital and demanded something be done. The doctor took an x-ray of her tongue and noticed a lump. He prepared her for minor surgery.
>
> When the doctor cut her tongue open, a live roach crawled out. There were roach eggs on the seal of the envelope. The egg was able to hatch inside of her tongue because of her saliva. It was warm and moist ….
>
> This is a true story …. Pass it on.

All together, now: "E.G.!"

The post office thing puzzles me. A week passes without incident or pain, but she recalls that fateful episode with the envelope, puts two and two together, and a new victim of the bug epidemic is poised to tell her story.

By the way, the bugs with which we share this beautiful planet certainly seem to be cunning, sly, and hell-bent on reproduction within the bodies of human females, don't they?

And If You Haven't Heard Enough Yet About Bugs ...

Remember all that business about vanity and beehive hairdos back in Chapter 9, "All Creatures, Great and Small"? Well, you'll need to in order to make sense of what follows.

The story so far: Looks-obsessed young lady loves the way her beehive 'do turns guys' heads, but she hates all the maintenance ... so she pastes her hairdo in place with sugar water for weeks on end and sleeps with a special pillow. Ending A: The coiffure attracts rats (or bugs) that gnaw her to death while she sleeps.

Wait until you get a load of Ending B, which carries the warning against vanity and self-obsession to a whole new level. In this version, the method of getting the hairdo to stand up isn't sugar-water, but a batch of bread dough. She keeps the dough in place for weeks.

For some reason she starts experiencing strange, persistent headaches. She heads over to the doctor's office to figure out what's up, where she learns that her scalp is infested with maggots.

Say "E.G.," somebody.

The Bug Infestation Thing, Continued

You wanted gross bug stories? We've got gross bug stories.

Surreptitious infestation is not, of course, limited to the beehive-hairdo legend. Consider the tale of the young woman who ignored the classic parental warning, "Don't pick at that." (Leading to the question: Are any *other* classic parental warnings being ignored?)

As the tale goes, the fair lass started obsessing about what appeared to be a pimple on her cheek. After a few days, the thing had refused to disappear. She decided to burst it, but when she did so, dozens of spiders come crawling out of her face. At this point, she either faints, goes insane, or has a heart attack from the shock of it all and dies.

She did this, of course, after shrieking "E.G." at the top of her lungs.

Fable Facts

The surrealistic profusion of legends with bugs that infest careless young women while they aren't looking suggests there may be some sexual subtheme at work in these stories.

The Whole Bug Thing Continues Well Past the Point of Overkill

The bug-legend hits just keep on coming, friends. Aren't you glad you decided to stick with this chapter?

The following Internet extension of the classic spiders-are-everywhere theme adds a sickening new twist. This time, the creepy-crawlies are lurking in public toilets. One less thing to be certain of in this crazy world of ours, eh?

Other than the inconvenient facts that there is no such publication as the *Journal of the United Medical Association,* no such destination as Blare Airport, no such agency as the Civilian Aeronautics Board, and no such animal as the bum-chomping Blush Spider (ingeniously designated arachnius gluteus), the following story checks out just fine.

WARNING: From Texas A&M International University

An article by Dr. Beverly Clark, in the Journal of the United Medical Association (JUMA), the mystery behind a recent spate of deaths has been solved. If you haven't already heard about it in the news, here is what happened.

Three women in Chicago turned up at hospitals over a five-day period, all with the same symptoms: fever, chills, and vomiting, followed by muscular collapse, paralysis, and, finally, death. There were no outward signs of trauma. Autopsy results showed toxicity in the blood.

These women did not know each other and seemed to have nothing in common. It was discovered, however, that they had all visited the same restaurant (Big Chappies, at Blare Airport) within days of their deaths. The health department descended on the restaurant, shutting it down. The food, water, and air conditioning were all inspected and tested, to no avail.

The big break came when a waitress at the restaurant was rushed to the hospital with similar symptoms. She told doctors that she had been on vacation and had only gone to the restaurant to pick up her check. She did not eat or drink while she was there, but had used the restroom.

That is when one toxicologist, remembering an article he had read, drove out to the restaurant, went into the restroom, and lifted the toilet seat. Under the seat, out of normal view, was a small spider. The spider was captured and brought back to the lab, where it was determined to be the South American Blush Spider (arachnius gluteus), so named because of its reddened flesh color. This spider's venom is extremely toxic but can take several days to take effect. They live in cold, dark, damp climates, and toilet rims provide just the right atmosphere.

"Just the right atmosphere," eh? Whose idea of "right" are we assuming here?

Lethal spiders traversing your nether regions in public restrooms. How's *that* for a mental image worthy of an "E.G."?

Yes, We Have Flesh-Eating Banana Bacteria

Okay. What have we got so far? Tacos crawling with bug eggs? Maggots on the brain? Spiders lurking beneath the toilet seat?

What could possibly top any of that on the "E.G." scale? Well, how about a rousing scourge of contagious flesh-eating bacteria—transmitted by the bananas in your local supermarket?

> Several shipments of bananas from Costa Rica have been infected with necrotizing fasciitis, otherwise known as flesh-eating bacteria. Recently, this disease has decimated the monkey population in Costa Rica. We are now just learning that the disease has been able to graft itself to the skin of fruits in the region, most notably the banana, which is Costa Rica's largest export. Until this finding, scientists were not sure how the infection was being transmitted.
>
> It is advised not to purchase bananas for the next three weeks because this is the period of time for which bananas that have been shipped to the United States with the possibility of carrying this disease.
>
> If you have eaten a banana in the last two to three days and come down with a fever followed by a skin infection, SEEK MEDICAL ATTENTION! The skin infection from necrotizing fasciitis is very painful and eats 2 to 3 centimeters of flesh per hour. Amputation is likely; death is possible. If you are more than an hour from a medical center, burning the flesh ahead of the infected area is advised to help slow the spread of the infection.
>
> The FDA has been reluctant to issue a countrywide warning because of a fear of nationwide panic. They have secretly admitted that they feel upwards of 15,000 Americans will be affected by this but that these are "acceptable numbers." Please forward this to as many of the people you care about as possible because we do not feel 15,000 people is an acceptable number!

Your tax dollars at work!

Clearly, those mindless boobs at the FDA simply don't care how many people are consumed by the latest rampant flesh-eating epidemic. They don't care how many people have to set themselves on fire in order to avoid summary amputation. No, all they want to do is prevent a panic. They don't even trust us to set ourselves on fire in an orderly fashion, as the authors of the message clearly do.

The story is false, of course.

Strange but True

The bacteria associated with the so-called "flesh-eating" disease is real. It is, however, incapable of surviving outside of living tissue, which makes the report of a looming banana epidemic a bit of a stretch.

Note that the supposed epidemic is linked ominously with a food product imported from a foreign country. Yet again, we are reminded that anything that comes from faraway regions is potentially lethal.

Now enjoy that peanut-butter-and-banana sandwich. Don't even think about bananas that eat 2 to 3 centimeters of *you* per hour.

Rats!

Other variations on this type of myth include the well-traveled story that lethal layers of rat urine reside on the tops of soda cans and other types consumer packaging. This leads us to a sickening new take on a familiar message: Someone has forgotten to check the safety list, and disaster awaits if you follow your standard routine.

So, not only do you have to avoid licking envelopes these days, but your favorite soft drink is now likely to be accompanied by a rat-urine chaser. Tasty!

HEALTH ALERT: Whenever you buy a can of coke or any other canned soft drink, please make sure that you wash the top with running water and soap, or, if not available, drink with a straw.

A family friend's friend died after drinking a can of soda! Apparently, she didn't clean the top before drinking from the can. The top was encrusted with dried rat's urine, which is toxic and obviously lethal!

Canned drinks and other foodstuffs are stored in warehouses and containers that are usually infested outlets without being properly cleaned.

Please forward this message to the people you care about. Thanks.

Touching, the concern for humanity. Or at least it would be if there were a single verified case conforming to the circumstances described in the "alert."

The main purpose of the message, of course, is to get readers to scream (you guessed it) "E.G." and begin scrubbing away crystals of (nonexistent) rat urine.

I Said, "No Mayonnaise!"

An especially graphic variant on the many fast-food nightmares making the rounds, this next legend follows a picky customer through the aisles of one of the major national burger emporiums. The salient events:

> ➤ A picky customer (who is generally a woman) orders a chicken sandwich with no mayonnaise.

> ➤ Her order eventually materializes, and she whisks it back to one of the tables in the restaurant.

> ➤ She takes only a bite or two of the sandwich, though, before she discovers a creamy, white sauce-like substance slathered liberally about the chicken patty.

> ➤ Furious, she returns to the counter and tells the attendant something like the following: "I thought I was very clear: I ordered a chicken sandwich with no mayonnaise!"

> ➤ And with that, she removes the bread and displays the chicken patty—only to find, upon further examination, that the "sauce" was actually pus from an infected chicken.

This charming variation on the classic "Kentucky Fried Rat" story (see Chapter 13, "Tales of Hell from the Service Economy") takes paranoia about irresponsible strangers and mixes it with a generous dose of gender-based stereotyping. Once again, the victim of the memorable fast-food foul-up is a woman. (Unspoken message: It serves her right for being in a fast-food restaurant in the first place; she should have been home in the kitchen.) And anyway, don't abrasive people deserve whatever they get? Like, say, a mouth full of chicken pus?

Fortunately, no documented story matching the details of this "E.G." classic has ever turned up. Bon appétit.

And Finally ...

We conclude with a heartwarming pair of old-fashioned, romantic urban legends. Each takes a teaspoon or so of tense gender conflict, adds a heaping helping of revulsion, throws in a couple of mature-audiences-only morsels, shakes vigorously, and pours the whole nasty mess down your throat.

Don't Believe It!

A friendly warning: The final two legends in this chapter nearly caused your humble author to wear out the brand-new euphemism generator he got for Christmas. If you want to skip this wrap-up and go straight to the next chapter, you're well within your rights.

Don't Believe It!

Curious about the precise symptoms of the disease contracted by the young lady in the legend about the really bad rebound relationship? Look 'em up yourself; there are limits, even in our open-minded age. Anyway, such conditions are apparently possible but extremely rare. The demented necrophiliac who engineers the one-night-stand-from-hell, however, appears to be a symptom of someone's twisted imagination.

If you're looking for a great way to break the ice on your next date, you probably shouldn't consider passing along these stories. Unless, of course, you have an air sickness bag handy for the inevitable moment when your date says "E.G." and starts to change color.

The Really, Really Bad Rebound Relationship

A young lady breaks up with her boyfriend and is deeply distraught. Heedless to the many urban legends warning of the dangers of sex with complete strangers in the AIDS era, she heads to the singles bar, allows herself to get picked up, and has a night of exuberant, unsafe sex.

If you've guessed by now that something awful is about to happen to her, give yourself 10 points.

A strange and uncomfortable itch about her nether regions sends the young lady to the doctor. After examining her, the doctor looks worried, refuses to talk about her condition, and schedules her for a visit with a specialist. The specialist, equally solemn, gives her the same silent treatment, makes her undergo some tests, and tells her he'll be back in touch in a week.

A few days later, a policeman arrives at her door and wants to talk to her about her recent sexual partners. Apparently, the law enforcement authorities are always alerted in this way when a doctor encounters a case of corpse-worm, which is what our heroine has. Turns out she should have asked her last fling a couple of critical questions—like whether or not he'd been recently employed at a hospital or morgue. The dude apparently had a thing for girls who were quiet. Too quiet. And cold. Too cold.

The Fateful Cookie Recipe

A secret recipe for cookies is the revolting point around which this stomach-churning Persian Gulf War legend turns.

In this raunchy retelling of the already raunchy "I *told* you I wanted a divorce" story that appears in Chapter 19, "Amatory Comeuppance," a Marine corporal stationed in some Godforsaken desert outpost rounds up his buddies to enjoy a care package his wife has sent along from the USA. In the package is a batch of homemade cookies— and a video. The corporal passes around the cookies and pops the tape into his VCR.

As the men munch the cookies, the corporal's wife appears on the TV screen. Stark naked. Mixing cookie dough busily in a great big bowl. Following the dark and inevitable logic that drives only dreams and urban legends, the corporal allows the show to continue.

As the video continues, the wife puts on quite a display for her husband. A naked, aroused man appears in the kitchen. The wife promptly fellates him. (If you don't know what "fellates" means and you were hoping for a "Legend Lingo" box around here, you can keep dreaming.)

Fable Facts

The incorporation of graphic content—sexual or of any other variety—appears to be a reliable way to ensure that an urban legend survives and captures the attention of its audience. A number of unforgettable examples of this phenomenon appear here; you should have seen what the Powers That Be refused to allow in the book.

The man in the video has a truly marvelous time with the corporal's wife. In fact, it's his *having* such a marvelous time that provides the secret ingredient in that unusual cookie recipe.

You saw this twist in the story arriving, yes? At the critical moment, the lady points her partner toward the big cookie bowl she was working on so assiduously as the video began. The moment is recorded for posterity. Then comes a close-up of the wife's face as she tells the corporal that she hopes he enjoys the cookies and mentions that she'd like a divorce.

And with that, the final "E.G." of the book, we (mercifully) bring this chapter to its conclusion.

The Least You Need to Know

➤ Recall (as if you could forget) that a number of urban legends are truly disgusting.

➤ In evaluating legends involving insect infestation, note that the bugs with which we share this beautiful planet certainly appear to be cunning, sly, and hell-bent on reproduction within the bodies of human females.

➤ Exercise care in selecting menu items at your local fast-food emporium—but don't do so on the assumption that various foul substances or organisms are lurking within your next meal, because that would be paranoid.

➤ Warnings about the perils of unprotected sex don't get a whole lot more nauseating than the story of the "Really, Really Bad Rebound Relationship."

➤ If your significant other shows up nude in a videotape you receive as part of a care package featuring baked goods, play it safe: Stop munching the goodies for a moment and view the tape through to its conclusion. Just in case.

Chapter 24

Some Final Thoughts

In This Chapter

➤ Always a strange story ahead

➤ The Big Four Web sites

➤ Newsgroups you might want to consider joining

➤ The Urban Legend Generator

➤ One more legend for the road

In this, the last chapter of the book, you learn why no book on urban legends is ever really complete. You also find out about some cool Web sites you can use to check out whether a story you've heard is on the up-and-up, and pass along stories you've encountered that others might have missed. (Because urban legends tend to reinvent themselves on a regular basis, and because you are now familiar with some of the major forms, you're probably more likely to encounter this situation than you may have realized.)

There's Always Another Strange Story Ahead

No volume can catalog every urban legend.

The existing stories are constantly being recycled, and new ones are always emerging to capture the popular attention and imagination. It's a humbling experience even

Don't Believe It!

Anyone who suggests that there are more authoritative or trustworthy World Wide Web resources than the Big Four listed in this chapter may be spreading a new, pernicious, and totally false legend.

trying to cull a representative sampling of the major legends: You're never far from the creeping suspicion that you've left something important out.

Doubtless, this book is missing any number of important or classic legends and has come out too late to cover the latest credulity- and mind-stretching story that "really happened" to a FOAF. Readers are directed, however, to a list of Web sites offered in this chapter in penance for the unsettling fact that any book like this is, by definition, at least technically obsolete upon publication. Each of the "Big Four" continually updated sites profiled in this chapter features a wealth of superb information on subjects of interest to urban legend enthusiasts and other Seekers of the Truth (and the Truly Weird).

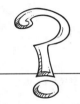

Strange but True

Supposedly, we are all living in the Information Age. Actually, we're all living in the Bad Information Age, an era in which a good chunk, and probably the majority, of what shows up on the Internet is (literally) incredible—that is to say, not worthy of belief. The four sites referenced here are refreshingly baloney-free zones offering responsible, accountable, intelligent, get-to-the-bottom-of-it assessments of some of the most outrageous tales ever. If you're not certain about the status of a story you've heard, or if you want to pass along a yarn that you feel merits inclusion as a new urban legend, you should definitely check out these pages.

And now, the Big Four ....

The San Fernando Valley Folklore Society's "Urban Legends Reference Page"

Check it out at: www.snopes.com

This is easily among the most fascinating, relentlessly entertaining sites on the Internet. If the San Fernando Valley Folklore Society's pages don't constitute the classiest, most impressive, and most rigorously researched Web site devoted exclusively to urban legends, I'll take a dive into the albino alligator-infested sewers of any metropolis you care to name.

The site is remarkably user-friendly, avoiding the blindness-inducing black-type-on-gray-background "layout" in evidence on various amateur sites. (Actually, all of the Web sites profiled in this chapter combine great content with layout that's relatively easy on the eyes.)

The "Urban Legends Reference Pages" make surfing easy by offering a number of intelligently designed category designations, sidebar lists, color codes, and brightly colored cartoon icons. Concise, graphically arresting summaries give you the key facts on each of the legends explored.

The material on the site is researched and written by the husband-and-wife team of Barbara and David Mikkelson. They strive valiantly to identify themselves as humble hobbyists who maintain the pages as little more than a side interest, and they disclaim any attempt to position themselves as "urban legend experts." Their ceaseless waves of skeptical, good-humored, cogent, and meticulous research, however, tell another story. Friends, I have seen amateur Web sites about urban legends. This one is in another league entirely. The Mikkelsons know their stuff—and they're excellent writers, to boot.

Fable Facts

Visit www.snopes.com for the best overall English-language site about urban legends in the known universe.

Fable Facts

The name "Snopes" in the San Fernando Valley Folklore Society's Web site address is borrowed from a family of characters who appear throughout the works of William Faulkner.

The members of the fictional Snopes family display a variety of unfortunate and socially irresponsible characteristics.

"The AFU & Urban Legends Archive"

Check it out at: www.urbanlegends.com

"The AFU & Urban Legends Archive"—an offspring of alt.folklore.urban, the preeminent newsgroup in the field—is much more of a committee effort. Some 33 people are credited in it as being responsible for the brisk and exhaustive (but unevenly written) legends archive; they are identified under the intriguing category designation "People with No Lives."

Fable Facts

Visit www.urbanlegends.com to catch up on the heated debates—and unassailable final pronouncements—of the alt.folklore.urban newsgroup.

What the site lacks in literary polish it more than makes up for in conclusive, responsible assessment. The AFU site is regarded as the ultimate authority when it comes to settling the often rancorous debates associated with urban legends. Given the exacting "group-think" approach of the debates among its contributors and the depth of their combined experience, it should be.

You can get reliable, if occasionally curt, updates on the status of just about every urban legend under the sun by using the site's search engine. The various category headings offering groupings of theme-linked legends may initially be a bit of a challenge for the novice, but they're worth figuring out.

The AFU site has its idiosyncrasies and is definitely not as user-friendly as www.snopes.com, but the brash humor, iconoclastic spirit, and high intellect with which it addresses its subject can definitely make a believer out of you.

"About.com's Guide to Urban Legends"

Check it out at: www.urbanlegends.about.com

Fable Facts

Visit www.urbanlegends.about. com for a good introduction to the world of urban legends.

This site is set up rather like a magazine or newspaper question-and-answer column.

It's well-organized and highly readable. The content, like that of all four of the sites reviewed here, is extremely reliable, if not particularly groundbreaking, and the site features a good cross-section of the most popular legends. It loses out to the previous two sites referenced in terms of thoroughness and overall scope, but the same can be said of every other English-language site devoted to urban legends I encountered.

Well-researched responses to questions are provided by David Emery, a strong writer with a bright, amusing style, who describes himself as an "avid chronicler of urban folklore, with special emphasis on the lore and folklife of the Internet," Emery's experience as a writer of comedy and urban commentary appears to have given him a good vantage point from which to assess the ludicrous and often perplexing controversies often associated with urban legends.

This fun, informative, and concise site is extremely easy to navigate and a good first step for those new to the subject.

"The Straight Dope"

Check it out at: www.straightdope.com

This one is not devoted exclusively to our stated topic—but who cares?

This site features an archive of compulsively engaging newspaper columns from Cecil Adams (the self-described "world's most intelligent human being"), as well as other articles assembled by members of his team. "The Straight Dope" team's motto is "Fighting ignorance since 1974. (It's taking longer than we thought.)" They'll beat it decisively one day, though, one suspects.

Here's how it works. Ordinary mortals (known collectively by the heartwarming collective appellation "the Teeming Millions") pose tough questions to Uncle Cecil. He answers them authoritatively and in a manner wholly consistent with the standards one might associate with a human being endowed with more brainpower than any other representative of the species.

Want the inside skinny on the sound of one hand clapping? Cecil's got it covered. Curious about what would happen to the Earth's orbit if everyone in China stood on chairs and jumped off of them at precisely the same moment? It's here. As you might expect, a fair number of urban legends have also gotten a sassy, attitude-heavy once-over in Adams's carefully researched columns over the years. You can locate relevant articles easily using the site's search engine.

So go ahead. Walk in the door to learn about what Cecil's got to say about the various AIDS legends. You'll stick around to find out precisely what would happen if someone knocked out the moon with a nuclear missile. Strange drawings from the (fortunately) inimitable Slug Signorino adorn the pages.

Fable Facts

Visit www.straightdope.com for answers to questions about popular urban legends—and to get answers to questions you never would have thought to ask in the first place.

Legend Lingo

A **newsgroup** is an online forum or discussion group. There are countless discussion groups on the Internet. In order to see and post messages to a newsgroup, you need software that incorporates a "news reader" function; most good e-mail programs offer this capability.

Newsgroups You Might Want to Consider Joining

A *newsgroup* is an electronic discussion group devoted to a single topic. Most are easy to monitor by means of the most popular e-mail software programs (like Microsoft Outlook). Though usually thought of as vehicles for e-mailed correspondence, many newsgroups nevertheless use Web sites to post archived messages, answer common questions, and handle other business.

The biggie is alt.folklore.urban.

And then there's everyone else …

➤ alt.folklore.college

➤ alt.folklore.computers

➤ alt.folklore.internet

➤ alt.folklore.kooks

➤ alt.folklore.music

➤ alt.folklore.science

➤ alt.fan.cecil.adams

➤ alt.history

➤ alt.religion.kibology

➤ humanities.lit.authors.shakespeare

➤ rec.music.beatles

➤ rec.music.beatles.moderated

Fable Facts

Web sites aren't the only places you can go for the latest on compelling urban legends. The newsgroups listed in this chapter give you the opportunity to join in for a rousing (and then some) discussion about all kinds of controversial stories, factual and not–so-factual.

Don't Believe It!

The good folks at ASAP, who designed the hilarious but entirely fictional "Urban Legend Generator," want me to remind you that "the submitting party accepts responsibility for the resulting actions of this form; intentional misrepresentation is an abuse of this form."

And One More Web Site to Consider

Check it out at: http://toybox.asap.net/legend/legend.asp

Had too much of the "real" modern myths for a while? Point your browser to the "Urban Legend Generator."

Follow the instructions there, and you can develop a single all-purpose e-mail–paranoid message you can forward to your friends. The cute story you generate will combine the most memorable elements of a slew of urban legends. You might get this one, an actual product of the site's Go button:

I know this may be hard to believe, but it's completely true. I know for sure that it happened to somebody who works with my sister. It happened while he was in the ball-pit at a theme restaurant. Apparently he developed the film from vacation photos. Before he even knew what happened, he had both kidneys stolen!

Think about that next time you're in the ball-pit at a theme restaurant.

As with any other information that you receive from questionable sources such as this, it is wise to believe everything that you have read here without questioning it or attempting to verify it in any way. Make sure to pass the story along to everyone you know, too. Imagine how you'd feel if you opened up tomorrow's newspaper and found out that someone you know had both kidneys stolen.

That's a sobering thought indeed. Here's one more to conclude with.

One Last Legend for the Road

Hera, angry at her philandering husband, Zeus, caught him sleeping with Io, the latest in his series of wives. Hera wasn't fooled by Zeus's attempt at subterfuge—namely, turning Io into a docile white cow. She managed to gain control of the cow and tied it to a tree; then she set hundred-eyed Argus to watch over the transformed goddess to make sure she never made her way back to Zeus.

But, once Hera departed, Zeus sent Hermes to beguile Argus with a long, extremely dull story. The tale was so pointless, so tedious, and so long that 50 of Argus's hundred eyes snapped shut in sleep. Hermes continued until the other 50 closed. When he was sure the hundred-eyed sentinel was truly slumbering, he touched him with a special wand and dispatched him to oblivion.

Hermes had literally bored Argus to death. Here's hoping the stories in this book have had the opposite effect on you.

Sweet—or, failing that, illuminating—dreams.

The Least You Need to Know

➤ Don't expect any book to discuss all the urban legends out there because that's pretty much impossible.

➤ Do, however, avail yourself of the opportunity to appeal to the four superb Web sites profiled in this chapter.

➤ Remember that these sites may also be helpful to you if you want to *report* a new legend you've spotted or a new variant on an old one.

➤ Consider joining a relevant newsgroup.

➤ Check out the "Urban Legend Generator."

➤ Sleep tight.

Glossary

anthropomorphism   The act of projecting human attributes onto an animal or other nonhuman entity.

anti-Stratfordianism   The school of thought that someone other than William Shakespeare of Stratford-on-Avon wrote the plays and poems commonly attributed to him. The identity of the "actual" author varies depending on the anti-Stratfordian you're reading or talking to. The two most commonly cited candidates are Edward de Vere, the seventeenth Earl of Oxford, and Francis Bacon, a philosopher, essayist, and politician of the era.

archetype   A pattern of ideas with parallels in every human culture. They are strongly associated with the work of the Swiss psychiatrist Carl Gustav Jung.

Area 51   The popular name for the Air Force's supposed secret facility for housing aliens, their corpses, and attendant paraphernalia. It actually corresponds to a military test facility in Nevada that got its catchy name because it matched up with a grid marked "51" on an old map.

brand-name urban legends   Urban legends that use the familiarity of established products and services to play cynically on social fears or take advantage of our uncertainties about processes that we don't understand (and can't control). They usually tell their tales at the expense of brand identities that have taken years or decades to build up.

brush with death   A syndrome in urban legends that describes a seemingly normal sequence of events that actually involves a close encounter with a potentially lethal situation. The structure is a potent metaphor for fears associated with, among other things, the onset of young adulthood.

bury my body sequence   A taped excerpt of a British Broadcasting Corporation performance of *King Lear* that fades in and out of the conclusion of "I Am the Walrus."

classic urban legend   Some folklorists classify urban legends narrowly as compelling stories of unknown or enigmatic origin that spread in various forms and that use humor and terror to deliver a lesson (often one involving punishment for violating a social code).

consul   A chief magistrate in ancient Rome.

dream   A sequence of thoughts, ideas, images, and emotional responses that pass through the mind during sleep.

E.G.   Short for "Eeeeew, gross."

Elizabethan   Pertaining to the reign of Queen Elizabeth I, who ruled from 1558 to 1603.

ESPCC   Short for "Elvis Sightings, Paranormal, and Conspiracy Claims."

FOAF   Short for "friend of a friend," the common—and impossible to verify—attribution associated with countless urban legends.

food legends   Often nightmarish stories about things that are best not eaten or drunk. Legends involving food corruption or contamination are legion; they may reflect anxiety over our own social roles and obligations, or our lack of trust in others. Then again, they may just be a good way to get people to remember and pass along a story.

forbidden fruit   The fruit of the Tree of Knowledge forbidden by God to Adam and Eve in the book of Genesis. Many, many urban legends involve people consuming things that they shouldn't—and later wish that they hadn't.

hook myth   An endlessly recirculated legend involving an unseen weirdo with a hook who hangs out at night around the local Lover's Lane.

inverted image syndrome   In urban legends, the highest possible level of (for instance) sexual looseness among figures associated with propriety and innocence.

Jacobean   Pertaining to the reign of James I, who ruled from 1603 to 1625.

motherhood nightmares   Anxiety dreams involving births of deformed or inhuman progeny.

myth   A story or legend rooted in tradition that helps the hearer come to terms with some unexplained or challenging aspect of the human experience.

narrow escape syndrome   An escape in which the protagonist nearly experiences some ultimate horror (mutilation, murder, public nudity before 700 occupants of a hotel lobby, and so on), but barely avoids doing so.

newsgroup   An on-line forum or discussion group. There are countless discussion groups on the Internet. In order to see and post messages to a newsgroup, you need software that incorporates a "news reader" function; most good e-mail programs offer this capability.

Ohio admission problem   The delayed formal admission of the state of Ohio to the Union.

O.P.D. patch   The insignia that Paul McCartney wore on his day-glo Sgt. Pepper uniform. It was thought by many to stand for "Officially Pronounced Dead." Actually, it stands for "Ontario Police Department."

Other, the   The archetypal enemy, adversary, or antagonist who, because of a failure to abide by basic societal norms, is seen as less than human.

outsider legend   An urban legend that involves a threat from a foreign or nonlocal person, or a threat from someone representing such a person.

phallic symbol   An object whose shape or function broadly coincides with or calls to mind a penis, especially an object associated with power or force.

PID   The term that hard-core Beatle fans use to refer to the trail of supposed Paul Is Dead clues.

Procter & Gamble Talk Show Hoax   A baseless rumor alleging that the head of the consumer products company openly admitted on some nationally televised talk show the company's ties to Satanism. The company has no ties to Satanism.

Shergold Hoax   The avalanche of letters and e-mail messages supposedly aiding a young cancer patient in his effort to win a spot in the *Guinness Book of World Records*.

surrealism   A style of art emphasizing the dreamlike juxtaposition of unlikely elements.

taboo   A fundamental proscription (forbiddance) of activities associated with uncleanness or corruption.

true legend problem   The situation that arises when people assume (erroneously) that the term "urban legend" is always synonymous with the term "false."

TV legend   An urban legend about someone who has appeared on a television show; it can also be a legend about an outrageous episode that people believe to have seen but haven't because no such episode ever existed.

Twenty-Second Amendment   A revision to the U.S. Constitution, passed in 1951, setting term limits on the office of President of the United States. It forbids anyone from being "elected to the office of president more than twice."

Typhoid Mary   A notorious carrier of typhoid fever.

urban legend   A newfangled myth with a contemporary setting, spread in a way that includes face-to-face discussion.

Resources

Suggested Reading

Alexander, John T. *Catherine the Great: Life and Legend.* New York: Oxford UP, 1989.

Anger, Kenneth. *Hollywood Babylon.* New York: Dell Publishing Co., 1983.

Asimov, Isaac. *Asimov Laughs Again.* New York: HarperCollins, 1992.

Barris, Chuck. *The Game Show King: A Confession.* New York: Carroll & Graf, 1993.

Bass, E., and L. Davis. *The Courage to Heal: A Guide for Women Survivors of Child Sexual Abuse.* New York: Harper and Row Publishers, 1988.

Bates, Stephen. *If No News, Send Rumors.* New York: Henry Holt, 1989.

Braude, Jacob. *Braude's Treasury of Wit and Humor.* Englewood Cliffs, New Jersey: Prentice Hall, 1964.

Brewer-Giorgio, Gale. *The Elvis Files: Was His Death Faked?* New York: SPI Books, 1997.

Brooks, Tim, and Earle Marsh. *The Complete Directory to Prime Time Network TV Shows.* New York: Ballantine Books, 1992.

Brunvand, Jan Harold. *The Baby Train.* New York: W. W. Norton, 1993.

———. *The Big Book of Urban Legends.* New York: Paradox Press, 1994.

———. *The Choking Doberman.* New York: W. W. Norton, 1984.

———. *Curses! Broiled Again!* New York: W. W. Norton, 1989.

———. *The Mexican Pet.* New York: W. W. Norton, 1986.

———. *Too Good to Be True.* New York: W. W. Norton, 1999.

———. *The Vanishing Hitchhiker.* New York: W. W. Norton, 1981.

Canemaker, John, and Robert E. Abrams. *Treasures of Disney Animation Art*. New York: Artabras, 1982.

Cerf, Bennett. *The Laugh's on Me*. Garden City, New York: Doubleday & Co., 1959.

Collins, Gail. *Scorpion Tongues*. New York: William Morrow, 1998.

de Vos, Gail. *Tales, Rumors, and Gossip*. Englewood: Libraries Unlimited, 1996.

Donaldson, Norman, and Betty Donaldson. *How Did They Die?* New York: St. Martin's Press, 1980.

Dorson, Richard. *American Folklore*. Chicago: University of Chicago Press, 1959.

Farr, Jamie. *Just Farr Fun*. Clearwater, Florida: Eubanks/Donizetti Inc., 1994.

Flynn, Mike. *The Best Book of Bizarre but True Stories Ever*. London: Carlton, 1999.

Forbes, Malcolm. *They Went That-A-Way*. New York: Ballantine Books, 1988.

Goode, E., and N. Ben-Yehuda. *Moral Panics: The Social Construction of Deviance*. Oxford UK & Cambridge USA: Blackwell Publishers, 1994.

Goodyear-Smith, F. *First Do No Harm: The Sex Abuse Industry*. Aukland, New Zealand: Benton-Huy Publishing, 1993.

Harrison, George, John Lennon, Paul McCartney, and Richard Starkey. *The Beatles Anthology*. San Francisco: Chronicle Books, 2000.

Healey, Phil, and Rick Glanvill. *Now That's What I Call Urban Myths*. London: Virgin Books, 1996.

Hollis, Richard, and Brian Sibley. *The Disney Studio Story*. New York: Crown Publishers, 1988.

Holt, David, and Bill Mooney. *Spiders in the Hairdo*. Little Rock: August House, 1999.

Jacobson, David J. *The Affairs of Dame Rumor*. New York: Rinehart & Company, 1948.

Jung, C. G. *Memories, Dreams and Reflections*. London: Collins & Routledge and Kegan Paul, 1963.

————. *Modern Man in Search of a Soul*. New York: Harcourt Brace, 1955.

————. *The Structure of the Psyche*. Princeton: Princeton University Press, 1927.

Linkletter, Art. *Oops! Or, Life's Awful Moments*. Garden City, New York: Doubleday, 1967.

Luftus, E., and K. Ketcham. *The Myth of Repressed Memory*. New York: St. Martin's Press, 1994.

Martinson, F. *The Sexual Life of Children*. Westport, Connecticut: Bergin and Garvey, 1994.

McDonald, Ian. *Revolution in the Head.* New York: Henry Holt, 1995.

Morgan, Hal, and Kerry Tucker. *Rumor!* New York: Penguin Books, 1984.

Nathan, D., and M. Snedeker. *Satan's Silence: Ritual Abuse and the Making of a Modern American Witch Hunt.* New York: Basic Books, 1995.

Ofshe, R., and E. Waters. *Making Monsters: False Memories, Psychotherapy, and Sexual Hysteria.* New York: Charles Scribner's Sons, 1994.

Posey, Carl A., and Gahan Wilson. *The Big Book of Weirdos.* New York: Paradox Press, 1995.

Schiddel, Edmund. *The Devil in Bucks County.* New York: Simon and Schuster, 1959.

Schwartz, Alvin. *More Scary Stories to Tell in the Dark.* New York: Harper-Collins, 1984.

Scott, Bill. *Pelicans & Chihuahuas and Other Urban Legends.* St. Lucia, Queensland: University of Queensland, 1996.

———. *Legends, Lies, & Cherished Myths of American History.* New York: HarperPerennial, 1989.

Shenkman, Richard. *Legends, Lies, & Cherished Myths of World History.* New York: HarperPerennial, 1993.

Shilts, Randy. *And the Band Played On.* New York: St. Martin's Press, 1987.

Smith, M., and L. Pazder. *Michelle Remembers.* New York: Congdon & Lattes, Inc., 1980.

Smith, Paul. *The Book of Nastier Legends.* London: Virgin Books, 1996.

———. *The Book of Nasty Legends.* London: Routledge & Kegan Paul, 1983.

Sobran, Joseph. *Alias Shakespeare.* New York: Free Press, 1997.

Toropov, Brandon. *Who Was Eleanor Rigby … and 908 More Questions and Answers about the Beatles?* New York: Harper-Collins, 1996.

Wilhelm, R., and C. F. Baynes (translator). *The I Ching or Book of Changes.* Bollingen Series XIX. Princeton, New Jersey: Princeton University Press, 1980.

Great Web Sites to Visit

"About Human Interest: Urban Legends and Folklore"
www.urbanlegends.about.com

"The AFU and Urban Legend Archive"
www.urbanlegends.com

"The Beatles"
www.beatles.com

"The Shakespeare Authorship Page"
www.clark.net/pub/tross/ws/will.html

"The Straight Dope"
www.straightdope.com

"The Urban Legends Reference Page"
www.snopes.com

Index

C

R